D0169111

CITY MAKING

CITY MAKING

BUILDING COMMUNITIES WITHOUT
BUILDING WALLS

Gerald E. Frug

PRINCETON UNIVERSITY PRESS   PRINCETON, NEW JERSEY

Frug, Gerald E., 1939–
City making : building communities without building walls / Gerald
E. Frug.
p. cm.
Includes bibliographical references and index.
ISBN 0-691-00741-1 (cl. :a lk. paper)
1. City planning—United States. 2. Urban policy—United States. 3.
Zoning law—United States. 4. Social classes—United States. 5. Land
use, Urban—United States. 6. Community development, Urban—
United States. 7. Community organizations—United States. 8.
United States—Social conditions. 9. United States—Race relations. I.
Title
HT167.F78 1999
307. 1′216′0973—dc21
99-12209
CIP

This book has been composed in Galliard

The paper used in this publication meets the minimum
requirements of ANSI/NISO Z39.48-1992 (R1997)
(*Permanence of Paper*)

http://pup.princeton.edu

Printed in the United States of America

10 9 8 7 6 5 4 3 2

For Stephen and Emily

Contents

Acknowledgments

WHILE writing this book, I have been informed, encouraged, prodded, inspired, and subjected to helpful criticism by dozens of colleagues and students. I regret that I cannot name them all in these acknowledgments because I am very indebted to them all. In what I consider a minimal gesture, I would like to express my appreciation to David Barron, Gary Bellow, Nathaniel Berman, Richard Briffault, Jim Brown, Tracy-Elizabeth Clay, Chris Desan, Richard Ford, Mary Joe Frug, Morton Horwitz, David Kennedy, Duncan Kennedy, Youngjae Lee, Frank Michelman, Martha Minow, Kathleen Sullivan, David Troutt, and Roberto Unger for their contribution to my work. And I would especially like to single out my assistant, Elizabeth Sponheim, who has been extraordinarily helpful with the preparation of the manuscript from beginning to end.

This book includes substantially revised versions of four articles that I originally published in law reviews: "The City as a Legal Concept," 93 *Harvard Law Review* 1057 (1980), "Decentering Decentralization," 60 *University of Chicago Law Review* 253 (1993), "The Geography of Community," 48 *Stanford Law Review* 1047 (1996), and "City Services," 73 *New York University Law Review* 23 (1998). As is the style in law review publishing, these articles were extensively—one might say excessively—footnoted. I have radically reduced the number of footnotes for this book, but scholars interested in further citations for any of the matters discussed in the following pages can find them in the law review versions.

CITY MAKING

Introduction _____

EVERY American metropolitan area is now divided into districts that are so different from each other they seem to be different worlds. Residential neighborhoods are African American, Asian, Latino, or white, and upper-middle-class, middle-class, working-class, or poor; many are populated by people who share a single class and racial or ethnic status. Traveling through this mosaic of neighborhoods, metropolitan residents move from feeling at home to feeling like a tourist to feeling so out of place that they are afraid for their own security. Commercial life provides a similarly wide range of experiences. In one spot, a shopping center offers Louis Vuitton or Hermès; in another, small stores are deteriorating or empty; in a third, the sidewalks are crowded with street vendors; in a fourth, a strip mall features Staples or Toys"R"Us. Some sections of the metropolis are even distinctive because they are integrated along some or all of these lines of race, ethnicity, class, and variety of commercial life. Still, everyone knows that Armani isn't located next to Kmart. Everyone knows which parts of the metropolitan area are nice and which are dangerous. We all know where we don't belong.

This pervasive urban landscape is not simply the result of individual choices about where to live or create a business. It is the product of a multitude of governmental policies. In this book, I focus on one such policy: the ways in which the American legal system has empowered—and failed to empower—cities. American law treats cities as subdivisions of the states, and the states have organized them in a manner that has helped separate metropolitan residents into different, sometimes hostile, groups. The design of cities' power to control land use provides an example of this phenomenon. Most American metropolitan areas are now splintered into dozens and dozens of cities, and for decades state governments have authorized these cities to wield their zoning and redevelopment authority to foster their own prosperity even if it is won at the expense of their neighbors. This pursuit of prosperity has usually involved trying to attract the "better kind" of commercial life and the "better kind" of people while, simultaneously, excluding the rest. Everywhere in the nation, some cities are understood as having succeeded in this effort, while others are understood as having failed. Those that have succeeded have enticed millions of people to escape the problems associated with America's central cities by crossing the city/suburb boundary. In response, central cities have sought to curb this exodus by exercising their own power over land use. Although no central city has attempted to prevent people from becoming city residents, many have used their ability to zone and condemn property to concentrate upscale commercial and residential uses in particular city neighborhoods. These zoning and redevelopment policies have had a powerful impact both on the allocation of resources in America's metropolitan areas and on the relationships among the different kinds of people who live within them. Across the country, they have segregated metropolitan areas into "two nations," rich and poor, white and black, expanding and contracting.[1] And they have undermined the ability of metropolitan residents even to understand each other, let alone to work together on the region's problems. The purpose of this book is to examine the ways in which the legal system has fostered this dynamic, and to propose changes in the structure of city power that would reverse it.

This focus on the legal system is unusual. Many books have been written about the impact of land-use policies on metropolitan fragmentation and, more generally, about the effects of suburbanization on American life. These books have concentrated on history, sociology, political theory, urban design, literary theory, or economics, and collectively they constitute an immensely valuable literature. I rely on many of them in the pages that follow. But none of these books has highlighted the role that the legal system has played in fostering the suburbanization of America or in the other aspects of urban life—like the unequal distribution of city services— that I discuss below. Yet it is the legal system that determines the kind of power that cities can exercise, and, I argue in this book, the way it has done so has had destructive consequences for American society. Prosperous suburbs have been able to enrich themselves at the expense of their neighbors because they have been empowered to defend their borders through autonomy-enhancing local government law rules, such as exclusionary zoning, protections against annexation, and the allocation of property tax revenues solely to those who live within the city borders. At the same time, local government law has denied American cities, central city and suburb alike, other powers—such as the authority to mount an adequate program to combat violence—that could help overcome the divisions that now characterize American metropolitan areas. To change American urban policy, we need to change the current legal definition of city power, replacing one that has intensified the tensions between metropolitan residents with one that will reduce them. As John Dewey put it long ago,

> Failure to recognize that general legal rules and principles are working hypotheses, needing to be constantly tested by the way in which they work out in application to concrete situations, explains the otherwise paradoxical fact that the slogans of the liberalism of one period often become the bulwarks of reaction in a subsequent era.[2]

This book offers a proposal for a local government law for the twenty-first century.

It begins with a discussion not of the exercise of city power but of the opposite phenomenon: in our highly urbanized country, the American legal system has chosen to create cities that are powerless to act on their own initiative. By this I mean not that cities are unable to exercise power at all—everyone is familiar with the zoning authority just mentioned, as well as with cities' ability to tax and regulate their residents—but something more fundamental. A city is the only collective body in America that cannot do something simply because it decides to do it. Instead, under American law, cities have power only if state governments authorize them to act. To appreciate the significance of the difference between these alternative sources of power, consider how other organizations in our society, such as corporations, unions, or churches, obtain the authority they need to take action. These organizations do not have to rely on grants of power from the state; instead, they have general authority, derived from their members, to do what they want to do unless prohibited by state law. Imagine the impact on the power and freedom of these organizations if they could do nothing without the permission of the state government. Imagine as well the impact on your own power and freedom if you were able to engage only in those activities that state law has allowed you to perform.

There is nothing unique about cities that required them to be powerless in this way. Of course it is possible to understand cities—like the state departments of education and transportation—as subdivisions of state governments. But they can also be understood, like other collective bodies, as created not by state governments but by their members—created, in other words, to pursue the interests of the people who live within them rather than those of the state. This second understanding of city power, in fact, informed the legal conception of cities for hundreds of years. In Part One I trace how, in the nineteenth century, the legal system undermined this alternative conception of cities' legal status while, simultaneously, giving another entity in our society, the private corporation, not only considerable authority to act on its own but legal protection from state control. To some readers, this comparison between cities and private corporations may seem surprising. What do these two kinds of organization have in common? The answer is that, before the nineteenth century, there was no legal distinction in England or in America between so-called public and private corporations—between cities (municipal corporations) and business corporations. All corporations had the same rights, and all of them were subject to the same protections against national and state control. In Part One, I describe how the legal system made the distinction between public and private corporations, and analyze how it relied on the public nature of cities to undermine cities' ability to wield significant power in America.

The comparison between public and private corporations is not the only one that the reader should keep in mind when considering the legitimacy of state control over cities. Although I claimed above that cities are the only collective body in America that derive their power solely from the states, that statement is not quite true. In legal thought, another entity is also sometimes understood as obtaining its power from the states: the federal government. Yet, as the twentieth century has demonstrated, this understanding of the source of federal power has had little effect on the scope of the federal government's authority. As the Constitution is now interpreted, it has the power to do virtually anything it likes. One of the ways to appreciate the extent of city powerlessness in America is to compare the legal interpretation of cities' authority with that of the federal government. As we shall see, city power has been interpreted very narrowly, while federal power, with rare exceptions, has been interpreted very broadly. What does this comparison say about the understanding of the comparative desirability of centralized and decentralized power adopted by American law?

It's not that centralization is widely considered to be preferable. On the contrary, the fear of making the national government the predominant power in the country is as old as America. The problem has been that many people think that decentralization of power is no longer possible: the world is too complex, local resources too inadequate, local power too threatening to minorities, and the country's problems too interconnected to permit reliance on local decision making. If most government decision making were decentralized today, the argument runs, cities would selfishly seek to evade responsibility for problems ranging from the disposal of toxic waste to the location of centers for the homeless ("Not In My Backyard"). They would attempt to enhance the prosperity of their own residents regardless of whether their actions threatened the national economy. They would invade the rights of their most powerless citizens. And they would be unable even to address issues that cut across local boundaries, such as the protection of the environment and transportation, let alone pay for the necessary programs. From this perspective, decentralization of political power is either an impossible dream—nostalgia for a past long since overtaken by events—or a nightmare that would quickly undermine the country's power and efficiency.

This argument against the decentralization of power relies on a particular conception of what city power is. It attributes to cities the power of self-assertion associated in our culture with an autonomous individual. It presents cities as able to do whatever they want to do as long as they stay within their sphere of delegated authority: they can act in their own self-interest, cooperate with others on their own terms, and cause harm to those who disagree with them. The political term for this form of autonomy is "sovereignty." The traditional understanding of city power envisions cities as sovereign in this sense: they are entitled to be selfish, like national governments, on a collective rather than an individual basis. It should not be surprising that the possibility of decentralizing power becomes severely limited once this conception of cities is adopted. No one could trust such an entity to exercise unsupervised power. It presents too much danger to outsiders and to its own members. As Michel Foucault suggests, fear of sovereign power is so common that it is routinely converted into a subjected sovereignty, a sovereignty limited by some other sovereignty.

> Humanism [has] invented a whole series of subjected sovereignties: the soul (ruling the body, but subjected to God), consciousness (sovereign in the context of judgment, but subjected to the necessities of truth), the individual (a titular control of personal rights subjected to the laws of nature and society), basic freedom (sovereignty within, but accepting the demands of an outside world and "aligned with destiny").[3]

Cities have a similarly subjected sovereignty: they can exercise power but are simultaneously subjected to the power of the state.

Those who have sought to defend city power against centralized control have not questioned this equation of city power with the notion of sovereignty. On the contrary, they have attempted to wrest from the state a sphere of local autonomy that would enable them to decide for themselves how to govern their own affairs. Nowhere has this effort been more successful than in America's most prosperous suburbs. Like business corporations in the nineteenth century, these cities have had to overcome the widespread reluctance to allocate power to decentralized groups, and, like business corporations, they have done so by relying on the public/private distinction. They have associated themselves not with the exercise of political power but with private values. In America today, suburban power is usually seen not as a threat to local residents or outsiders but as a vehicle for the protection of home and family and of private property. This privatized picture of suburban life not only has helped convince the states to grant these cities significant power over zoning, education, and resource allocation but has helped persuade the courts to defend their power against attacks by insiders and outsiders alike. Moreover, local government law has enabled these cities to pursue their own self-interest regardless of the impact on their neighbors because it has adopted a privatized conception of the boundary lines between the central city and its suburbs—and between the suburbs themselves. Like the boundary lines that separate one private property–owner from another, city borders have become a vehicle for dividing us from them, our problems from their problems, our money from their money, our future from their future. Those who can afford it can therefore assure themselves of better schools, safer streets, and more homogeneous neighborhoods simply by moving from one side of the line to the other.

This privatized conception of city power has done little for America's central cities. No one is excluded from living within their borders. They remain the primary example in America of public places: often on a daily basis, central-city residents encounter people radically different from themselves whether they like it or not. Because of their open, public nature, central cities cannot easily be imagined, in the manner of the prosperous suburbs, as vehicles for the protection of private values such as home and family and private property. Instead, the task of making public policy decisions for diverse cities such as these seems unmistakably governmental. Under current local government law, however, state power over cities cannot be curbed by a defense of the public values that heterogeneous cities have the potential of fostering, such as those derived from participation in the democratic process or from the kind of life experience that preservation of public space provides. To be sure, the states have allowed even these cities to make some decisions about local policy. Yet not only are their decisions less defensible in court but their scope is limited by the power granted to neighboring suburbs. Central-city decisions have to be made with the suburbs in mind, because the privatized interpretation of the city/suburb boundary line provides an easy way to immunize oneself from their impact. The legal system's decision to build local power on the protection of local autonomy and associate autonomy with private values, in short, has had an unequal effect on metropolitan residents: it has enhanced the power of America's prosperous suburbs at the expense of its central cities.

Even more fundamentally, the manner in which local government law has empowered cities and the curbs that it has placed on them, taken together, have limited the scope and promise of decentralized power in America. Local government law's conceptions of city power and city powerlessness are complementary, not antithetical: both undermine the fundamental democratic experience of working with different kinds of people to find solutions to common problems. State control has reduced the importance of cities as instruments of public policy and thereby diminished the opportunity for widespread participation in public decision making, a form of participation that is achievable only at the local level. At the same time, local government law's privatized version of local autonomy has channeled the decisions that cities are allowed to make into vehicles for separating and dividing different kinds of people rather than bringing them together, withdrawal from public life rather than engagement with others, and the multiplication of private spaces instead of walkable streets and public parks. Local government law's conceptions of city power and city powerlessness have also played a decisive role in enabling state control over city decision making. This impact becomes clear if we return, once again, to the legal rule that permits cities to exercise power only if the state gives it to them. Of necessity, this has meant that each city's energy has focused on convincing the state to do so. And because each city is simply trying to advance its own self-interest in this process, the radical difference between cities has provided little incentive for intercity cooperation. Quite the contrary: it can be—and has been—to the advantage of some cities to gain power from the state at the expense of their neighbors. Yet cities could control state policy rather than being subservient to it if they could learn to work together by resolving their conflicts through negotiation and compromise. States, after all, are nothing more than the combination of all the localities within them. Any policy agreed to by the cities collectively is virtually certain to become state policy. Of course, the prospect of such an intercity agreement now seems remote. But the reason it does is that cities are treated as if they were autonomous individuals, entitled to walk away from the negotiations whenever it seems in their self-interest to do so.

In this book, I seek to defend a version of city power that does not rely on the notion of local autonomy. In my view, the fear of self-aggrandizing autonomous entities articulated by critics of decentralization—particularly, collective groups of individuals like cities—is not unreasonable. Prosperous suburbs, after all, have exercised their zoning authority and other local powers in precisely the selfish way that opponents of decentralization claimed they would. But decentralization of power need not be understood in the privatized manner that local government law now embraces. City power can become a vehicle for facilitating the ability of different kinds of people—of strangers who share only the fact that they live in the same geographic area—to learn to live with, even to collaborate with, each other. Its value can be seen in terms of connecting metropolitan residents rather than separating them. Reconceiving city power in this way requires rethinking the legal conception of a city from the ground up. And this involves, first of all, rejecting the legal system's attempt to build city power on the image of the autonomous individual and the nation-state. The legal system treats autonomous individuals and nation-states not only as interested in pursuing their own self-interest but as able to discover what their self-interest is in an unproblematic way: they can do so simply by looking within themselves. In other words, it treats them as having what theorists have called a "centered" sense of self. By adopting a similar understanding of city power, local government law has imagined that power can be decentralized in America by moving a portion of it from the national government to the local level without changing its nature. It seeks to decentralize power simply by recentering it—by moving its location—rather than by decentering it, that is, by questioning the sharp self/other distinction embodied in the notion of the centered subject.

In Part Two, I describe another way to decentralize power, one that redefines decentralization by building on the vast literature of critique of the centered subject, a literature that to date has focused primarily on the individual rather than on collective entities such as cities. My redefinition offers a legal conception of cities that is not based on the notion of sovereignty. It is based instead on the recognition of the impact that cities within a single metropolitan area have on each other, as well as the links that metropolitan residents have to cities other than their place of residence. By building decentralization on theories of the subject other than that of the autonomous individual, I seek to defend what I consider to be the values of decentralization: the freedom gained from the ability to participate in the basic societal decisions that affect one's life, the creativity generated by the capacity to experiment in solving public problems, and the energy derived from democratic forms of organization. I do so, however, not by protecting local selfishness but by making interlocal connection part of the definition of what a city is. As we shall see, this can be accomplished either by a requirement that cities take regional considerations into account in their decision making, or by a de-emphasis on the importance of the boundary lines that mark the separateness of the cities located within a single metropolitan region. The reason that the legal definition of a city should be changed in one of these ways is not simply that it would promote, rather than frustrate, regional solutions to metropolitan problems. The divisiveness fostered by the traditional conception of city power has become self-reinforcing: the more a city's sense of self is based on separation from its neighbors, the more important such a separation becomes. A redefinition of city power also has another advantage: it has the potential of reducing the demand for constraints on city authority. There is no need for state or federal control of cities if they act together to solve interlocal problems rather than define themselves against each other. The states and the federal government are themselves organized by bringing local representatives together, with interlocal compromise understood as the foundation of public policy.

Currently the most important intercity relationship is not at the state or federal level but at the regional level: most metropolitan residents cross city lines within their metropolitan area virtually every day. Thus it is within America's metropolitan regions that, in Part Three, I locate a new role for cities in American life, one enabled by my reconception of city power. The name I give to this new role is community building. I use the word "community" in this book with a good deal of hesitation. The term has often been invoked to refer to a group of people who share things in common—a sense of identity or history or values—and who seek to foster the bonds they have with each other. This is not the meaning of the term "community" I have in mind. Instead, I use the word as synonymous with what Iris Young calls "the ideal of city life":

> By "city life" I mean a form of social relations which I define as the being together of strangers. In the city persons and groups interact within spaces they all experience themselves as belonging to, but without those interactions dissolving into unity or commonness. . . . City dwelling situates one's own identity and activity in relation to a horizon of a vast variety of other activity, and the awareness . . . [of] this unknown, unfamiliar activity affects the condition of one's own. . . . City dwellers are thus together, bound to one another, in what should be and sometimes is a single polity. Their being together entails some common problems and common interests, but they do not create a community of shared final ends, of mutual identification and reciprocity.[4]

Young has advanced this notion of "city life" not as a definition of community but as an alternative to it. She rejects what she sees as communitarians' emphasis on the bonding of homogeneous groups rather than on "the being together of strangers." Unlike Young, I do not cede the term "community" to those who evoke the romance of togetherness. Communities—the gay community, the black community, the professional community—seem to me more accurately understood in terms of the being together of strangers than in terms of feelings of identity or unity. True, members of these communities have something in common. So do those who live in the same geographical area. But the aspect of their lives that members of any of these groups have in common is simply a starting point. The hard work in community building—and the task I think cities should undertake—is to deal with the differences within the group. For me, this task requires not cultivating a feeling of oneness with others but increasing the capacity of all metropolitan residents—African American as well as white, gay as well as fundamentalist, rich as well as poor—to live in a world filled with those they find unfamiliar, strange, even offensive. Many people consider such a goal to be utopian. But no one thinks that it is unimportant. One reason that it seems necessary is to decrease the level of tension that the differences between the people who live in America's urban areas now generate. But there is a positive objective as well, one I describe at length in Part Three: heterogeneity stimulates learning, growth, adventure, fun.

There is no institution in American life that is now devoted to community building. What kind of institution could do so? The most powerful private institutions in America—private corporations—are unlikely to be a helpful mechanism for addressing the divisions that now fracture American society or for stimulating the ability of metropolitan residents to profit from the diversity of their region. Cities, by contrast, offer a good deal more promise. The cities that constitute America's metropolitan areas contain within their collective borders all of the distinctions that now characterize American life, whether these distinctions are understood in terms of political beliefs, religion, race, ethnicity, class, sexual orientation, gender, or values. This range of diversity is considerably broader than that offered not only by private corporations but also by voluntary associations and family life. Moreover, cities are not simply governments, indistinguishable from the states and the federal government. Unlike central governments, cities can provide the kind of personal, day-to-day contact among citizens and between citizens and their elected officials that community building requires. In Parts Three and Four, I suggest how cities can be organized to take advantage of their capacity to foster community building by focusing on two specific city functions. The first, mentioned at the outset of this introduction, involves a transformation of cities' land-use, zoning, and redevelopment policies. The second is a revision of the ways in which cities deliver city services—above all, education and police services. By discussing these two city functions in some detail, I seek to illustrate the ways in which the reformation of the legal concept of the city could transform the day-to-day operation of city governments.

Reinventing city power along the lines I propose in this book will not be easy to accomplish. But it is not impossible. It will take no more governmental intervention and individual initiative to bring it about than has the creation of America's current urban landscape. The endless suburban sprawl, the distance between jobs and those who need them, the isolation of poor African American neighborhoods and privileged white suburbs, the increasing disparity between rich and poor cities, the mounting suspicion and distrust of unfamiliar strangers—none of this would have been possible without the extraordinary amount of federal, state, and local intervention I describe below in Part Three. What kind of America has this astonishing feat of social engineering produced? What kind of America will result from a continuation of an urban policy that fosters separation and division? At the moment, the *New York Times* reports, "the fastest-growing residential communities in the nation are private and usually gated, governed by a thicket of covenants, codes and restrictions."[5] Together with the consolidation of the political power of the outer suburbs, this development suggests that the kind of divisiveness that community building is designed to combat may be intensifying.

This book is written for those interested in exploring alternatives to an America built on the separation of different kinds of people. I would like what I say below to be of interest to legal specialists and to academics who study urban problems. But I have written the book in a way that, I trust, will not seem technical or legalistic—even when I discuss topics as abstruse as postmodern theory—in order to describe to general readers the impact of the legal concept of the city on their own lives.

Part One

THE CITY AS A LEGAL CONCEPT

1

City Powerlessness

The Current Legal Status of Cities

American cities do not have the power to solve their current problems or
to control their future development. Cities have only those powers delegated to them by state governments, and traditionally these powers have
been rigorously limited by judicial interpretation. Even if cities act pursu-
ant to an unquestionable delegation of power from the state, their actions
remain subject to state control. Any city decision can be reversed by a
contrary decision by the state, a process the legal system calls "preemption." Moreover, state power is not limited simply to the ability to determine the scope of city decision-making authority or to second-guess the
exercise of that authority whenever it seems appropriate to do so. States
have absolute power over cities, and the extent of that power has been
extravagantly emphasized by the Supreme Court of the United States:

> The State . . . at its pleasure may modify or withdraw all [city] powers, may take
> without compensation [city] property, hold it itself, or vest it in other agencies,
> expand or contract the territorial area, unite the whole or a part of it with an-
> other municipality, repeal the charter and destroy the corporation. All this may
> be done, conditionally or unconditionally, with or without the consent of the
> citizens, or even against their protest. In all these respects the State is supreme,
> and its legislative body, conforming its action to the state constitution, may do
> as it will, unrestrained by any provision of the Constitution of the United States.

In an attempt to limit this subservience to the state, most state constitutions have been amended to grant cities the power to exercise "home
rule." But cities are free of state control under home rule only on matters
purely local in nature. And, nowadays, little if anything is sufficiently local
to fall within such a definition of autonomy. As a result, cities are generally
treated by American law as "creatures of the state."[1]

This firm state control of city decision making is supplemented by federal restrictions on city power. Over the course of the twentieth century,
the federal government has taken an increasing part in determining city
policy, sometimes by mandating city action but more often by attaching
strings to federal grants-in-aid. The importance of these grants-in-aid illustrates another source of city powerlessness, a declining ability to gener-

ate income. City income is largely based on something cities cannot control: the willingness of taxpayers to locate or do business within city boundaries. Everyone is familiar with the exodus of wealthy taxpayers, including businesses, from the nation's central cities. Yet even if cities could ensure that taxpayers remained within their borders, it would not mean that they would have the power to tax them. A city's decision to increase taxes must be expressly authorized by the state, and some states have a constitutional limitation on the amount of taxes permitted. The Commerce Clause and the Fourteenth Amendment of the federal Constitution also limit the kinds of taxes cities can impose. And even more stringent restraints curb the cities' ability to borrow money. Cities' borrowing authority is usually limited to a fixed percentage of its property base, their use of borrowed money is normally restricted to "capital" as opposed to "operating" expenses, and the borrowing itself often requires a popular referendum to authorize the debt. Given these limits on cities' taxing and borrowing ability, city dependence on state and federal financial aid is not surprising.[2]

City power is limited in other ways as well. Cities, unlike states, are not general lawmaking bodies. State constitutions have been interpreted to deny cities the authority to define individual rights or alter the basic legal structure of society by making what is called "private" or "civil" law. As a result, cities' ability to regulate private activity is more like that of an administrative agency than that of the state itself. Cities are also not allowed to exercise the economic power of private corporations. In many states, cities have no authority to engage in a business activity unless it is not-for-profit; in the states where profit-making activities are permitted, their scope is severely limited. City business functions are thus largely reduced to the provision of traditional municipal services. Yet today many of these services, such as education, transportation, and water supply, are provided not by cities but by special districts or public authorities that are organized to cut across city boundaries, and over which cities have no control.[3]

These limits on city power usually seem natural and uncontroversial. They appear simply to follow from cities' status as junior members of the governmental hierarchy. This sense of naturalness keeps us from questioning them or trying to think of ways to change them. It is difficult even to imagine what another legal status for cities would look like. Of course, sharply different legal powers are imaginable for private corporations. The limitation of city powers to those delegated by the state is clearly inapplicable: private corporations can be organized to pursue any legal purpose merely by filing papers in whatever state the incorporators choose. The restrictions imposed on cities by the federal Constitution also do not apply to private corporations; on the contrary, while cities are restrained by the Constitution, corporations are protected by it. Nor do the limits on city taxing and borrowing power and on city business opportunities have an analogue for private corporations. Their revenue-raising capacities are instead governed by the market. To be sure, federal and state governments have extensive constitutional authority to regulate private corporations, and they have exercised this power to a considerable degree. Still, the widespread agreement that private corporations should remain independent of state power restrains its exercise. No one thinks that corporate property rights, like city power, should be fully subject to state control. On the contrary, their protection from governmental regulation is widely understood as the cornerstone of the "free enterprise" system.

The point of this comparison between the law for cities—municipal corporations—and the law for private corporations is that we never think to make it. The differences between the two types of entities are simply too obvious: one is public, the other private; one governed by politics, the other by the market; one a subdivision of the state, the other a part of civil society. In the modern development of the law governing cities, the historical connection between public and private corporations has been forgotten in favor of an automatic incantation of the distinction between them: city discretion is the exercise of coercive power and must be restrained, while corporate discretion is the exercise of liberty and must be protected. Our conceptual framework, based on the public/private distinction, thus helps confirm the current powerlessness of cities. City powerlessness appears to be an inevitable and desirable feature of modern life. The idea of local power conveys a picture of the strangulation of nationwide businesses by a maze of conflicting local regulations and the frustration of national political objectives by local selfishness and protectionism. Far from seeming a political choice, the rejection of local power seems implied by the needs of modern large-scale organizations, both public and private. A widespread distrust of city power buttresses this image of necessity. Many people think that while cities are supposed to protect the public interest, they cannot actually be depended on to do so. City discretion of any kind evokes images of corruption, patronage, even foolishness. This combined sense of necessity and desirability has made local powerlessness part of our definition of modern society. Advocates of the decentralization of power seem naive: they fail to understand the world as it really is.

Why City Powerlessness Matters

Our ideas about the powerlessness of cities are so well settled that it is difficult to see why city powerlessness matters. It is tempting to try to attribute the reason to the so-called crisis of the cities. But exactly what this crisis is, or why we should care about it, is uncertain. It may be the need to improve the quality of life for those—often poor, often African American or Latino—who live in the nation's major cities, or the need to encourage greater concentrations of people because of the environmental damage produced by the suburbanization of the countryside, or the need to preserve city institutions important to the nation as a whole, such as trade or cultural centers. Yet if the "crisis of the cities" means no more than these kinds of problems, an increase in city power does not seem necessary for their solution. Many of these problems might be solved more quickly if city governments were abolished and replaced by federal officials authorized to implement a national urban policy. The need for city power does not rest on the view that local decision making is the only, or even the most efficient, way to solve local problems. Indeed, if we focus on cities as they are presently organized and managed, we will not see the argument for city power. Cities as they currently exist should not simply be made more powerful. The argument for city power rests on what cities have been and what they could become.

Cities have served and might again serve as vehicles for the achievement of purposes that have been frustrated in modern American life. They could respond to what Hannah Arendt has called the need for "public freedom": the ability to participate actively in the basic societal decisions that affect one's life. This conception of freedom as a positive activity designed to create one's way of life differs markedly from the currently popular idea of freedom as merely (in Arendt's words) "an inner realm into which men might escape at will from the pressures of the world," or a "*liberum arbitrium* which makes the will choose between alternatives." The basic critique of the development of Western society that has emerged since the beginning of the nineteenth century has emphasized the limited ability of individuals to control their own lives. This development is sometimes attributed to the growth of bureaucracy: an individual's work is increasingly governed by a distant, hierarchic chain of command, and an individual's political destiny decided by distant government officials. Others attribute the development to the evolution of the capitalist system to a stage in which the few individuals who control the bulk of productive property directly make the economic decisions, and indirectly make the political decisions, that determine a society's future. Still others emphasize the organization of society to conform to the utilitarian view of the individual as a consumer of satisfactions: economic freedom is defined as the ability to choose from an array of products and jobs, political freedom as the ability to choose among political candidates, and intellectual freedom as the ability to choose opinions from the "marketplace of ideas." There is little opportunity, in each case, for individuals to create their own material life, determine their own political future, or form their own ideas from personal experience. For our purposes, the important point is that all of these critiques stress the need for the individual to gain control over those portions of his or her life now determined by others.[4]

Since absolute individual self-determination is pure fantasy, these critiques have focused on a more limited objective: reorganizing society to increase the degree of individual involvement in the decisions that shape it. One step toward meeting that objective is the reduction of the scale of decision making. Limited size seems to be a prerequisite to the ability of ordinary citizens to participate in public life. Those who seek to expand this kind of participation do not imagine that every citizen has to be involved in every political decision, or that there is no role for elected officials in American democracy—let alone that every issue has be to decided in one big meeting. There is no single mode of decision making, called "democracy," that specifies how much participation is required, the amount of time people need to spend in meetings, or the role of experts in the resolution of political problems. The amount of citizen participation can vary from issue to issue, and there are many ways to involve people in public decision making and still budget their time. What advocates consider important is not the extent of participation but the impact derived from engagement in the decision-making process. Only this engagement, proponents have argued, can overcome what Tocqueville called "individualism." Individualism, he said, is

> a calm and considered feeling which disposes each citizen to isolate himself from the mass of his fellows and withdraw into the circle of family and friends; with this little society formed to his taste, he gladly leaves the greater society to look after itself.

Tocqueville feared that this kind of privatization would foster a yearning for conformity and, with it, a willingness to yield public affairs to an omnipotent, efficient, albeit gentle, centralized despotism. For him, an essential antidote to this danger was the learning experience and stimulation provided by involvement in local government. More than a century later, John Dewey called the demise of participatory local government the central evil of the modern era. Popular participation, he contended, was the way to replace reliance on the mass media with personally acquired information and to create the sense of a common venture necessary for any meaningful definition of the "public interest." More recently, Hannah Arendt argued that no one can be truly free or happy without recapturing the meaning of freedom as active participation in public decision making and the meaning of happiness as public happiness, the sharing of public power. Freedom is cheapened, she said, when it is defined merely as a source of protection for our private lives, rather than as a creative form of control over our lives.[5]

Many who write in this tradition have treated the identity of those entitled to participate in public affairs to be as obvious as the constituency of
the polis was to Aristotle. But it is no longer possible simply to assume
that city boundaries define the right constituency. Metropolitan fragmentation has created too many cities that feel more like a private, gated community than an open and diverse public forum. While participation in
these homogeneous cities certainly has its value, its effect is likely to be
considerably different from one built on engagement with people representing a variety of backgrounds and perspectives. The community-building efforts that I describe below would thus affect the nature of the public
freedom that cities have the potential of fostering. Community building
would allow the creation of a wider public, one that would produce a
more meaningful experience of public freedom than is now available in
many contemporary suburbs and city neighborhoods. Contact with this
wider public would enable disparate strangers to work together to solve
common problems, a process that can change not only their relationship
with each other but their understanding of their own self-interest. The
experience gained from this kind of interaction cannot be delegated to
elected officials or experts: it needs to touch the lives of ordinary citizens.
Only in the places where daily life is centered—in the cities in which they
live, work, shop, and go out—can people learn to be comfortable with
those different from themselves.

This vision of civic life will appear utopian to many readers. Indeed it
is if we define utopia, as did Karl Mannheim, as a vision of the world
derived from unrealized and unfulfilled tendencies in current society that
threaten to break through the existing order and cause its transformation.
The idea of freedom as participation in the exercise of power has been a
persistent and persistently revolutionary idea in Western social thought. It
was, according to some scholars, the purpose of the American Revolution
until the reaction against mass democracy in the 1780s; it was also, according to others, the central core of Marxism prior to the Leninist addition of the priority of organization. What makes the concept seem so unrealistic these days is the strength of our conviction that all decision making
requires specialization, expertise, and a chain of command. Currently,
small units are organized like large ones: cities are just another version of
bureaucratic government. Local democracy survives only as a faint echo,
discernible in the remnants of the New England town meeting and in the
sense that, somehow, the bureaucratic governments of most localities are
still more accessible, controllable, and amenable to popular direction than
is the federal bureaucracy. Why are cities today governed as bureaucracies
rather than as vehicles for encouraging the exercise of public freedom?
The answer cannot simply be that they are too large. When the bureau-

cratic form of city government spread across the country in the late nineteenth century, there were only two cities in the United States with over
one hundred thousand people. Even today many cities are as small as Ath-
ens was in classical times.[6]

Instead, the answer must be sought in the fact that our accommodation
to bureaucracy has made it hard to take the prospects of democracy
seriously. Our adjustment to bureaucratic forms has fostered a belief in
their inevitability and, with it, a widespread distrust of democracy. Even
if the size of an entity is small (as in a workplace or small town), even if
the level of general education is high (as in most industrialized countries),
even if solving the problem in question plainly requires the kind of judgment expertise cannot possibly provide (as is true for most policy making),
democracy is treated as not an option. People are too lazy or too busy, it
is said; they won't participate. People are too stupid; they won't know
what to do. Meetings will go on forever; no decisions will ever be made.
And, besides, people *want* to have experts make decisions for them; they
don't even *want* democracy. These antidemocratic sentiments—like
countless others—are endlessly repeated, although they are rarely based
on empirical evidence or a theoretical explanation of the reasons for different levels of popular participation. They are also not likely to be based on
personal experience. They are usually voiced by people who have had no
personal experience whatsoever engaging in collective decision making on
an issue of public policy. Rather than reflecting an insight into "human
nature," as is often claimed, these sentiments are an expression of antidemocratic prejudice. This form of prejudice shares many of the ingredients classically associated with other kinds of prejudice: the objects of the
prejudice are often depicted as lazy, ignorant, and appropriately kept in
their place. And it thrives in an environment in which experience with
democracy is rare.

We cannot overcome this attitude simply by changing our minds. Nor
is a reduction in the size of decision-making units enough, standing alone.
There must also be a genuine transfer of power to cities. No one is likely
to participate in the decision making of an entity of any size unless that
participation will make a difference in his or her life. Power and participation are inextricably linked: a sense of powerlessness tends to produce
apathy rather than participation, while the existence of power encourages
those able to participate in its exercise to do so. State control of city decision making has thus not only prevented cities from experimenting in
democratic forms of organization but has helped make experiments seem
less appealing. City power would not ensure the success of efforts to increase the level of popular participation, but it would be an important
ingredient of it. Indeed, a powerful city is desirable, in my view, only if

it becomes transformed, modifying not only its ability to foster greater participation in its decision making but also its ability to engender more openness to unfamiliar strangers.

The Role of Law in City Powerlessness

Nothing in the development of modern political thought necessitated the place that cities now occupy in American society. On the contrary, over time political thinkers have adopted changing, often contradictory, answers to the persistent question of the proper role of cities in social life.[7] The principal puzzle that has affected the extent of cities' power has been their relationship to the state.[8] Cities have been seen both as vehicles useful for the exercise of the coercive power of the state and, like voluntary associations, as groups of individuals seeking to control their own lives free of state domination. Cities, in other words, have been understood both as creations of the state and as creations of the individuals who lived within them. Cities have therefore failed to fit neatly into the development of modern political theory, which for centuries has sought to make a distinction between the actions of the government and the actions of individuals—to make, in short, the public/private distinction.[9]

Gradually, however, a process of working out a solution to the status of cities has been developed, a process that has, to a large extent, been carried on by the formulation of legal doctrine. For centuries courts have wrestled with cases requiring them to decide whether cities are an exercise of individual freedom or a threat to that freedom analogous to that posed by the state. In the seventeenth century, for example, England's highest court was asked to decide whether city charters could be revoked by the king. To resolve this question, the court had to decide whether cities threatened individual rights, thereby justifying centralized control of their charters, or protected individual rights, thereby justifying protection from the king. As I describe in the next chapter, the court's answer was to subject the city to centralized control; indeed, the general answer developed by the legal system has been to identify the city with the state and to conceive of it as a threat to freedom. But legal theory is still working out the exact relationship between the city, on the one hand, and the state and the individual, on the other. Thus it is now settled law, for the purposes of the Fourteenth and Tenth Amendments to the federal Constitution, that cities are just like state governments. They can no more deny due process or the equal protection of the laws than can the states, and they are just as entitled as the states to Tenth Amendment protections from excessive federal control. But it is equally well settled, for the purposes of federal antitrust law and the Eleventh Amendment to the federal Constitution (dealing with sover-

eign immunity), that cities are not states. Unlike states, they are not ex-
empt from federal antitrust laws or entitled to constitutional sovereign
immunity; indeed, for antitrust purposes, they are treated like private corporations.[10] Even today, then, courts are in the business of classifying cities
within the public/private distinction. To understand how these decisions
are being made, we must explore the history of the city as a legal concept.

2

A Legal History of Cities

THE BEST WAY to understand a legal concept is to analyze it the way a geologist looks at the landscape. For a geologist, any portion of land at any given time is "the condensed history of the ages of the Earth and a nexus of relationships."[1] The current legal status of cities is similarly the remnant of a historical process, so that its meaning cannot be grasped until the elements of that process, and their relationships, are understood. This chapter is an effort to describe how people at different points in history have interpreted the question of city power—that is, the proper relationship of the city, the individual, and the state. Each attempt to resolve the question has had a cumulative effect on our current understanding of how to think about the issue; each stage in the process has added to, not replaced, its predecessor.

A brief road map might be helpful before we begin. I turn first to the medieval town, not only because it is the ancestor of the modern city but also because it presents a conception of a status for cities that has been the persistent focus of attack ever since. The medieval town was a corporate entity intermediate between the state and the individual, an entity that was not classifiable as political or economic, as public or private. It was understood instead as enabling the exercise of the power of groups, as distinguished from that of the individual or the state, in social life. The group that medieval towns empowered consisted of merchants, and they were able to resist centralized control because they exercised economic power, and because the towns, as corporations, had rights protected against the king. Over time, the nature of these rights became the subject of a major controversy between cities and the king, a controversy that was resolved by the Glorious Revolution of 1688. The question presented in this dispute required determining the rights of all corporations—the entities that exercised economic power in society—when challenged by the king. The outcome increased the protection of corporate rights, and thus city rights, against the king. But cities' relationship to the legislature remained unsettled. Moreover, the task of defining that relationship remained difficult because, like all corporations, cities continued to be understood as entities intermediate between the state and the individual. In the nineteenth century, American courts created a public/private distinction for corporations in order to define the relationship between corporations and the legislature. Thus, as in England, the legal system in America formulated the rights of cities in the process of establishing the general relationship between corporations and the state. American courts used the public/private distinction to solve the difficulty generated by the intermediate nature of corporations by dividing them into two categories, placing cities in the sphere of the state and private corporations in the sphere of the individual in civil society. For the first time, cities became sharply defined public, political entities, and decisions about the extent of city power came to be understood as establishing the proper role of decentralized political activity within a unified nation with a private economy. The chapter concludes with a discussion of the articulation of the public/private distinction in an important late-nineteenth-century treatise on municipal corporations by John Dillon, and the unsuccessful criticism of that articulation by other writers and by political activists. Despite this criticism, Dillon's insistence on strict state control of city decision making has remained largely intact: it is the basis of the current legal status of cities in American society.

The Medieval Town

Its Status as an Association

Our ideas about the promise and the dangers of local autonomy derive from those that emerged, after the decline of Roman cities, with the revival of European towns in the eleventh century.[2] These medieval towns established a degree of autonomy within their society that has been the goal of advocates of local power and the target of its critics ever since. The autonomy of the medieval town, however, was the autonomy not of a political institution like a modern city but of a complex economic, political, and communal association. Rather than being an artificial entity separate from its inhabitants, the medieval town was a group of people seeking protection against outsiders for the interests of the group as a whole. The merchants who created the towns used them as a means of seeking relief from the multiplicity of jurisdictional claims to which they, and their land, were subject. They were able to gain autonomy by utilizing their growing economic power to make political settlements with others in the society, specifically the king and the nobility. And they achieved a freedom from outside control that was made possible by, and that allowed to be enforced, a strong sense of community within the town. It was this autonomy for the merchants and their ability to establish their own communal rules that were recognized in the legal status of the town.

City autonomy thus meant the autonomy of the merchant class as a group. But the medieval town protected these group rights without distinguishing them from the rights of the individuals within the group. The status of an individual merchant was defined by the rights of the group to which he belonged, namely, the medieval town. As a result, the medieval town had features that for us are unrecognizable: a strict identity between individual interests and the town's interest as a whole, a lack of separation between individual property rights and town sovereignty rights, and a mixed political and economic character. Not only were the interests of the merchants the goal of town autonomy, but they provided the rationale for its functions. The town controlled individual commercial conduct with a thoroughness unmatched in history. It protected the worker from competition and exploitation, regulated labor conditions, wages, prices, and apprenticeships, punished fraud, and asserted the town's interests against neighboring competitors.

It is important that we understand the aspect of "freedom" that was achieved by the autonomy of the medieval town. It was, in essence, the ability of a group of people to be governed at least to some extent by their own rules, free of outside interference. As Fernand Braudel described it, with some exaggeration:

> The medieval city was the classic type of the closed town, a self-sufficient unit, an exclusive Lilliputian native land. Crossing its ramparts was like crossing one of the still serious frontiers in the world today. You were free to thumb your nose at your neighbour from the other side of the barrier. He could not touch you. The peasant who uprooted himself from his land and arrived in the town was immediately another man. He was free—or rather he had abandoned a known and hated servitude for another, not always guessing the extent of it beforehand. But this mattered little. If the town had adopted him, he could snap his fingers when his lord called for him.[3]

In some areas, particularly Italy, Flanders, and Germany, this autonomy allowed the towns to lead a fully separate life for a long time. But even where such a separate life was not achieved, as in England, the structure of the towns provided their inhabitants shelter to pursue, largely on terms defined within the towns, their own economic interests.

This autonomy by no means created the medieval town as an idyllic oasis of freedom in a world of feudal bondage. Internally, often from the outset, the towns were not democratic but hierarchical: they operated under the strict control of an oligarchic elite. Far from achieving communal bliss within the towns, the exercise of hierarchic power (to quote Braudel again) "quickly set in motion their class struggles. Because if the towns were 'communities' as has been said, they were also 'societies' in the modern sense of the word, with their pressures and civil wars: nobles against bourgeois, poor against rich ('thin people,' *popolo magro*, against 'fat people,' *popolo grasso*)."[4] Thus if we could look today at a medieval town, the idea of the town as a community would appear to us largely as a cover for the advancement of particular interests, and the value of town autonomy, although apparent, would be overshadowed by real and potential internal conflicts. But although the conflicts within the town surely were apparent to its inhabitants, they could see an importance and value in the communal association that we do not. We must try to understand how those subjected to the power of others within the town could look at their town, describe it as a community, and defend the importance of its autonomy.

The identification of the individual with the town as a whole was based on the role of the town in the life of its inhabitants. The town defined their place in society, defended them from outsiders, and enabled them to pursue their livelihood. As a result, they felt patriotism and loyalty to the town. (Braudel characterized medieval towns as "the West's first 'fatherlands.' ") In addition, their sense of community was maintained by the complex idea of "city peace":

> [C]ity peace was a law of exception, more severe, more harsh, than that of the country districts. It was prodigal of corporal punishments: hangings, decapitation, castration, amputation of limbs. It applied in all its rigor the *lex talionis*: an eye for an eye, a tooth for a tooth. Its evident purpose was to repress derelictions, through terror. All who entered the gates of the city, whether nobles, freemen or burghers, were equally subject to it. Under it the city was, so to speak, in a permanent state of siege. But in it the city found a potent instrument of unification, because it was superimposed upon the jurisdictions and seigniories which shared the soil; it forced its pitiless regulation on all. More than community of interests and residence, it contributed to make uniform the status of all the inhabitants located within the city walls and to create the middle class. . . . [T]he peace created, among all its members, a permanent solidarity.[5]

This power to discipline its inhabitants did not undermine the town's value as an association because the town's legitimacy, like that of any other group, did not depend on the protection of individuals from collective power. It depended instead on the medieval conception of the role of the individual in society. The medieval idea of city autonomy—the relationship of the town to the rest of society—was itself legitimated by the overall organization of the medieval world.

A classic description of the medieval conception of society is contained in the work of Otto Gierke. According to Gierke, in medieval political thought the relationship within each association was an example, in microcosm, of the relationship between the association and all others in society, and this in turn was understood as a harmony whose individual parts com-

plemented each other as do the parts of the human body. Indeed, each
form of association, like social life and like man himself, was understood
as a diminished copy of the divinely instituted harmony of the universe.
This harmony was not conceptualized as noncoercive collective action or
as individual coordination. No part of society represented the product of
individual agreement; hierarchy was everywhere. God ruled the world, so,
naturally, the king ruled his realm, the lord ruled his manor, the elite of
the town ruled the town, and the father ruled his family. Each organization allowed its members, and the group as a whole, to contribute something to the working of society and to be a constituent part of the harmony of the whole. But no organization required equality of its members
any more than the working of the human body or of the universe itself
requires equality of its parts. Rather than seeking to distinguish the separate interests within the town or to differentiate the town from the rest
of society, medieval political thought sought to analyze their harmonious
unity. Neither the idea of an individual identity separate from the town nor
that of town autonomy separate from others in society required a notion of
opposition between the parts and the whole. Since preserving the integ-
rity of the parts was necessary to preserve the whole, the protection of
town autonomy was thought to enable the town's inhabitants to contribute to the functioning of the society at large. The autonomy of the medieval town cannot be understood, then, in terms of our modern insistence
on separating individual interests from town interests and town interests
from the "state" interests. Instead, the idea of the autonomy of the town
and of its citizens merged; as Frederic Maitland saw in the English medieval borough, the distinctions we recognize as fundamental—between
personal property rights and town sovereignty rights, between the town
as a collection of individuals and the town as a collective whole—were
absent.[6]

The Early Modern Attack on Group Identity

Slowly, however, an entity separate from its membership—the town, as
Maitland put it, with a capital *T*—"struggles into life." This emergence
of the town as an entity with rights and duties independent of, even opposed to, its inhabitants, this creation of the town as "a person," occurred
long before the first corporate charter was granted by King Henry VI in
1439. It grew with the idea, in Maitland's words, that "[t]he 'all' that is
unity will not coincide with, may stand apart from, the 'all' of inhabitants."[7] Only once this was established could the effect of the king's actions
with respect to the towns become distinguishable from its effect on the
towns' citizens. Only then was it possible to conceive of the king's attempt

to control the towns as liberating, and not restricting, the individual. The separation of the individual's interest from town unity, and the increase of the king's power over the town, were thus part of the same process.

The dissolution of the medieval town as an organic association and the accompanying increase in the power of the king over the town were part of the general unraveling of medieval society. A similar process has been traced within medieval rural society. In fact, the creation of modern society can itself be understood, as Gierke saw it, as a progressive dissolution of all unified structures within medieval society—the feudal manor, the medieval town, even the king himself. Instead of seeking to understand the harmonious working of the whole, emerging political thought separated out from each aspect of life an individual interest as contrasted with a group interest and, at the same time, consolidated all elements of social cohesion into the idea of the nation-state. With the development of modern political thought, according to Gierke, "[the] Sovereignty of the State and the Sovereignty of the Individual were steadily on their way towards becoming the two central axioms from which all theories of social structure would proceed, and whose relationship to each other would be the focus of all theoretical controversy." Modern political philosophy thus undermined the vitality of all groups that had held an intermediate position between what we now think of as the sphere of the individual and that of the state. The unity of the church, the feudal manor, and the medieval town dissolved into entities separate from, and opposed to, the interests of their members, and each of them established separate relationships with the emerging nation-state. The king himself became divided into his "individual" and "State" parts, a division "between his private property and the State's property which was under his care."[8]

Much of Gierke's analysis of the development of modern political thought is stated in terms of legal doctrine, particularly the development of the legal status of corporations. The king, the church, the university, and the medieval town were the principal examples of medieval corporations, and many of these institutions were, together with the feudal manor, the principal objects of attack. For Gierke, changing the conception of the corporation was the means by which early modern thinkers undermined the status of these groups. To show how this was done, Gierke contrasts two conceptions of the corporation, the Germanic and the "antique-modern." In the Germanic conception, the corporation is an organic unity that is not reducible to a collection of individuals or to an artificial creation of the state. Rather, its existence is seen as "real in itself." The "antique-modern" conception, on the other hand, views the corporation as merely the sum of its individual members and, simultaneously, as a "fictional person" created by, and therefore subject to, the state. This contrast reflects the distinction that Gierke suggests between the

medieval belief in unity and the fracturing of that unity by modern political theory through a focus on the individual and the state. The movement
from the Germanic to the antique-modern conception of the corporation,
he argues, facilitated the undermining of the corporate entity by the development of individual freedom from corporate unity and of state power
over corporate unity. Entities like the medieval town, "formed and interpreted as a fraternal association," with autonomous power for the unity as
a whole, could gradually become mere locations for individual effort and
mere "creatures of the state."[9]

For early modern thinkers, such as Suarez, Grotius, Bodin, and Hobbes,
the attack on the autonomy of medieval corporations, including the medieval town, was necessary to protect what they considered the vital interests
of individual liberty and of the emerging nation-state. Their perspective
was the predecessor of our own: they sought to eliminate the domination
of individuals within the town by the town oligarchy and to establish the
rule of law over all centers of power. So important was the need to restrict
the towns' control of individual activity and their irresponsible local protectionism that the increase in the power of the nation-state necessary to
achieve these objectives seemed benign. In other contexts, thinkers such
as these viewed increasing the power of the state as a threat to individuals—one interest advanced only at the expense of the other. But increasing
the power of the state over the towns was understood as simultaneously
advancing both state and individual interests. This viewpoint encouraged
early modern thinkers, as it encourages us, to see the eradication of the
power of the towns as a step forward in the progress of freedom. Yet the
defense of the power of the town was itself based on the notion of freedom.
In fact, as we have seen, it was the idea of freedom from feudal restrictions
that was the basis for the creation of the town. Elimination of the town
as an entity intermediate between the state and the individual could,
therefore, threaten the way of life—the freedom—of those protected by
town autonomy. Both the efforts to destroy the town and the efforts to
preserve it were made in the interest of freedom.

The Early Modern Town

Its Relationship to the King

In spite of the efforts to undermine them, the towns retained much of
their autonomy and power, at least until the beginning of the nineteenth
century.[10] The primary explanation for this fact in the case of English
cities, the models for the American law of cities, was the retention of a
major aspect of their medieval identity. The towns remained economic

corporations whose franchises provided protection against control by the king and fracturing by individuals. Commerce was the basic activity of municipal corporations, and the power of the economic elite, which played an increasingly dominant role in the towns, was both the force behind, and the result of, the protection afforded by corporate charters. An understanding of the nature of city autonomy in England prior to the nineteenth century therefore involves an examination of the relationship between this economic elite and the king.

That relationship was one of mutual dependence as well as mutual suspicion. The fact that the towns were controlled by a largely self-perpetuating oligarchy created a conflict between the towns' elite merchants and their craftsmen and commoners, a conflict that dominated the towns' political life. The economic elite was thus forced to seek outside support for their privileges, particularly from the king. The elite also increasingly looked to the king for social advantages and legal protection. The king, for his part, favored control by a small group on whom he could depend for financial and administrative support. This mutuality of interest became a centerpiece of mercantilism. As Perry Anderson describes it:

> Economic centralization, protectionism and overseas expansion aggrandized the late feudal State while they profited the early bourgeoisie. They increased the taxable revenues of the one by providing business opportunities for the other. The circular maxims of mercantilism, proclaimed by the Absolutist State, gave eloquent expression to this provisional coincidence of interests.[11]

Yet the king remained suspicious of the independent power wielded by the economic oligarchy and persistently sought to bring them under his control. They, in turn, resisted royal interference as an inroad on the basic rights of Englishmen, since the liberty of the towns and the protection of freehold interests, such as the corporators' freehold interest in the corporate franchise, had been established by the Magna Carta. The issue of royal power and of corporate freedom was also entangled with another central issue of the time, the relationship between the king and Parliament. From the fourteenth century, municipal corporations were represented in Parliament, where they became a dominant influence. This parliamentary role provided an alternative forum for protecting city interests and made unnecessary the search for the kind of political autonomy asserted by cities elsewhere in Europe. Moreover, since the rural upper classes were themselves developing commercial interests, they tended to align with city interests against the king rather than, as elsewhere, with the king against the cities. Thus the limitations on the king's power with respect to Parliament and with respect to the cities were two aspects of protecting the same interest: that of the commercial class.

The Attack on City Charters

The uneasy alliance between the king and the commercial oligarchy broke down in the late seventeenth century, thereby precipitating royal conflicts with both the cities and Parliament. The dispute with the cities took the form of an attack by the king on their corporate charters, since the charters defined both the power of the corporate elite over ordinary citizens and their relationship to the king. As far back as the thirteenth century, the king had asserted the power to revoke these charters for wrongdoing. The issue became increasingly sensitive, however, because city officials had begun to determine not only the identity of city representatives in Parliament but the identity of the juries upon which the king depended to enforce the law. The question of the status of corporate charters became the focus of what has been called the "most important case in English history," the quo warranto brought in 1682 by Charles II in which he challenged the legitimacy of the corporate status of the city of London.[12] The arguments made in the case are significant because they illustrate how people conceived of the issue of city autonomy near the close of the seventeenth century.

The king, believing that centralized control was necessary to prevent social conflict, asserted the right to revoke the charters of cities and the other economic corporations later formed on the model of the cities, such as the East India Company, the Hudson Bay Company, and some of the American colonies. If their charters could not be forfeited for wrongdoing, they would become "so many commonwealths by themselves, independent of the Crown and in defiance of it." This view of the need for royal power echoed Hobbes:

> Another infirmity of a Common-wealth, is the immoderate greatnesse of a Town, when it is able to furnish out of its own Circuit, the number, and expence of a great Army: As also the great number of Corporations; which are as it were many lesser Common-wealths in the bowels of a greater, like wormes in the entrayles of a naturall man. To which may be added, the Liberty of Disputing against absolute Power, by pretenders to Politicall Prudence; which though bred for the most part in the Lees of the people; yet animated by False Doctrines, are perpetually medling with the Fundamentall Lawes, to the molestation of the Common-wealth. . . .[13]

For the cities, however, corporate power was liberty itself, the corporate charter being evidence of rights vested in the corporation by the king. If the wrongdoing of an individual could be treated as if it were that of the corporation and thus result in the forfeiture of the corporate charter, the vested rights on which the members of the corporation relied would be rendered valueless. In short, the vested rights acquired by the corporate franchise were rights of property and must be protected to ensure the liberty of all Englishmen. This argument anticipated Locke:

> [T]he supreme power cannot take from any man any part of his property without his own consent. For the preservation of property being the end of government, and that for which men enter into society, it necessarily supposes and requires that the people should have property, without which they must be supposed to lose that by entering into society which was the end for which they entered into it; too gross an absurdity for any man to own. Men, therefore, in society having property, they have such a right to the goods, which by the law of the community are theirs, that nobody hath a right to take them, or any part of them, from them without their own consent; without this they have no property at all.[14]

Thus the conflict over whether the city charter was a revocable franchise or a vested right represented, in microcosm, the fundamental split in modern political theory between positivism, the Hobbesian view that individual interests are subordinate to the command of the state, and natural rights theory, the Lockean view that the state reaffirmed, and was limited by, the natural rights of man.

The king's victory in the London case represented a victory for the positivist position and established the legal principle of royal control of the cities for a time. Many other city charters, as well as the charters of some American colonies, were surrendered to Charles II and James II under the threat of further quo warranto proceedings. Yet the royal conflict with the commercial class merely shifted its location to Parliament. Finally, in 1688, the Glorious Revolution ended the Stuart reign. As a result, the London case was reversed, the surrender of other city charters was undone, and the immunity of corporate charters from royal abrogation was reestablished. But the Glorious Revolution did not lead to the adoption of a Lockean protection for corporate rights as we would understand it today. Although the revolution protected corporate charters from the only source then thought to threaten them—the king—it did not resolve the extent of Parliament's power over those charters. The revolution was a victory for both Parliament and the cities: increasing the power of one secured the interests of the other. Hence one could support the victory for both Parliament and the cities without conceiving of Parliament as exercising "state" power that could invade corporate "rights." Almost a century later, William Blackstone shared the same view. He did not see Parliament as a threat to corporate freedom, even though it had absolute power to dissolve corporations, because, he argued, Parliament itself considered corporate charters inviolate.[15]

At the time of the American Revolution, then, corporate liberty was protected against royal attack, but the extent of its vulnerability if Parliament became hostile remained unresolved. The resolution of this issue—the confrontation of legislative power and corporate rights—produced for the first time a legal distinction between public and private corporations. Until the early nineteenth century, no such distinction between cities and other mercantile entities chartered by the king existed either in England or in America. Neither Blackstone nor Stuart Kyd, who authored the first treatise on corporations in 1793, mentioned the idea of public and private corporations.[16] We turn, therefore, to the question of how in America the public/private distinction became decisive in resolving the issue of legislative control over corporations, a resolution that left public corporations in the Hobbesian sphere of command and private corporations in the Lockean sphere of rights. Before this question may be answered, however, a preliminary issue must be explored: why were American cities even viewed as corporations for purposes of determining the scope of their rights against the state?

The Early American City

Its Corporate Status

Since the important English cities were corporations indistinguishable as a legal matter from any other commercial corporation, English law naturally treated the question of the power of cities as being synonymous with that of the power of corporations. In colonial America, however, most cities were not corporations at all. Nevertheless, the issue of city power was resolved in America as in England in the form of the question of corporate power. Why American cities were treated as corporations is a puzzle that deserves further scrutiny.[17]

Prior to the Revolution, there were only about twenty incorporated cities in America. In New England, where local autonomy was most fully established, no city possessed a corporate franchise; the power of the New England towns was based instead on their role as the vital organizing unit in social life. Although originally subordinate to the colonial government, the towns increasingly established their power on the basis of the direct popular sovereignty exercised in town meetings. By the late eighteenth century, colonial legislatures were far from being considered a threat to town liberty—a role assigned to the English king and his colonial representatives—since these legislatures were composed of representatives of the towns who were under explicit instructions to represent the towns' interests. Proposals to turn New England towns into corporations were denounced as attempts to weaken the towns by substituting elitist English boroughs for direct democracy.

In the South, Charles Town, South Carolina, was the only major city. Although it had "many of the characteristics of a city-state," it too was not a corporation. Its power was based not on town meetings as in New England but on the influence of its merchants. These merchants dominated both the colonial legislature and the complex of organizations that ran the town. In 1723, Charles Town successfully resisted attempts to transform the city into a corporation. Even in the mid-Atlantic region, in which incorporated cities were most numerous, the corporation was not always the basis of a town's governance. For example, in Philadelphia, one of the two major corporate cities in colonial America, special purpose commissions and voluntary associations progressively assumed duties previously entrusted to the corporation, which was considered archaic and aristocratic. By the late eighteenth century, the Philadelphia corporation was "a club of wealthy merchants, without much purse, power, or popularity."[18]

In general, then, colonial towns did not have the formal corporate structure of the English cities. Instead, they bore a resemblance to the kind of associations that created the medieval towns, and thus their power could have been perceived as based on the freedom of association rather than on corporate rights. Both medieval and colonial towns were established by people who broke away from existing social restraints, and who formed relatively closed societies with new social structures. Moreover, the relationship in colonial America between the aspects of association represented by the town and the aspects of association represented by the family and by religion was often quite close. Conceiving of colonial towns as associations was, therefore, by no means impossible. As in the case of medieval towns, however, we must be careful not to confuse the concept of association with that of democracy or equality. Although some towns operated on the basis of popular participation (at least for those then considered eligible), hierarchical relationships existed in most colonial towns, just as in the family and the church.

Despite the evidence that the towns were associations, they were treated by the courts as if they were corporations. We can only speculate why the towns were viewed in this manner. One possible explanation is that, at the time, many people saw no radical distinction between a corporation and an association. Even colonial religious bodies often considered themselves corporations, their corporate nature seen as affirming and strengthening their associational ties. While from a lawyer's point of view a corporation could be formed only by a grant of a corporate charter from the Crown, an alternative conception was that a corporation existed whenever a group possessed and exercised power. It was thus not dispositive to say that the towns had no corporate charters, since medieval cities had also been considered corporations long before they had received charters. Many medieval cities—London being the most prominent—became corporations by prescription rather than by grant because they had existed as corporations "time whereof the memory of man runneth not to the contrary."[19]

The important point about colonial towns and cities was that they exercised power as a group: as a group they had rights; as a group they had powers. Such an association would be a corporation, or "quasi-corporation," since the corporation was the dominant way of asserting group authority and protecting group rights. The towns were "bodies politic," and all bodies politic—English cities, colonial towns, churches, the states themselves—seemed to be corporations. If this hypothesis about the creation of the corporate status of colonial American cities is true, it would explain how historians could describe eighteenth-century New England towns as corporations long before the first charter was granted.[20] Whatever the explanation, the rejection of corporate charters by most early American towns prevented their transformation into the kind of closed corporation that governed English cities or Philadelphia, but it did not prevent them from being conceived of as corporations.

The City's Relationship to the Legislature

The question of the appropriate extent of legislative power over the cities was therefore decided as part of the larger issue of the desired extent of legislative power over all corporations, whether cities or other mercantile bodies. In late-eighteenth-century America, the larger issue was deeply troubling. On the one hand, corporate rights had been protected from the king by the Glorious Revolution; these rights, once recognized, seemed to deserve protection from legislative infringement as well. America had rejected the English notion of legislative supremacy in favor of the Lockean concept of a legislative power limited by natural rights. Legislative denial of these rights could be tolerated no more than executive denial. On the other hand, corporations exercised power in society that seemed to limit the rights of individuals to earn their livelihood, and this power, wielded by an aristocratic elite to protect their monopolistic privileges, needed to be controlled by popular—that is, legislative—action. Thus while the exercise of legislative power was perceived as a threat to corporate rights, the exercise of corporate rights risked the curtailment of legislative power thought necessary to protect the welfare of the people.

On a deeper level, the corporation represented an anomaly to political thinkers who envisioned the world as divided between individual rightholders and state power, the ruled in conflict with the ruler. The corporation exhibited traits of both poles: it was part ruled and part ruler, both an association of individuals and an entity with state-granted power. It thus was a feudal remnant, a vestige of the medieval town. Its continued existence demonstrated that the effort to undermine the intermediate forms of medieval social life had not succeeded. Even more troublesome, the corporation was in some respects a protector of, while in other ways a threat to, both individual rights and the state. In one capacity, the corporation not only protected individual property rights but also served as a useful vehicle for the exercise of state power. Yet at the same time the corporation, like the medieval town, restricted the freedom of individual enterprise and operated as a miniature republic, impervious to state control. The dilemma created by the corporation, then, could be solved neither by retention of its present form nor by abolition in favor of individual rights, as urged by Adam Smith, or in favor of the state, as advocated by Hobbes.[21]

The Adoption of the Public/Private Distinction

The Development of the Distinction

To solve the problem created by the intermediate status of the corporation, early-nineteenth-century legal doctrine divided the corporation into two different entities, one assimilated to the role of an individual in society and the other assimilated to the role of the state. The corporation as an entity that was simultaneously a right-holder and a power-wielder thus disappeared. In its place emerged the private corporation, which was an individual right-holder, and the public corporation, an entity that was identified with the state. The very purpose of the distinction was to ensure that some corporations, called "private," would be protected against domination by the state, and that others, called "public," would be subject to such domination. In this way, the corporate anomaly was resolved so that corporations, like the rest of society, were divided into individuals and the state.[22]

This public/private distinction for corporations was not purely a legal invention. The distinction had been generally emerging since the American Revolution, and both the newly created identities, public and private, were the product of a pervasive attack on the exclusive privileges and oligarchic power wielded by corporations. The attack that established the "private" character of business corporations developed as their number expanded, rising from only eight in 1780 to several hundred by the time of the critical *Dartmouth College* opinion in 1819.[23] Even though these business corporations were public service enterprises, such as canals, bridges, water supply companies, and banking enterprises, their creation raised troubling questions concerning the amount of protection afforded their investors and participants. As the courts gradually developed protections for the investors' property, pressure mounted on the legislature to extend the opportunities for incorporation from a favored few to the more general population. Yet as the legislature yielded to this drive for more incorporations, the demand for protection of property rights for those involved itself increased. As Oscar and Mary Handlin note, "The process which multiplied the institution [of the corporation] and the unfoldment of its private character reacted upon each other in a reciprocal, accumulative fashion. Every new grant strengthened the grounds for considering it private; every new affirmation of privateness strengthened the hands of those who demanded new grants."[24] This process gathered momentum, culminating in the middle of the nineteenth century in the Jacksonian effort to pass general incorporation laws, thus allowing the "privilege" of incorporation to be exercised by all.

The attack on the exclusiveness of city corporations worked in another direction. With the sovereignty of the people becoming the emerging basis of republican politics, and with population growth fueling a need to add new functions to city corporations, the pressure for state legislation to expand participation in corporate governance mounted. The most important closed corporation in America, that of Philadelphia, was abolished by radical republican legislators in 1776, and it was replaced several years later with a modified, more broadly based, corporation. This attack on the privileged control of city corporations and the simultaneous expansion of participation in corporate decision making made it increasingly difficult to separate the city corporation from the people as a whole, that is, to view city corporate rights as distinct from the rights of the public at large. The movement toward what was then considered universal suffrage, in the 1820s and 1830s, helped confirm the emerging public character of city corporations, thus setting them in contrast to "private" business corporations.

The Protection of Property

Despite these developments, American courts in the early nineteenth century had great difficulty in establishing the public/private distinction for corporations. All corporations continued to have similar characteristics. Corporations, whether cities or mercantile entities, were chartered only to further public purposes, and many of their functions overlapped. All corporations were in one sense created by individuals and, in another sense, created by the state through the award of the franchise. Many mercantile corporations wielded the same powers as cities, such as eminent domain, while many cities received their income from the same sources as mercantile corporations, primarily commerce and trade. Both cities and mercantile corporations served to protect the private investments of individual founders and allowed those active in their governance a large degree of self-determination. Many cities and mercantile corporations were controlled by an elite, and consequently both were subject to popular attack. Finally, cities and mercantile corporations alike could be viewed as associations of individuals organized to achieve commercial ends. In short, all corporations wielded power and all corporations protected rights. The concepts of power and rights, so fully merged in the medieval town, had not yet been segregated into their public and private identities. In determining where to draw the public/private distinction for corporations, the courts first had to decide what was important to protect against state power. In *Trustees of Dartmouth College v. Woodward*, decided in 1819, the United States Supreme Court gave its response to this question, an answer that came straight from Locke: what needed protection was property. The scope of property rights divided private from public corporations, private corporations being those founded by individual contributions of property, and public corporations being those founded by the government without such individual contributions.

Having decided the importance of property rights, the Court then sought to determine the status of cities under the public/private distinction. While three major opinions were delivered in the case, Justice Story, who had four years earlier first made the public/private distinction for corporations in a Supreme Court opinion, presented the most complete discussion of the issue:

> Another division of corporations is into public and private. Public corporations are generally esteemed such as exist for public political purposes only, such as towns, cities, parishes, and counties; and in many respects they are so, although they involve some private interests; but strictly speaking, public corporations are such only as are founded by the government for public purposes, where the whole interests belong also to the government.[25]

This passage is ambiguous. Justice Story may have been arguing that the critical distinction between private and public corporations was whether they were founded by individuals or "founded by the government for public purposes, where the whole interests belong . . . to the government." This seems close to the positions taken in the case by both Chief Justice Marshall and Justice Washington. Only if the corporation were completely a state creation, Justice Washington argued, would there be a diminished need to protect property rights from state domination; protection of rights would be unnecessary if there were but one party, the state, involved in the foundation of the corporation. Yet if that were the definition of public corporations, most cities could not be public corporations: most were not founded by the government, nor did they belong wholly to the government. Alternatively, Justice Story may have accepted what was "generally esteemed" at the time, if not "strictly speaking" true: that all cities were public corporations. He twice referred to "towns, cities, and counties" as examples of public corporations. Which of these positions Justice Story held with regard to the place of cities within the public/private distinction is unclear. Moreover, the notion of property rights could not, in itself, distinguish cities from other mercantile corporations. Many cities possessed property contributed by individual founders, and mercantile corporations could readily be created by governments for their own purposes. In fact, Justice Story recognized in *Dartmouth College* that cities possessed certain property rights, although he did not indicate what, if any, additional legal protection from legislative interference cities should receive.

Seventeen years later in his *Commentaries on American Law*, Chancellor Kent offered his own view of the status of cities within the public/private distinction:

> Public corporations are such as are created by the government for political purposes, as counties, cities, towns and villages; they are invested with subordinate legislative powers to be exercised for local purposes connected with the public good, and such powers are subject to the control of the legislature of the state. They may also be empowered to take or hold private property for municipal uses, and such property is invested with the security of other private rights.[26]

In this passage, Chancellor Kent apparently rejected the notion that, in order for an entity to constitute a public corporation, the "whole interest" must belong to the government. He simply asserted that cities were "created by the government," thus denying their actual history both in England and in America. Having taken that step, Kent then divided city authority into two parts: legislation for the public good, and the possession of property for municipal uses. Of these, only city property received protection from state control. Just as public and private corporations are distinguished by the need to protect private property, cities themselves became bifurcated by the same need—self-determination was retained only for the protection of their private property. It is this view that became, and remains, the law concerning the status of cities in the United States.

The Subordination of the City to the State

It is by no means self-explanatory why, once corporate property rights were protected, early-nineteenth-century writers like Chancellor Kent seemed to think it obvious that the other functions of cities would be subordinate to state power. Cities, like other corporations, had never based their resistance to state control simply on the protection of property. Freedom of association and the exercise of self-government had also been values protected by the defense of the corporation. It did not follow from the need to protect property that property alone needed protection, and that these other values could be sacrificed to state domination. Even at the time, these other values were seen as part of the definition of liberty, their importance being most clearly articulated in the defense of state power against federal control encapsulated in the doctrine of federalism. Indeed, the subordination of cities to the state turned the political world as it then existed upside down. New England towns had controlled state legislatures since prior to the Revolution, and the move in other sections of the country to end aristocratic city governance in favor of democracy was not made with the intention of establishing state control over cities. Nor was the subservience of cities to the state inevitable. The proper relationship of city to state was a hotly contested political issue. Some argued that the sovereignty of the people required control at the local level, but others feared the power of democratic cities. Aristotle, Montesquieu, and Rousseau could be invoked in favor of power at the local level, while Madison and Hume could be cited to show the danger of local self-government.[27] The fact that legal theorists could classify cities as public corporations and thereby subject them to state control thus requires an explanation.

In seeking to understand why cities became subordinate to state power, I will not seek to isolate some factor as the "cause" of this change in city status. I will suggest instead how an early-nineteenth-century thinker could have conceived of state control of cities as a defense, rather than as a restriction, of freedom. Such a thinker could acknowledge city rights, once the cities became synonymous with the people within them, only if he were willing to recognize the right of association and self-determination for any group of people, however large. This recognition would threaten many other important values. It would limit the nation's ability to establish a unified political system under the federal Constitution, thereby preventing the needed centralization of authority and perpetuating the idea that the nation was merely a loose federation of localities. Moreover, these groups, particularly small groups, could be seen as "factions" dangerous to the individuals within them, inhibiting the individual's free development and threatening his property rights. In other words, recognizing the rights of the city as an exercise of the freedom of association would frustrate the interests both of the state and of individuals. Recognizing the rights of the city as an association would thus bring to the surface what political theorists sought to deny: that corporations represented the continuation of the group rights of the medieval town, protecting both the associational and the property rights of their members. Recognition of city rights would also bring to the surface the conflict between the values of association and of property rights themselves, a conflict that had been hidden by the fact that both values had traditionally been protected by the corporate form. Prior to the emergence of the public/private distinction, there was no difference between a corporation's property rights and its rights of group self-government. But now group self-government—or popular sovereignty—seemed a threat to property rights, and property rights seemed a necessary limit to popular sovereignty. Any recognition of the rights of the city would therefore require the courts to choose between associational rights and property rights in particular cases, rather than simply protecting property rights against the power of "governmental" collective action. All these problems seemed to disappear, however, if recognition of the rights of cities were avoided.

The amount of emphasis to put on the fear of democratic power in explaining the judicial decision to limit the power of cities is a matter of conjecture. Such a fear plainly existed, even in the minds of such champions of local power as Jefferson and Tocqueville. While Jefferson saw towns as the "elementary republics" of the nation that must be preserved so that "the voice of the whole people would be fairly, fully, and peaceably expressed . . . by the common reason" of all citizens, he also saw them as objects to be feared: "The mobs of great cities add just so much to the support of pure government, as sores do to the strength of the human body." For Tocqueville, "the strength of free peoples resides in the local community," giving them both the "spirit of liberty" and the ability to withstand the "tyranny of the majority." But he also thought that the size of American cities and the nature of their inhabitants were so threatening to the future of the republic that they required "an armed force which, while remaining subject to the wishes of the national majority, is independent of the peoples of the towns and capable of suppressing their excesses." This vision of cities as the home of "mobs," the working class, immigrants, and, finally, racial minorities, is a theme that runs throughout much of nineteenth- and twentieth-century thought. Chancellor Kent's own fears of the democratic cities were certainly no secret.[28]

Yet one need not rely on the assertion that the subordination of cities was the product of unwillingness to protect the cities' rights of association and fear of democratic power. Since the issue of city power was decided as part of the issue of corporate power, the threatening ideas associated with the rights of association did not need to be brought to consciousness. It is for this reason that the classification of American cities as corporations mattered. It can be understood as helping to obscure the notion that associational rights were being affected in the process of defining the laws governing city rights. No rights of association needed to be articulated when the rights of "private" corporations were discussed, since property rights were sufficient to protect them against state power. There was also nothing that required rights of association to be imagined when the subordination of "public" corporations was discussed. Yet if no rights of association were recognized, cities, increasingly deprived of their economic character—the basis of their power for hundreds of years—had little defense against the reallocation of their power to the individual and to the state. There was nothing left that seemed to demand protection from state control.

The developments in legal doctrine that led to the public/private distinction for corporations did not immediately alter the allocation of power between American states and cities. In fact, prior to the 1850s, local autonomy remained largely intact. The impetus for the assertion of state political power to curb local autonomy finally came when the desire to restrict city activity in favor of private activity increased. In light of the new conception of public and private activities, the investment by cities in business enterprises no longer seemed an appropriate "public" function, and local regulation of a city's business community seemed to invade the "private sphere." Hence state control over these city activities was invoked. But state control of cities during this period was by no means limited to the assurance of a "laissez-faire" policy designed to prevent both cities and states, as governments, from intervening in the private sector. Much state legislation compelled the cities to raise and spend money for state-supported causes, including the promotion of economic enterprise. Other state legislation—so-called ripper legislation—simply sought to transfer control of the city government to state-appointed officials. For a wide variety of purposes, state power to control cities could be exercised, and was exercised, as a matter of law.[29]

The Modern Law of Municipal Corporations

Dillon's Treatise

The legal doctrine that cities are subject to state authority was enthusiastically endorsed by John Dillon, who in 1872 wrote the first and most important American treatise on municipal corporations.[30] Dillon did not seek to disguise the values he thought important in framing the law for municipal corporations. In speeches, law review articles, and books, Dillon eloquently defended the need to protect private property from attack and indicated his reservations about the kind of democracy then practiced in the cities.[31] It would be a mistake, however, to read Dillon's defense of strict state control of cities as simply a crude effort to advance the interests of the rich or of private corporations at the expense of the poor inhabitants of cities. Instead, it is more plausible to interpret Dillon as a forerunner of the Progressive tradition: he sought to protect private property not only against abuse by democracy but also against abuse by private economic power. To do so, he advocated an objective, rational government, staffed by the nation's elite—a government strong enough to curb the excesses of corporate power and at the same time help those who deserved help. It is important to understand how Dillon could consider state control of cities as a major ingredient in accomplishing these objectives.

According to Dillon, a critical impediment to the development of a government dedicated to the public good was the intermingling of the public and the private sectors. Strict enforcement of a public/private distinction, he thought, was essential both to protect government from the threat of domination by private interests and to protect the activities of the private economy from being unfairly influenced by government intervention. Moreover, to ensure its fully "public" nature, government had to be organized so that it could attract to power those in the community best able to govern. Class legislation in favor of either the rich or the poor had to be avoided—neither a government of private greed nor one of mass ignorance could be tolerated. Instead, it was the role of the best people to assume responsibility by recognizing and fulfilling their communal obligations: "It is a duty of perpetual obligation on the part of the strong to take care of the weak, of the rich to take care of the poor." This vision pervades Dillon's work on municipal corporations. From his perspective, cities presented problems that seemed almost "inherent" in their nature. By merging the public and private spheres, cities had extravagantly invested in private businesses, performing functions "better left to private enterprise." As both a state and federal judge, Dillon saw firsthand the problems engendered by municipal financing of railroads. He therefore advocated constitutional limitations and restriction of the franchise to taxpayers to prevent such an expenditure of money.[32]

At the same time, Dillon believed that all of the functions properly undertaken by cities should be considered "public." He therefore criticized the courts for contributing to the division of city activities into public and private spheres. For half a century, courts had distinguished the city's governmental functions, which were subject to absolute state power, from its proprietary functions, which received the constitutional protection afforded to rights of private property. While conceding that such a distinction was "highly important" in municipal corporation law, Dillon found a city's retention of any private identity "difficult exactly to comprehend." Since a city was by definition created by the state, "which breathed into it the breath of life," there seemed nothing private about it at all. Most troubling of all, according to Dillon, cities were not managed by those "*best fitted* by their intelligence, business experience, capacity, and moral character." Their management was "too often both *unwise* and *extravagant*." A major change in city government was therefore needed to achieve a fully public city government dedicated to the common good.[33]

But how could this be achieved? To Dillon, the answer seemed to lie in state control of cities and in judicial supervision of that control. State control, though political, was purely public, and the "best fitted" could more likely be attracted to its government. Moreover, enforcement of the rule of law could play a role, since law was "the beneficence of civil society acting by rule, in its nature . . . opposed to all that [was] fitful, capricious, unjust, partial or destructive." The state and the law working together could thus curb municipal abuse by rigorously enforcing the public/private distinction. In his treatise, Dillon could not have more broadly phrased the extent of state power over city functions. State power "is supreme and transcendent: it may erect, change, divide, and even abolish, at pleasure, as it deems the public good to require." In addition to legislative control, he argued for a major role for the courts:

> The courts, too, have duties, the most important of which is to require these corporations, in all cases, to show a plain and clear grant for the authority they assume to exercise; to *lean against constructive powers*, and, with firm hands, to hold them and their officers within chartered limits.

Once all these steps were taken, Dillon argued, the cities' governance could properly be left to democratic control.[34]

These days, it is hard fully to comprehend Dillon's confidence in noblesse oblige and in the expectation that state and judicial control would help ensure the attainment by cities of an unselfish public good. The late-nineteenth-century legislature now seems as unwise and extravagant as the late-nineteenth-century city, and the contemporary definition of law is somewhat more restrained than Dillon's. The important point, however, is that the legal doctrines emphasized by Dillon—state control of cities, restriction of cities to "public" functions, and strict construction of city powers—are not necessarily tied to his vision of society. While for Dillon the law of cities and the goals of public policy formed a coherent whole, he stated the law so broadly and categorically that it could simply be extracted from its context and applied generally. Dillon's vision of society may be gone forever, but his statement of the law of municipal corporations, stripped of its ideological underpinnings, largely remains intact. For example, in the current edition of his treatise, Professor Antieau's articulation of the subservience of cities to state power (absent specific state constitutional protection for cities) is no less emphatic than Dillon's in 1872. His emphasis upon the strict construction required of grants of power is simply a paraphrase of the so-called Dillon's Rule. He too criticizes the public/private distinction within municipal corporation law as "difficult to draw," although, like Dillon, he has no difficulty with the distinction between public and private corporations themselves. Only his statement of the law of what are now called public utilities seems more accepting than Dillon's.[35]

Attempts to Establish a "Right to Local Self-Government"

Dillon's thesis did not go unchallenged at the time. The major challenge was launched by Judge Thomas Cooley, only three years after he published his celebrated *Treatise on Constitutional Limitations.* In a concurring opinion in *People ex rel. LeRoy v. Hurlbut,* Cooley denied the existence of absolute state supremacy over cities. Relying on American colonial history and on the importance of political liberty in the definition of freedom, he argued that local government was a matter of "absolute right," a right protected by an implied restriction on the powers of the legislature under the state constitution. Amasa Eaton advanced the same thesis in a series of articles entitled "The Right to Local Self-Government." Eaton canvassed English and American history to demonstrate that this "right to local self-government" existed prior to state incorporations and could not be subjected to state restriction.[36]

The most extensive rebuttal to Dillon was published in 1911 by Eugene McQuillin in his multivolume treatise, *The Law of Municipal Corporations.* In an exhaustive survey, McQuillin traced the historical development of municipal corporations and found the essential theme to be a right to local self-government. He rejected the suggestion that cities were created by the state, arguing that "[s]uch [a] position ignores well established, historical facts easily ascertainable." McQuillin strongly criticized courts that failed to uphold the right of local self-government:

> The judicial decisions denying the right of local self-government without express constitutional guaranty, reject the rule of construction that all grants of power are to be interpreted in the light of the maxims of Magna Carta, or rather the development of English rights and governmental powers prior to that time; that is, the common law transmuted into our constitutions and laws. They ignore in toto the fact that local self-government does not owe its origin to constitutions and laws. . . . They disregard the fact that it is a part of the liberty of a community, an expression of community freedom, the heart of our political institutions. They refuse to concede, therefore, that it is a right in any just sense beyond unlimited state control, but rather it is nothing more than a privilege, to be refused or granted in such measure as the legislative agents of the people for the time being determine.

McQuillin sought to buttress his argument by inventing a new rationale for the public/private distinction within municipal corporation law, the distinction that had so confused other writers. There was a general consensus, McQuillin noted, that absolute state power could be exerted only over a city's "public functions." Those functions, he argued, were those that in fact had been given the city by the state. Since the justification for state supremacy depends on the idea of state creation, state control must be limited to those things so created. Powers not derived from legislative action must therefore be "private" and subject to the same constitutional protection as other private rights. The power of the locality that historically was exercised prior to a state charter—the right to local self-government—was, then, a "private" right and could not be subject to state supremacy.[37]

History has not been kind to the Cooley-Eaton-McQuillin thesis. In a later edition of his treatise, Dillon denied the theory's usefulness and noted its lack of judicial acceptance. In a similar vein, Howard Lee McBain, a noted municipal law authority of the time, argued that most courts had properly rejected the right of local self-government. In discounting the thesis, McBain seized upon the weak links in the way the proponents framed the right. He denounced the idea of an "implied limitation" on legislative power as dangerous and unworkable. He argued that even if the right to local self-government were a common law right, it would not therefore be beyond the legislative power to change the common law. He also denied that there was in fact a historical right to self-government, at least if interpreted as the right to democratic, popular control of local officials. McBain's arguments were cleverly aimed at the phrasing, and not the substance, of the Cooley-Eaton-McQuillin thesis. The proponents of the thesis could have responded that the power of public corporations was a "liberty" interest expressly protected by the Due Process Clause in the same way that the "property" interests of private corporations were protected. They could also have explained that this liberty interest was not the democratic control of corporations as understood in the nineteenth century but the kind of local autonomy all corporations had exercised before the ideas of property and sovereignty were separated in the late eighteenth and early nineteenth centuries. They did not make these arguments. But it would not have mattered if they had. By the time of McBain's attack, courts were not willing to question the distinction between public and private corporations—even Cooley, Eaton, and McQuillin did not challenge that distinction. The idea that state power over cities was different from state power over corporations had become an automatically accepted part of legal thought.[38]

In 1923, William Munro, in his classic work, *The Government of American Cities*, stated that Dillon's position on state control of cities was "so well recognized that it is not nowadays open to question." McQuillin's thesis, on the other hand, has been substantially revised even in his own treatise by its current editor:

> [U]nless granted by the state constitution, the general rule is that a municipal corporation has no inherent right of self-government that is independent of legislative control. . . . Distinction should be made between the right of local self-government as inherent in the people, and the right as inherent in a municipal corporation; while as to the people, the right has quite commonly been assumed to exist, but as to the municipal corporation the right must be derived, either from the people through the constitution or from the legislature.

No other serious academic challenge to the Dillon thesis has ever been made.[39]

There was, however, a political challenge to state control of cities, launched in the late nineteenth century under the rallying cry of "home rule." Once state invasion of city authority became a common occurrence, it became apparent that cities were not faring well under the doctrine that purported to give private enterprises rights and public bodies power. Although by 1886 private corporations had become "persons" whose rights were constitutionally protected,[40] public corporations no longer had the sovereign power they once exercised. Their remaining power derived only from specific state authorizations, and even these were strictly construed by the courts. To reverse the cities' loss of self-government, late-nineteenth- and early-twentieth-century reformers proposed the amendment of state constitutions, and, in fact, they achieved the enactment of a wide variety of constitutional amendments designed to prevent the invasion of city autonomy. But these constitutional amendments have failed to achieve their objective. The reason for this failure lies in the legal system's continuing unwillingness to grant autonomy to an intermediate entity that appears to threaten the interests of both the state and the individual.

One common constitutional amendment, for example, required states to pass only "general," rather than "special" or "local," legislation. This requirement was designed to curb the states' ability to control a single city's decision making by legislation. Yet if the states' ability to deal with substate, or local, problems were prohibited altogether, individuals could be subjected to irresponsible local action or neglect without any means of correcting it. Some targeted legislation thus seems necessary to protect not only the states' interests but individual rights. As a result, these constitutional restrictions have been interpreted to permit "general" legislation aimed at a class of cities, even if the "class" is composed of only one city (even, in fact, if it is a class of cities defined as having a population between 29,946 and 29,975). Restrictions on special legislation have, in other words, become no more than weak equal protection clauses, requiring only that the state have a rational basis for its classification of cities. The weakness of these clauses stems from the fact that there is nothing suspect about state restrictions on city decision making and nothing fundamental about the invasion of local autonomy. Without one or the other of these ingredients, constitutional protections of equality are usually ineffective in limiting state power.[41]

Another important state constitutional restriction granted cities "home rule," meaning both the ability to enact legislation without specific state permission and the ability to prevent state invasions of local autonomy. At times, these home rule amendments have been useful in expanding the cities' ability to exercise their powers by seeking general, rather than detailed, state authorization. But they have not successfully created an area of local autonomy protected from state control. Local self-determination has been thought appropriate only for local matters, and state courts have therefore had to decide whether issues are of "statewide concern" or are "purely local" in nature. Given the fact that virtually every city action affects people who live in neighboring cities, as well as nonresident visitors, any of them can easily be seen as frustrating state objectives. And given the fact that local regulations typically affect the rights of individuals, the immunization of city decision making from state control is possible only if courts have a strong sense that the local values being advanced outweigh the state's determination to protect the individual interests involved. Yet the history of city power has provided the courts little basis for such a preference for local rather than statewide democratic decision making. Thus it is not surprising that the interests of the state and the individual have generally been upheld at the expense of city power, notwithstanding the existence of state constitutional protections of home rule.[42]

Cities Become Businesses Again

A look at one final late-nineteenth-century development will conclude this history of the development of cities' current legal status. Major changes in city organization resulted from reformers' attempts to eliminate corruption in city politics. The importance of this problem is so well known that, in the popular American mythology, the history of cities in this period is often modeled on the chapter headings of Samuel Orth's book *The Boss and the Machine*: "The Rise of the Machine," "Tammany Hall," "The Awakening," and "The Expert at Last." Recent historians have sought to revise this version of history, substituting a more complex view of what was at stake in the movement to replace city machines with what were called more "businesslike" forms of city government. To the immigrant, they argue, the machines responded to vital needs for jobs and services in a manner that was corrupt but humane. For the "reformer-individualist-Anglo-Saxon," whose goals were "citizenship, responsibility, efficiency, good government, economy, and businesslike management," on the other hand, the machine represented an evil that had to be curbed.[43]

In 1890, Dillon himself referred to the need to make city governments more businesslike:

> In many of its more important aspects a modern American city is not so much a miniature State as it is a business corporation, its business being wisely to administer the local affairs and economically to expend the revenues of the incorporated community. As we learn this lesson and apply business methods to the scheme of municipal government and to the conduct of municipal affairs, we are on the right road to better and more satisfactory results.[44]

Despite this rhetoric, the attempt to eradicate city corruption did not transform cities into businesses. Although the reformers dealt with corruption in a way that made city governments less political, they added controls on city operations that would be unthinkable for any American business. These controls—such as civil service tests for employees, competitive bidding requirements for city contracts, and the appointment of city managers not removable by the chief executive officer—reinforced, rather than undermined, the public/private distinction. They also helped exacerbate the powerlessness of cities because they further eroded any connection between cities and the exercise of public freedom. Today, almost half of American cities have "nonpartisan" elections, commission governments, or city managers.

The reforms did have one curious side effect. If cities were to be considered businesses, some argued, they should own and operate some vital city services, such as public utilities. This concept of the city as a business is far from Judge Dillon's, but it was the centerpiece of the solutions to city corruption offered by other reformers (such as Frederick Howe). Eliminate the corrupt businessman seeking city contracts, they argued, and you eliminate the principal source of corruption; with municipal ownership, no such corrupt contracts would exist. Advocates of this vision achieved a limited amount of municipal ownership as part of transforming the city into "a business."[45]

This review of the history of the city as a legal concept makes clear that a complex transformation occurred over a period of hundreds of years, a transformation that increasingly narrowed the definition of the city's nature to that of a state subdivision authorized to solve purely local political problems. The city changed from being an association promoted by a powerful sense of community and by an identification with the defense of property to a unit that threatened both the members of the community and their property. It is not just that cities became subject to state control—although that in itself is important. Cities also lost their economic strength and their connection with the freedom of association, elements of city life that had formerly enabled cities to play an important part in the development of Western society. It should not be overlooked that this process reached its culmination at the very time that popular participation in city affairs had at last become generally possible. Indeed, it seems ironic that city powerlessness became firmly established as a legal principle during the last few decades of the nineteenth century, the period described in Arthur Schlesinger's seminal history of cities entitled *The Rise of the City*.[46] On the other hand, it may not be ironic at all. As Schlesinger argues, urbanization reinforced the felt need for controls over city power. The fear of the changing nature of the city population generated political support for controls at a time when that support could not be countered with any effective notion of a city's right of self-determination.

3

Strategies for Empowering Cities

The Difficulty of Decentralizing Power

The history of city power just recounted illustrates the precariousness of establishing any form of group power in modern society. Every example of group power—whether political or economic, public or private—permits the power-wielder to invade the spheres of the individual and the state and thus is subject to the same kind of attack as the one waged against cities. Yet most modern political thinkers seem convinced that the creation of a world without any intermediate organizations—a world in which the state is the only power-wielder other than individuals themselves—would leave individuals unable to prevent the state from threatening their liberty.[1] The history of cities illustrates how entities intermediate between the state and the individual can serve as a defense of freedom. The creation of the medieval town as a protection for the merchants' way of life, the defense of the English corporation against the king in the name of rights of property, the vitality of the colonial town as an association, the defense of a "right of local self-government" against Dillon's support of state control of the cities, and the effort to gain "home rule" can all be seen as attempts to preserve intermediate organizations in order to protect individuals from the power of a centralized state. These examples demonstrate that many definitions of freedom—not only public freedom but freedom of choice and the maintenance of civil liberties—can be tied to the defense of some form of independent corporate life.

In supporting the need for decentralized power, however, one must avoid making the mistake of denying the force of the attack against it. Immunizing, even to a limited extent, any definition of group power is dangerous. We have seen examples of the threat that corporate power poses to individual freedom in the history of the city. Similar examples can be drawn from the more recent history of private corporations or even from the history of the family, which in ancient times was itself considered a corporation. These include the need to protect employees from corporate managers' ability to engage in race and gender discrimination and the need to impose state-created restraints on child abuse within the family.[2] Our choice whether or not to have strong intermediate bodies is not a choice between vulnerability and protection. Although the exercise of state power infringes individual rights protected by independent groups, the exercise of group power infringes individual rights protected by the state. Every time we seek state help to protect us from a group's invasion of our rights, we strengthen one threat to liberty at the expense of another. But every time we prevent the state from protecting us against group power, we accomplish the same result.

To decentralize power to cities, we must find a way to enable them to retain their power when challenged by individuals or by the state. Such a strategy cannot be based on the creation of a zone of absolute immunity from state control. We know this not only from the history of the subordination of cities but also from the failed attempt to protect private corporations from state enforcement of wage and hour legislation through constitutional interpretation. Ceding to any corporate body absolute power over the individuals who constitute it poses too much danger to individual liberty. The strategy also cannot rely purely on a concept of political decentralization. The undermining of intermediate entities has nowhere been more effective than in presenting the danger involved in genuine decentralization of power to a purely political, purely governmental organization. Decentralization of power to such an entity would make it, to the extent of its independence from state power, a sovereign political body. But to permit two sovereigns to function within the same state would create what is called an *imperium in imperio*, "the greatest of all political solecisms." The need for a single unified sovereign has become a fundamental premise of Western political thought.[3]

The decentralization of power to cities, however, need not be based on a zone of immunity from state control or on the equation of cities with purely political power that Dillon and others sought to establish. It can be based instead on the reestablishment of their importance in the lives of their inhabitants. All powerful local units have combined their political identity with other forms of religious or fraternal cohesion or economic power. The role of the polis in Greek life was so central that Aristotle described man as a political animal. Medieval towns, as we have seen, were powerful because they represented an economic-political-communal unit that allowed their citizens to achieve a new status within feudal society. New England towns, at the height of their power, were religious and fraternal communities, and their ability to represent what seemed to be the fundamental interests of their citizens enabled the towns to control the state, rather than the other way around. Even now, the organizations that wield decentralized power in America base their power on their ability to establish an indispensable place in American society. The current power of private corporations is an example of this phenomenon. More important than their legal rights is their role in the nation's economic system: any political or legal attempt to destroy their power would create what would seem to most people to be frightening instability. This kind of power can be self-protecting.

The Disappearance of the Group

Still, the question remains: how can intermediate groups, even those important to their constituents and to society as a whole, defend themselves against the power of the centralized state? In the twentieth century, there has been one principal answer to this question: obscuring the entity's connection with group power and associating it instead with individual rights. Defenders of private corporations, for example, have been able to assuage people's fear of the power of intermediate groups by creating the impression that a corporation is the collective embodiment of the desires of the individuals who constitute it rather than a collective threat to their liberty. As I have already mentioned, since the nineteenth century private corporations themselves have been treated as individuals—as "persons" protected from state control by the Fourteenth Amendment. Yet even when corporations are recognized as groups, their protection is widely associated with the preservation of individual freedom. Limiting state control over corporations is thought to protect property rights. Corporations' freedom to construct their relationship with their employees is seen as an example of the freedom of contract. The individuals who are conventionally considered the constituents of the corporation—the stockholders—are imagined as participating in its membership voluntarily ("if they don't like what the corporation is doing, they can sell"). They are also pictured as advancing democratic ideals ("shareholder democracy"). Decentralization of power to private corporations is thus routinely understood as a defense of private property and the freedom of association rather than as a collective threat to these freedoms. The original meaning of corporate power—group power—has largely been lost from view.[4]

Homeowners associations are another contemporary example of a form of group power that has successfully avoided being experienced as a threat to the freedom of its members. People buy a house within condominiums or other residential associations, it is often said, because they want the benefits these associations provide, and they agree to the restrictions that the associations impose on the use of their property in order to enhance its value. If they didn't want these restrictions, they wouldn't have agreed to them. This connection between homeowners associations and property rights—like the similar connection for private corporations—echoes the defense of the medieval town and of the city corporations at the time of the Glorious Revolution. Homeowners associations are also seen as embodiments of the freedom of association, even of democracy. Since those who live in a homeowners association govern themselves by electing a board of directors, the argument runs, the rules imposed upon the residents are self-imposed. This reference to self-rule tracks the defense articulated for the New England town. Some commentators also see homeowners associations as expressions of the notion of community historically connected with America's colonial towns.[5]

Private corporations and homeowners associations are not alone in their ability to defend their power by making the threat of group power seem to disappear. American suburbs have also been able to convince the state to delegate to them considerable power—such as the zoning power, control over school admission and funding, and defenses against annexation—by presenting themselves as vehicles for safeguarding the rights of their residents. In his mammoth article on local government law, Richard Briffault argues that courts and legislatures have defined the central function of the suburbs as the protection of "the home and family—enabling residents to raise their children in 'decent' surroundings, servicing home and family needs, and insulating home and family from undesirable changes in the surrounding area." This focus, he says, has led "to an association of the locality with individual autonomy." Joan Williams places the emphasis elsewhere, arguing that suburban power rests not on the notion of home and family but on the defense of property values. The United States Supreme Court's cases dealing with zoning and school financing, she says, have "served to protect private property (the taxpayer's wallet or the suburban enclave) against redistributive intrusions."[6] There is also a third possible explanation for the judicial and legislative solicitousness for suburban power: the concept of community. Consider, for example, Chief Justice Burger's defense of a suburb's decision to ban nude dancing:

> The residents of this small enclave chose to maintain their town as a placid, "bedroom" community of a few thousand people. To that end, they passed an admittedly broad regulation prohibiting certain forms of entertainment. Because I believe that a community of people are—within limits—masters of their own environment, I would hold that, as applied, the ordinance is valid. . . . Citizens should be free to choose to shape their community so that it embodies their conception of the "decent life." This will sometimes mean deciding that certain forms of activity—factories, gas stations, sports stadia, bookstores, and surely live nude shows—will not be allowed.[7]

This invocation of community relies on the romantic image commonly associated with the term. It evokes the idealized feeling of belongingness, oneness, solidarity, and affective connection that, it is imagined, were once fostered in traditional, face-to-face villages. Like the invocation of home and family, this image of community is reserved for the suburbs. For our purposes, it does not matter which of these three interpretations of suburban power seems most convincing. All three defend suburban power in the language of individual rights, thus presenting suburbs as enabling the protection of individuals from state control rather than as "creatures of the state" who themselves threaten individual freedom.

This is not to suggest that suburbs—or private corporations and homeowners associations, for that matter—have been able to escape altogether their association with group power. Suburbs have had their powers limited because of concerns about the protection of property rights and the rights of freedom of speech and religion, and in some states their zoning power and their authority over school financing have been subjected to state control because of the widespread impact of these aspects of local decision making. Private corporations have been regulated because of the threat they pose to their shareholders as well as to their employees, and some commentators have defended this kind of regulation on the grounds that private corporations now exercise the kind of power in modern society traditionally associated with the state. Homeowners associations have been attacked because of their intrusions on the liberty of the individuals who live within them, and, at least by commentators, as an exercise of power that is detrimental to the rights of outsiders.[8] None of this should be surprising. After all, these organizations are—in fact—examples of group power and thus present the dangers that all intermediate groups pose in a modern society. What is remarkable is the extent of their ability to withstand this attack by successfully identifying themselves with private values. Central cities, by contrast, have largely retained their association with the exercise of group power rather than with individual rights. In the popular mind, they remain examples of mini-sovereigns, linked more with the taxation and regulation of their residents than with their ability to protect them from state control. As a result of this contrast with the suburbs, the power of the nation's major cities has been subjected to persistent state intervention while suburban power has grown.[9]

The current power of American suburbs can be interpreted as a development of the public/private distinction discussed in chapter 2. This distinction, originally invoked to separate cities from private corporations, can now be seen as separating some cities from others, namely, the "private" suburbs from the "public" central cities. Once again, as was the case for private corporations, what needs protection is the private entity, with public power regarded as appropriately subject to state control. A more complex reading of the development of the public/private distinction is also possible. Rather than relying on a sharp public/private distinction, the suburbs, like private corporations and homeowners associations, can be seen as merging the notions of the public and the private while the central cities have remained more fully public. Suburbs, after all, are still governments. It's just that their governmental power is not seen as inconsistent with their role as instruments for the protection of property rights and the freedom of association. Similarly, while the managers of private corporations are clearly private individuals, they are also defended as exercising "public" responsibilities: they are seen as "trustees" for the shareholders or, more generally, as fulfilling public obligations to the society as a whole ("this broadcast has been brought to you by Texaco").[10] Even their single-minded pursuit of profits can be understood as simultaneously advancing the private interest of shareholders and the interests of the public at large. Homeowners associations represent yet another public-private mix: they are examples both of private associations and of democracy in action. As we have seen, this kind of merged image of public and private characterized all powerful corporations, including cities, before the nineteenth century. It is even more common today: administrative agencies (like the Federal Reserve Board), government corporations (like the Communications Satellite Corporation), public authorities (like the Port Authority of New York and New Jersey), and city managers are all imagined as combining businesslike rational decision making with state power. Central to the attractiveness of this merged public-private image is the combination of the positive associations with the notion of the private (privacy, individual liberty, business efficiency) with the positive images of the notion of the public (interest in others as well as oneself, serving the public interest). The merger helps suppress the negative associations with each of the two ingredients (private selfishness and the threat of state power).

Given this development, one option for decentralizing power to cities—all cities—would be for them to follow the lead of American suburbs and identify themselves with private values. It has been recognized since the adoption of the public/private distinction in the nineteenth century that all cities retain a private as well as a public character. All cities own property and contract with businesses for labor and materials in the same way that any corporation does. In fact, when they act in this capacity, the United States Supreme Court has held that the constitutional restrictions routinely applied to their public actions do not apply.[11] One way cities could expand this private capacity would be to become more like private corporations. They could run profit-making businesses and, thereby, rely on business income, rather than taxes, for support. Moreover, since all city services already have private counterparts (police/security guards, public education/private schools, courts/arbitration), they could either privatize city services or run them themselves as if they were privatized. Alternatively, cities could reject this corporate model and instead become more like homeowners associations. To do so, central cities could associate themselves with the values of home and family, private property, and community solidarity. After all, parents raise families in private homes in central-city neighborhoods as well as in suburbs and homeowners associations, and, even now, efforts are underway to erect gates across public streets to protect some of these neighborhoods. More generally, since no one is forced to move to a central city any more than to a homeowners association, those who do so can be treated as voluntarily agreeing to the applicable rules in the same way as they agree to a homeowners association's regulations. And the taxes they pay to the city can be understood to be just as voluntary—and just as mandatory—as the monthly assessments that are paid to homeowners associations. Actually, the connection between cities and voluntariness can be based on more than individuals' presumed agreement to abide by city rules when they move to town. It can also be based on the fact that popular control over taxes and governing rules is stronger in central cities (and suburbs) than in homeowners associations. Cities are managed according to the one-person, one-vote rule of democracy, while voting in homeowners associations is usually apportioned according to interests in property (with developers retaining a controlling share of the board of directors, at least at the outset).

For the reasons I explore in detail in chapter 6, these are not the routes to city power that I seek to defend. Although some aspects of these strategies may well be useful—I shall ultimately adopt a few of them myself—they all rely on the attempt to flee from the problematic nature of group power through an embrace of private values. No doubt these private values are important and worth defending. But there are many organizational forms that nurture them—not just private corporations and homeowners associations but countless nonprofit organizations and voluntary associations, ranging from private schools to country clubs. In my view, cities are valuable because they have the potential of offering something different: they offer the possibility of dealing with the problematic nature of group power by reinvigorating the idea of "the public." At present, the term "public" often refers to nothing more than the exercise of state power. The difference between public and private schools, for example, is commonly understood simply as distinguishing the schools run by the government from those that are run by nonprofit organizations. But the notion of the public need not be so limited. Two ingredients of a wider definition have already been mentioned: the idea of engagement in public life embodied in the notion of public freedom and the increase in the capacity to accommodate oneself to unfamiliar strangers that I have called community building. Another ingredient can be found in public parks and public streets: only in these kinds of public space do people come into contact with the diversity that characterizes our metropolitan areas in the ordinary course of daily life. Public freedom, community building, and public space can foster a sense of self not based on intimacy, privacy, or self-protection.

They can nurture the public aspect of the self, one derived from the stimulation and engagement that Tocqueville, Dewey, and Arendt (among many others) associate with the public realm. By fostering these ingredients of the self, cities need not threaten, let alone eliminate, the values associated with private life. When entering public space—or when engaging in public freedom or community building—people do not give up their private property, their attachment to home and family, or their ability to enjoy a zone of privacy. They gain something else: the possibility of a public-private mix different from the one currently embraced by private corporations, homeowners associations, and suburbs. The exploration of what this "something else" entails will occupy the remainder of this book. In the second half of the book, I describe how an emphasis on the value of public life can change the impact that cities have on the lives of their inhabitants. In the balance of this chapter and in the next two chapters, I turn to an important prerequisite to the creation of such an impact: the establishment of a more public relationship among the cities themselves.

The Structure of Local Government Law

The structure of local government law, through its conception both of city power and of city powerlessness, nourishes a privatized version not only of city life but of intercity relationships. Local government law empowers cities in individualist terms: the boundaries that separate cities from each other are treated as comparable to the boundaries that separate one property-owner from another. This understanding of city boundaries results from the equation of city power with city autonomy—that is, with the ability to act like a self-interested individual, albeit on a collective basis. The very purpose of obtaining power, from this perspective, is to allow the people within each city to choose for themselves the kind of life they want to live. In the making of this choice, it is considered obvious that the only relevant decision-makers are those who live within city boundaries, and that outsiders affected by the decisions have no voice in the decision-making process. One problem with this understanding of city power is that it has contributed to city powerlessness. Since cities are understood, like self-interested individuals, to threaten each other as well as the state, some entity other than the cities has to have the authority to resolve their conflicts. Under current law, this authority is exercised by the state legislature and state courts. But ceding to these state agencies the power to limit city autonomy in order to resolve intercity conflict simultaneously gives them authority to limit it for other reasons. The cities' effort to gain autonomy jeopardizes that very autonomy by empowering a central government to decide what it is.

The current definition of city power does more, however, than facilitate state aggrandizement. It also induces cities to abandon their own decision-making responsibilities. By treating cities as autonomous individuals, local government law fuels a desire to avoid, rather than to engage with, those who live on the other side of the city line. Especially in the prosperous suburbs, the equation of city boundaries with the boundaries of private property encourages city residents to think of the city line as separating "us" from "them": crime, bad schools, and inadequate resources across the city line, far from generating pressure for intercity negotiation, are dismissed as "their problem." Why engage in an intercity negotiation if it would jeopardize our own autonomy? Those who see themselves as better off than their neighbors also experience the powerlessness of other cities as a form of self-protection. Why should we be willing to help others gain power that might ultimately threaten us? This attitude reduces cities' experience of dealing with intercity conflict—particularly when the conflict requires one city to sacrifice its advantages in the interest of the group as a whole. Whenever a conflict arises, cities routinely feel that their only real choice is to ask the state to resolve it. Of course, such a dynamic is not inevitable. Cities might understand, and act to reverse, a trend toward city subservience to the state. To do so, however, will require a spirit of cooperation that, to a self-interested city, might rub against the grain.

Local government law reinforces this privatized relationship between cities by organizing the decentralization of power solely in terms of a vertical relationship between individual cities and the state. Because cities are "creatures of the state," the relationship with the state is the only meaningful one cities have. If a city can strike a deal with the state and thereby obtain the power it wants, the impact on those who live outside the city's borders can simply be considered irrelevant. What has been lost in this vertical conceptualization of the decentralization of power is the possibility of building the decentralization of power on the relationship among the cities themselves. Because the state is no more than the collected representatives of the localities—the state legislatures themselves are elected locally—cities could control state policy, rather than being subservient to it, if they could forge an intercity alliance. The power that can be generated by this kind of collective action is well recognized—so well recognized, in fact, that it regularly generates an effort by centralized authorities to limit it. The ability of employees to increase their power by forming unions—and the efforts of employers to prevent unionization—is one well-known example. The power that private corporations can create through agreements with each other—and the attempts to limit these agreements through antitrust laws—is another. Article I, section 10, of the U.S. Constitution is a third. That section provides: "No state shall, without the Consent of Congress, . . . enter into any Agreement or Compact with another State. . . . " Why did the federalists who framed the Constitution want centralized control of interstate cooperation? The reason, I suggest, is that they feared that interstate compacts could create a powerful counterforce to the national government. Action by the federal government, they realized, is not the same thing as action by the united states. These attempts to impose centralized control on collective action demonstrate its importance: organizing can strengthen the ability of individuals and groups to resist centralized power.

By equating the notions of city power and local autonomy, local government law has made this kind of collective action unlikely. Intercity agreements are now possible only if each participant believes that it would be in its own self-interest, as the participant itself defines it, to make them. Although some agreements can be made on this basis, it allows far too little room for compromise on critical intercity issues such as zoning, school financing, and crime control. To enable the creation of powerful intercity alliances, local government law's embrace of the notion of local autonomy needs to be abandoned. Rather than emphasizing the importance of the boundary lines that separate one city from another, the legal definition of city power should be based on strengthening the connections that cities have with each other. Cities can avoid dependence on state-granted delegations of power only by increasing their capacity to solve the problems generated by intercity conflict themselves. No one thinks that, in a world filled with others, individual cities can be allowed to determine their future on their own. Local government law now recognizes this fact by empowering the state to define city power. But local government law could replace this reliance on state power with rules that make intercity negotiation and compromise, rather than state control, the mechanism for curbing local selfishness. That way, cities could operate under rules that they themselves design. No doubt these intercity negotiations will sometimes fail. Some conflict will seem unresolvable, and the temptation to seek a solution to the conflict from a higher authority will not easily go away. But city residents need to learn that, to the extent that cities fail to agree among themselves, they will be subject to centralized control. The only way to escape centralized control is to come to an agreement. In a democratic society, cities, like individuals, cannot reasonably expect more power than the ability to participate with others—including those with whom they disagree—in a collective decision-making process.

The Centered Subject and Its Critique

Defining city power in terms of intercity collaboration rather than local autonomy requires rethinking what cities are and why we want to empower them. Currently, as we have seen, the legal system considers cities, like corporations, to be collective individuals: they are able to contract, own property, and otherwise act in their own self-interest in the same way that individuals do. Moreover, local government law has endowed these collective individuals with a particular conception of subjectivity, one that is commonly called a centered sense of self. One aspect of this sense of self is its emphasis on separateness: to be autonomous requires making a clear distinction between "self" and "other." Another aspect lies in its method for determining how to discover what one's self-interest is: one discovers it, according to this conception, by looking within oneself. Richard Briffault provides a good account of local government law's application of this picture of the self to cities, a position that he calls "localism." He defines localism as "a belief that land-use regulation, schools, and tax policy ought to be controlled locally, with the interests of local residents as the exclusive desideratum of local decision makers." Localism, he adds:

> reifies local borders, using invisible municipal boundary lines to delimit the range of local concern and the proper subjects of local compassion and treating the creation and maintenance of local borders as a basic right. . . . Local borders, once created, reinforce local identification, become a focus of sentiment and symbolism and create a powerful legal bulwark for the preservation of local interests.

This definition of localism contains all the ingredients of the centered subject: boundary lines separate one subject from another, each subject looks only within to determine its interests, and "preservation of local interests" is a meaningful goal.[12]

Briffault's definition of localism derives from his analysis of the power that courts and legislatures have given the suburbs. Relying on the examples of exclusionary zoning, school financing, and protection against annexation, he argues that adherence to localism has empowered suburbs, but not central cities, to shape their own social and economic development. But local government law's limits on city power also attribute to cities the subjectivity of the centered self, although they usually associate it not with localism but with the idea of sovereignty. The most common image invoked to control city decision making is the tyranny of the majority, an image epitomized in the modern imagination by *Brown v. Board of Education.* Like the ancient power of the king, this collective tyranny is pictured as the exercise of the passions and power of an uncontrollable and unpredictable sovereign subject. "What is a majority, in its collective capacity," Tocqueville asks, "if not an individual with opinions, and usually with interests, contrary to those of another individual, called the minority?" There is also another version of the centered subject that is sometimes invoked to limit city power. On occasion, the power of cities is restricted not because they are analogized to sovereign states but because they are understood to be like property-owners. Property-owners too, one should recognize, exercise power that can invade the rights both of their neighbors and of those who live on the property (hence nuisance law and landlord-tenant law). Thus the Supreme Court has denied cities the exemption from federal antitrust laws that it affords to states by associating cities with the dangers attributed to private property-owners (such as private corporations). Applying these laws to cities was necessary, the Court said, because of "the serious economic dislocation which could result if cities were free to place their own parochial interests above the Nation's economic goals reflected in anti-trust laws."[13]

In the two chapters that follow, I shall attempt to alter the current conception of city power and city powerlessness—and thereby strengthen the prospects for intercity cooperation—by proposing versions of the decentralization of power that do not envision cities as centered subjects. It is important to recognize that, since cities are creatures of the state under American law, the current identity attributed to them is itself a creature of the state. Even those who can't help thinking of individuals or the nation-state as having a "natural" subjectivity should realize that there is nothing natural about the subjectivity currently imagined for cities. States can create cities with any subjectivity they please. Local government law, having endowed cities with the subjectivity of the centered self, can just as readily endow them with one that is decentered, that is, with one that questions the sharp self/other distinction that now dominates legal decision making. That, I suggest, is what it should do.

Such a revision of local government law is long overdue. Comparable revisions have already taken place within many other branches of American law. In fact, the current disjunction between local government law and the legal system as a whole is striking. As I noted above, many American suburbs now rely on the privatized notions of home and family, property rights, and community solidarity to provide a coherent way to locate the "local interests" that city autonomy is designed to defend. These are the values that enable suburban residents to think of themselves as a single, unified group. But the suburbs have been able to create this sense of unity only by suppressing the deconstructive critique to which these values have been subjected elsewhere in the legal system. The blissful notion of home and family has had to omit any reference to divorce, child abuse, work-family conflicts, violence against women, and the like—a mainstay of the study of family law. The "one's home is one's castle" concept of property has had to mask the conflicts—over issues like economic growth or neighborhood preservation—that the modern "bundle-of-rights" definition of property now highlights throughout property law. The invocation of community has had to repress not only issues of race, gender, and the like but the friction generated by individualism itself, that is, by the entire modern critique of life in traditional face-to-face villages. No doubt, the idealized version of home and family, property, and community produces a familiar picture of American life, one ably captured by Norman Rockwell in the 1950s. But local government law is one of the few places in the legal system in which this picture is still presented as truth.[14]

My proposed revision of local government law is built on a well-developed critique of the notion of the centered subject. I turn to a sketch of this critique because, I suspect, some readers will think that cities simply *are* centered subjects: what else could they be? The answer that the critique has provided stems from an analysis of a version of the centered subject that these readers might think even less amenable to attack than collective groups like cities. It has concentrated on individuals. In this context, it has focused on the notion, essential to the image of the centered self, that an individual not only can distinguish herself or himself from others but has a sense of self determinate enough to serve as a touchstone for the pursuit of self-interest. One way critics have articulated the difficulties with pinning down such a notion of the self has been to point out that describing one's own sense of self—describing oneself, even *to* oneself—is a creative process. Identifying the self requires the invention of a narrative: the selection, editing, and unifying of countless aspects of memory and desire. It requires the transformation of the multiplicity of one's life into a single account—more accurately, into a series of accounts, since the attempt to establish one's identity has elements both of establishing a sense of identity at any particular moment and of establishing a sense of continuity over time. As Nietzsche put it in *The Will to Power*, "the 'subject' is only a fiction." It "is not something given, it is something added and invented and projected behind what there is."[15]

Critics have analyzed how individuals construct this narrative of the self in different ways. Some describe it in sociological terms:

> The human infant becomes a "self," a being capable of speech and action, only by learning to interact in a human community. The self becomes an individual in that it becomes a "social" being capable of language, interaction and cognition. The identity of the self is constituted by a narrative unity, which integrates what "I" can do, have done and will accomplish with what you expect of "me," interpret my acts and intentions to mean, wish for me in the future, etc. The . . . empiricist illusion of a substance-like self cannot do justice to those contingent

processes of socialization through which an infant becomes a person, acquires language and reason, develops a sense of justice and autonomy, and becomes capable of projecting a narrative into the world of which she is not only the author but the actor as well.[16]

Others have instead analyzed it in terms of political power:

The individual is not to be conceived as a sort of elementary nucleus, a primitive atom, a multiple and inert material on which power comes to fasten or against which it happens to strike, and in so doing crushes individuals. In fact, it is already one of the prime effects of power that certain bodies, certain gestures, certain discourses, certain desires, come to be identified and constituted as individuals. The individual, that is, is not the *vis-à-vis* of power; it is, I believe, one of its prime effects. The individual is an effect of power, and at the same time, or precisely to the extent to which it is that effect, it is the element of its articulation. The individual which power has constituted is at the same time its vehicle.[17]

Still others have located it in language:

All psychological categories (the ego, the individual, the person) derive from the illusion of substantial identity. But this illusion goes back basically to a superstition that deceives not only common sense but also philosophers—namely, the belief in language and, more precisely, in the truth of grammatical categories. It was grammar (the structure of subject and predicate) that inspired Descartes' certainty that "I" is the subject of "think," whereas it is rather the thoughts that come to "me": at bottom, faith in grammar simply conveys the will to be the cause of one's thoughts. The subject, the self, the individual are just so many false concepts, since they transform into substances the fictitious unities having at the start only a linguistic reality.[18]

Whichever of these explanations is adopted, the self is seen as contestable, as amenable to multiple interpretations. Although identity is usually defined in terms of sameness, it is actually constructed out of a series of differences: the difference between the aspects of one's life one attributes to the self and the aspects one associates with the actions of others; the difference between the self as described in the present and as seen in the past; the difference between the parts of oneself accepted into the narrative and those rejected; the difference between the describing self and the self being described. The creation of these differences cannot produce a centered subject because neither the interpreter nor the materials being interpreted have a fixed meaning. This is not just a problem of articulation. Determining how to express oneself and not just the demands of the culture, defining a sphere in which personal behavior is not subservient to political power, deciding how to give meaning to one's life—these are questions about how to become a person, how to form one's character.

But the "self" who must answer these questions is being challenged by them: the consciousness of the answerer is what is being questioned. Trying to live in a way that is different from, rather than controlled by, cultural or political commands—like trying to give meaning to a self read as a "text"—thus demands more than just continuous effort. It requires endless interpretation, and it is never possible to know for sure what to interpret or who is doing the interpreting. The Arabian poet Sama Ma'ari has described a version of this sense of self by saying: "Identities are highly complex, tension filled, contradictory, and inconsistent entities. Only the one who claims to have a simple, definite, and clear-cut identity has an identity problem."[19]

This brief account of the critique of the centered subject does not begin to capture the complexities of the topic, but it might nevertheless be adequate to introduce the related problem of group identity. The critique of the centered subject is more familiar when it is applied to groups rather than to the self. Treating individuals as a group plainly requires selecting, editing, and unifying disparate elements—the creation of a sameness out of a multitude of differences. Consider any group to which you belong. It doesn't matter whether the group is defined in terms of geography, race, ethnicity, gender, sexual preference, politics, or some other criteria. Defining what the group has in common and what distinguishes it from outsiders is always a contestable matter of interpretation. To say that one "is" an Asian American or a cross-dresser or a Democrat or a man or a Texan never means that one's self-image can be captured by any of these labels. It is common to feel both inside and outside these group identifications simultaneously. In part this is because each of these labels has meanings imposed by outsiders that a self-identified group member might reject: being called a queer by someone in a passing car does not have the same meaning as feeling identified with Queer Nation.

But there is no single group identity from an insider perspective either. Since everyone is a member of many groups, any particular group label falsifies to the extent that it suggests a sameness within the group. A group identity has to be forged out of differences that divide the group; it never simply exists. Every group member recognizes the problem of uniting all Asian Americans or cross-dressers or Democrats or men or Texans behind any single cause. But the multiplicity of group identifications also allows some group members to dispute the legitimacy of others' claim to membership: to some Asian Americans, an American from Sri Lanka is not a "real" Asian American; to some Texans, an Asian American is not a "real" Texan; to some men, a cross-dresser is not a "real" man; to some Democrats, Bill Clinton is not a "real" Democrat. As Barbara Johnson observes, "difference disliked is identity affirmed."[20]

This critique of the coherence of collective identity, often called "antiessentialism," has been elaborated extensively in literature denying that there is a core identity to being black or being a woman or being gay.[21] The argument applies equally to groups such as cities. Territorial boundaries circumscribe a very diverse group of people. For major American cities, this is obvious enough: race, ethnicity, class, politics, gender, sexual preference, and neighborhood, among other sources of identity, fracture the city in a multitude of ways. But suburbs are also not homogeneous. Although some city differences (such as class) may not exist in some suburbs, others plainly do. Concerns about politics, gender, sexual preference, and neighborhood—let alone the economy and the ozone layer—do not stop at the suburban border. Some suburban residents identify less with their neighbors than with people from another city who share their race or ethnicity or some other source of their identity. Other suburban residents are ambivalent about their locality: happy to have escaped the city and anxious to escape suburban boredom. Besides, most suburban residents have never even met each other. A suburb, like any city, is no more than an "imagined community": it consists of people who have only an image of their connection with each other.[22] This image is a "fiction": it "is not something given, it is something added and invented and projected behind what there is."

In the pages that follow, I do not intend to nail down exactly what a decentered subjectivity for a locality would look like. Doing so would entail giving the decentered subject a specific content—in other words, it would require finding a center for the decentered subject. The literature about the decentered subject does more than reject such a notion of a stable identity for the self. It provides many different notions about what a decentered self is. I suggest below two different ideas for a new subjectivity for localities in local government law. I call them the situated self and the postmodern self. But these ideas are my own creations, based loosely on a literature with an astonishing variety of ideas about decentered subjectivity. Countless other candidates for local government subjectivity can also be imagined. This multiplicity of possibilities for a city's subjectivity is not a problem that needs to be overcome; we do not need one test for cities' subjectivity. In this book, I hope to stimulate the production of multiple possibilities for city identity, as well as the production of a multitude of suggestions about how to redefine what cities are and what they can do.

Part Two

DECENTERING DECENTRALIZATION

4

The Situated Subject

ONE WAY of decentering cities' subjectivity would be to build on the literature that emphasizes that the self is formed only through a relationship with others. As Kenneth Gergen puts it, "it is not individual 'I's who create relationships, but relationships that create the sense of 'I.' "[1] This insight has stimulated a wide variety of communitarians, civic republicans, and feminists, among others. Although it would be impossible here to survey this extensive literature, or even to summarize the work of a single writer to whom I am referring, it is important that we take a brief look at the kinds of claims made by people who write in these traditions before turning to the changes I propose in local government law doctrine.

A Glimpse at the Literature

Michael Sandel, Charles Taylor, and Michael Walzer are examples of those often labeled communitarians. Sandel describes what he calls a situated or "constitutive conception" of the self.

> To say that the members of a society are bound by a sense of community is not simply to say that a great many of them profess communitarian sentiments and pursue communitarian aims, but rather that they conceive their identity—the subject and not just the object of their feelings and aspirations—as defined to some extent by the community of which they are a part. For them, community describes not just what they *have* as fellow citizens but also what they *are*, not a relationship they choose (as in a voluntary association) but an attachment they discover, not merely an attribute but a constituent of their identity.

In the same vein, Charles Taylor asserts that "our identity is always partly defined in conversation with others or through the common understanding which underlies the practices of our society." Taylor argues that the "autonomous individual" himself is a social construct: "the free individual of the West is only what he is by virtue of the whole society and civilization which brought him to be and which nourishes him." If so, the autonomous individual has to be interested in others, not as a matter of sentimentality or altruism but as a matter of self-interest. "Since the free individual can only maintain his identity within a society/culture of a certain kind,

he has to be concerned about the shape of this society/culture as a whole."
Similarly, Michael Walzer contends that everyone—liberal or communitarian—has to recognize the collective contribution to the constitution of the self. What people disagree about, in his view, is not the constitution of the self but "the connection of constituted selves, the pattern of social relations."[2]

As Walzer suggests, the recognition that the self is a product of human relationships does not endow the self with any particular identity. Quite the contrary: the multiple possibilities for human relationship produce multiple possibilities for the self. Liberalism, according to Walzer, is a theory of relationship "which has voluntary association at its center and which understands voluntariness as the right of rupture or withdrawal." Civic republicanism, by contrast, seeks to promote a different kind of human relationship and, thereby, to encourage a different kind of self-development. Frank Michelman describes this conception in terms of dialogue. The republican concept of the subject, he says,

> contemplates . . . a self whose identity and freedom consist, in part, in its capacity for reflexively critical reconsideration of the ends and commitments that it already has and that make it who it is. Such a self necessarily obtains its self-critical resources from, and tests its current understandings against, understandings from beyond its own pre-critical life and experience, which is to say communicatively, by reaching for the perspectives of other and different persons.

For Michelman and others who write in the republican tradition, this conception of the self transforms the meaning of the idea "that we are free only insofar as we are self-governing." The term "self-government" becomes a collective, not an individual, activity: "self-cognition and ensuing self-legislation must . . . be socially situated; norms must be formed through public dialogue and expressed as public law." Self-government, in other words, is the work of politics. In the strongest version of republicanism, Michelman says, "political engagement is considered a positive human good because the self is understood as partially constituted by, or as coming to itself through, such engagement." Michelman quotes Hannah Pitkin: "only in public life can we jointly, as a community, exercise the human capacity to 'think what we are doing,' and take charge of the history in which we are all constantly engaged by drift and inadvertence." Although Michelman does not embrace Pitkin's strong claim for the importance of politics, he, like others, defines republicanism in terms of the central importance of citizenship to human flourishing.[3]

Other writers do not accept this republican emphasis on—or definition of—politics. For example, although Roberto Unger defines the self in terms of relationship, his focus is on people's emotional connection with each other—their "experience of mutual longing"—together with their skepticism that "any particular framework of society and culture can give full expression to the opportunities of practical or passionate connection." This combined emphasis on personal encounters and cultural skepticism, which he calls the "Christian-romantic tradition," has led Unger to investigate the paradoxes of empowerment: how can we connect with others on whom we so depend yet who make us so vulnerable? And how can we break out of the social and cultural contexts that both define us as people and yet confine our ability for practical, passionate, and cognitive empowerment? In a series of books, Unger has explored these questions of personal and social connection in a wide variety of contexts: the nature of human passions, the organization of work, the structure of the economy, and the future of social theory, to name but a few. "To satisfy our longing for acceptance and recognition, to be intimately assured that we have a place in the world, and to be freed by this assurance for a life of action and encounter," Unger writes, "we must open ourselves to personal attachments and communal engagements whose terms we cannot predefine and whose course we cannot control." For Unger, personal and social transformation thus requires an understanding and revision of contexts considerably broader than the political sphere as the republican tradition defines it.[4]

A number of strands of feminism also embrace a version of the situated self. No doubt the most famous example is Carol Gilligan's *In a Different Voice*. Writing about theories of moral development, Gilligan draws a contrast "between a self defined through separation and a self delineated through connection, between a self measured against an abstract ideal of perfection and a self assessed through particular activities of care." For Gilligan, "the ideal of care is . . . an activity of relationship, of seeing and responding to need, taking care of the world by sustaining the web of connection so that no one is left alone." Defining the link between this notion of care and gender—even defining Gilligan's own link between the two—is, to put it mildly, a matter of considerable controversy. But Gilligan's book, at the very least, insists that a relationship-centered version of the self is an alternative to the traditional individualist conception of the highest form of moral development. "My own work," she writes, "indicates that the inclusion of women's experience brings to developmental understanding a new perspective on relationships that changes the basic constructs of interpretation. The concept of identity expands to include the experience of interconnection."[5]

Finally—to offer one last example—Martha Minow has argued that we should not consider legal reasoning the product of a centered subject, let alone the product of no subject at all. She insists that there is no such thing as impartiality: "impartiality is the guise partiality takes to seal bias against exposure." But, she continues, recognizing one's own partiality is not enough. It allows people either to ignore the experience of others or to appropriate others' experience into their own understanding of the world. We must do more—we must learn to "take the perspective of another."

> I must acknowledge and struggle against my partiality by making an effort to understand your reality and what it means for my own. I need to stop seeking certainty and acknowledge the complexity of our shared and colliding realities, as well as the tragic impossibility of all prevailing at once. It is this complexity that constitutes our reciprocal realities, and it is the conflict between our realities that constitutes us, whether we engage in it overtly or submerge it under a dominant view.

Minow contends that by exploring our own stereotypes, welcoming anomalies, trying to understand how others understand, and constructing new bases for connection, individuals—even judges—can begin to confront people's differences. Minow's emphasis, in short, is less on political or social transformation than on the transformation of consciousness. She seeks to change how people think.[6]

The Situated Subject as Local Government Law

The writers to whom I have just referred certainly do not form a single school of thought; indeed, they are likely to find it odd that I have grouped them together. But collectively, along with many others I haven't mentioned, they could be a source of ideas for a local government law based on a notion of the situated self. I explore some of these ideas below through two doctrinal examples: the laws dealing with exclusionary zoning and condominium conversion. Before turning to these examples, however, we must begin to understand cities as situated subjects. The easiest way to do so is to focus on the relationship between America's central cities and their suburbs; in this context, the mutually constitutive nature of municipalities seems virtually undeniable.

"Every true suburb," in Robert Fishman's words, "is the outcome of two opposing forces, an attraction toward the opportunities of the great city and a simultaneous repulsion against urban life."[7] The suburbs would not be what they are without this love-hate relationship with the central city. If the recent, extraordinary American migration to the suburbs were fully successful and the central city ceased to exist altogether, the character of the suburbs would be radically different. There would, for example, be no place for those excluded by exclusionary zoning to live except the suburbs. The identity of the modern central city has been equally affected by the presence of its suburbs. Although these cities existed before there were suburbs, the current social and economic problems of the modern central city are, in part, the result of what has happened beyond the city (to use the literal definition of the word "suburb"). This too can be illustrated by the impact on city life of exclusionary zoning: if no suburb excluded the poor or people of color, the nature of central cities would be radically different. There are also countless other illustrations of the fact that the relationship between central cities and suburbs (in Michael Sandel's words) is "not a relationship they choose (as in a voluntary association) . . . but a constituent part of their identity." Localities cause unemployment by attracting businesses from neighboring cities; they generate pollution that harms their neighbors as well as themselves; they zone for office complexes and shopping malls that change the lives of employees and customers in other towns; they educate people who move elsewhere in the area; they enact crime-control policies that cause criminals to move to new locations, thereby victimizing people who live across the border. This chapter builds on a recognition of this inextricable entanglement between central cities and suburbs.

Current local government law has rejected such an understanding of local identity in its treatment of exclusionary zoning. The United States Supreme Court and most state courts have allowed localities to decide their zoning policies in the interests of their own residents with little regard to their effect on outsiders. Residents who desire to make their suburb into what Gregory Weiher has called a "theme park"—"a place of escape, a place where worries and cares must remain outside the gate"— are entitled to do so as long as they do not intentionally discriminate on the basis of race and meet other minimal requirements. The impact of this aspect of local government law on America has been profound. It has fostered not only the suburbs' ability to exclude potential residents but also their ability to recruit them: in a country where people frequently move, racial, ethnic, and class segregation can survive only if there are clear boundary lines that indicate where "the right" kind of people live. Suburban boundaries have also helped to engender a suburban consciousness that has become part of the identity of millions of Americans—a consciousness that combines the felt legitimacy of suburban separation with an acceptance of the benefits of race and class privilege. Fears of racial and class integration, desires to protect "home and family, property, and community," and allegiance to suburban separateness have defined and reinforced each other. That's why many people would feel personally threatened by the blurring of suburban boundary lines that would result from a definition of cities as situated subjects.[8]

Geographic boundaries have helped organize America's metropolitan areas in terms of gender roles as well. Suburban consciousness emphasizes boundaries not only between central cities and suburbs but also between houses and between people. It nurtures what M. P. Baumgartner calls a "moral minimalism": an avoidance of conflict, an emphasis on privacy and separation, and distanced social ties. To put the matter in Carol Gilligan's terms, if the centered subjectivity of the suburb were an attribute of a person, that person would be gendered male:

> Men and women may perceive danger in different social situations and construe danger in different ways—men seeing danger more often in close personal affiliation than in achievement and construing danger to arise from intimacy, women perceiving danger in impersonal achievement situations and construing danger to result from competitive success. The danger men describe in their stories of intimacy is a danger of entrapment or betrayal, because caught in a smothering relationship or humiliated by rejection and deceit. In contrast, the danger women portray in their tales of achievement is a danger of isolation, a fear that in standing out or being set apart by success, they will be left alone.

Since both men and women can have suburban consciousness, we need not read Gilligan as suggesting that there is a single male or female reaction to relationships. We can understand her notions of relationship as gendered cultural stereotypes: separateness, self-interest, and competitiveness are commonly imagined as masculine while openness, caring, and vulnerability are treated as feminine.

The opposite gendered understanding of the city/suburb distinction is also possible. The suburbs can be understood not as male but as an extended women's sphere, a "sorority house with kids," as William Whyte called them in the 1950s. The classic suburb was created to foster the domestic virtues associated with the role of the mother in the traditional nuclear family; the traditional father, but not the traditional mother, commuted to the city to work. Moreover, the suburbs have contributed to the perpetuation of this cult of domesticity by making it more difficult for women to combine family life with working outside the home. This reading of the suburbs need not be understood as contradicting the Gilliganesque reading but can be combined with it: the cult of domesticity can itself be seen as male. But no matter which reading is adopted, it should be clear that confronting the issue of exclusionary zoning will challenge not only separation by race and class but also the ways in which our forms of urban life have built upon, and allocated, gender roles.[9]

One court has already taken a step toward recognizing the interdependence between suburb and city in the exclusionary zoning context. In the well-known case of *Southern Burlington Township N.A.A.C.P. v. Township of Mt. Laurel*, the Supreme Court of New Jersey refused to allow localities to base their land-use policy solely on the desires of local residents. Condemning the social consequences caused by the suburbs' effort to exclude the poor, the court held that every municipality in its zoning policy had to afford an opportunity for low- and moderate-income housing "at least to the extent of the municipality's fair share of the present and prospective regional needs therefor." On the question of "*whose* general welfare must be served . . . in the field of land use regulation," the court stated:

> Frequently the decisions in this state . . . have spoken only in terms of the interest of the enacting municipality, so that it has been thought, at least in some quarters, that such was the only welfare requiring consideration. It is, of course, true that many cases have dealt only with regulations having little, if any, outside impact where the local decision is ordinarily entitled to prevail. However, it is fundamental and not to be forgotten that the zoning power is a police power of the state and the local authority is acting only as a delegate of that power and is restricted in the same manner as is the state. So, when regulation does have a substantial external impact, the welfare of the state's citizens beyond the borders of the particular municipality cannot be disregarded and must be recognized and served.[10]

The extent to which *Mt. Laurel*'s notion of municipal legislation rejects the conception of the centered self is a matter of interpretation. One certainly can read the court's opinion as retaining the insider/outsider framework of the centered subject. The opinion allows cities to continue to serve the interest of the people who live within city boundaries unless there is a "substantial external impact" on outsiders. Thus the court might simply be requiring localities to pay attention to the injuries that self-interested activity causes others—in a way analogous to tort law or John Stuart Mill's *On Liberty*—rather than changing the conception of the municipal self. In Michael Sandel's terms, *Mt. Laurel* can be read as requiring localities to change merely the object and not the subject of their feelings and aspirations. It is also possible, however, to read the opinion as recognizing, in the context of exclusionary zoning, the regional construction of local identity. A locality's zoning policy, the court might be saying, affects not only its own identity but also the identity of other cities within the region. Suburban exclusiveness is dependent on the neighboring cities' refusal to exclude; some places have to be open for others to be closed. And just as the identity of the excluding suburb is enabled by its neighbors' openness, their identity as less "exclusive" is created by the exclusion. In Gregory Weiher's words, "one can only meaningfully speak of the type of people that live in a certain area because at the same time implicit reference is made to all the people who *do not* live there." Under this reading, *Mt. Laurel* requires localities to accept a fair share of regional needs for low- and moderate-income housing not out of sympathy or altruism but out of the recognition that they are defined by, and define, others.[11]

It should not be surprising that cities in New Jersey might have found such a change of perspective hard to pull off. Since they had previously acted as centered subjects—and were still permitted to exercise that subjectivity in all contexts other than exclusionary zoning—it would be quite an accomplishment for cities to rethink their identity in response to a court order on a single topic. And, as we've seen, the case can be read as not even demanding such a rethinking. As a result, the subsequent history in New Jersey of the *Mt. Laurel* litigation—one that led to greater centralization of zoning decisions—could readily have been anticipated.[12] The localities' subjectivity remained unchanged, and, as centered subjects, they had to be forced to behave altruistically. The literature of the situated subject suggests that endowing localities with a decentered subjectivity requires much more than the court order in *Mt. Laurel*. To overcome exclusionary zoning, current local government law—other than cases like *Mt. Laurel*—has to be recognized, and rejected, both as a social policy and as a contribution to the construction of personal identity. Current law not only has fragmented the metropolitan area but is perpetuated by the kind of person this fragmentation has nurtured. The problem with implementing *Mt. Laurel* or similar reforms is the power of this status quo. A central government's attempt to change it would be experienced by the people who benefit from it as an astonishing invasion of their personal freedom. Yet it is unlikely that those who profit from current law will undo it themselves. How, then, can centered subjects ever come to embrace a vision of themselves as decentered, as interdependent?

One way to answer this question would build on the civic republican emphasis on the political construction of identity. It would take seriously my earlier quotation from Hannah Pitkin: "only in public life can we jointly, as a community, exercise the human capacity to 'think what we are doing,' and take charge of the history in which we are all constantly engaged by drift and inadvertence." *Mt. Laurel*'s impact was limited by its strategy of treating every city as an individual decision-maker required to confront regional needs by itself as a matter of thought. From a republican perspective, understanding the mutually constitutive impact of zoning decisions instead requires intercity dialogue. "Feelings and ideas are renewed, the heart enlarged, and the understanding developed," Tocqueville observed, "only by the reciprocal action of men one upon another."[13] If so, zoning policies should be worked out not centrally or by each municipality alone but through regional negotiations. To establish such intercity negotiations, institutional innovations are necessary; I discuss below what they might be. But as republican writings emphasize, the success of intercity negotiations will also depend on the entitlements of the participants, the organization of the discussion, and the consequences not only of agreement but of failure to agree. The self may be formed through dialogue, but the dialogue will not change its participants if they can simply walk away because they don't like the deal. Not only is the experience of interdependence a prerequisite to changing legal rules but, paradoxically, changing legal rules is a prerequisite to creating the experience of interdependence. To eliminate exclusionary zoning and the consciousness that supports it, legal doctrine must recognize and break through this paradoxical structure. One ingredient in this effort is the expansion and development of existing alternative exclusionary zoning doctrines, such as the test expounded by *Mt. Laurel.* Another ingredient involves exposing and building upon the decentered nature not just of legal doctrine but of the suburban residents for whose benefit exclusionary zoning persists. Suburban residents not only disagree with each other on issues of race, class, gender, sexual orientation, the environment, population growth, and so forth, but they feel conflict themselves over these issues. Suburban self-protection might be undermined, therefore, if regional negotiations were organized not in terms of the suburb/city divide but in terms of the divisions that exist *within* both the suburbs and the central city. In order to examine this strategy, I need to introduce a second local government law doctrine, the law of condominium conversion.

Many cities have enacted legislation designed to limit the ability of landlords to convert rental housing into condominiums. This kind of legislation and exclusionary zoning raise comparable issues. Both restrict an owner's ability to control his property, and both do so in order to preserve an existing community by excluding outsiders. Exclusionary zoning enables suburbs to exclude the poor; condominium conversion legislation is an effort to protect low-income neighborhoods from gentrification. Indeed, condominium conversion legislation is one of the principal vehicles central cities use to preserve the neighborhood character of poor city neighborhoods. One could therefore imagine both being permitted (any community can control its own character) or both being forbidden (no community can exercise the right to exclude). As it turns out, however, suburban exclusion is easier to accomplish than urban exclusion because current local government law's treatment of condominium conversion legislation is radically different from its treatment of exclusionary zoning.

When dealing with condominium conversion legislation, courts have taken the need to protect the rights of property-owners from excessive governmental regulation much more seriously than they do when dealing with exclusionary zoning. In Massachusetts, for example, the Supreme Judicial Court has invoked several local government law doctrines to limit cities' power to prevent the conversion of rental housing. Although the Massachusetts state constitution allows cities to exercise home rule, the Supreme Judicial Court has held that the home rule power does not include the ability to pass condominium conversion legislation. Regulating the landlord-tenant relationship, the court has reasoned, falls within the exception to cities' home rule power that prevents them from enacting "private or civil law." Unable to use their home rule power, Massachusetts cities must therefore seek specific state authorization to pass condominium conversion legislation. But specific grants of authority to cities are narrowly construed under Dillon's Rule; accordingly, the court has held many specific state authorizations insufficient to permit condominium conversion legislation. These condominium conversion cases thus exemplify the aspect of local government law that curbs city power thought to invade individual rights, just as most exclusionary zoning cases exemplify the aspect of local government law that enhances suburban power. Moreover, the exclusionary zoning cases do not help central cities: city residents cannot challenge city zoning laws that facilitate gentrification on the grounds that they exclude the poor. As a result, those with enough money can profit from both doctrines: they can isolate themselves in the suburbs and they can buy up inner-city neighborhoods through gentrification.[14]

Examining exclusionary zoning and condominium conversion law together does more than simply provide an example of the social policy local government law now embraces. It can help us break out of the clichéd vision of open cities and closed suburbs often imagined in the context of exclusionary zoning. The effort to pass condominium conversion legislation demonstrates that the instinct for exclusion is not limited to the suburbs. Feelings of race and class privilege, desires to protect "home and family, property, and community," and allegiance to separateness exist on both sides of the central-city/suburb boundary. Many blacks would see the weakening of the city boundary line as an attack on the political power they have gained in central cities, and many residents of ethnic neighborhoods fear that rising housing prices will destroy their community. The prevention of gentrification, like exclusionary zoning, enables people to preserve comparatively homogeneous communities and advances the interests that the members of the community have in common. Central-city and suburban residents thus have similar reasons to protect territorial identity: racial pride, feelings of community, fear of outsiders, and preference for their own way of life over that lived on the other side of the border.

Examining exclusionary zoning and condominium conversion law together also helps demonstrate that there are people on both sides of the border who want to move to the other side. Some central-city residents may see the suburbs as a means of escape, but some suburban residents want to escape to the central city as well. Gentrification, like the move to the suburbs, reflects the desire for a better life. Moreover, exclusionary zoning limits the ability to escape in both directions. It prevents the poor from moving to the suburbs, and it contributes to the decay of the inner cities that restricts the possibilities for gentrification. Like the urban poor, suburban residents who would prefer to live across the border often can't find an acceptable place to live. A different local government law could enable greater mobility in both directions, a mobility that even some who wouldn't move would like to encourage. Gentrification brings an increase in the tax base and spending in the central city; integration brings values of diversity that some suburbanites favor. Of course, these feelings of openness to newcomers exist alongside the desire to exclude them that I have already mentioned, just as the urge to locate elsewhere coexists with the feeling of comfort associated with staying put.

This conflict between the desires to exclude others and to integrate with others replicates the structure of identity formation described in the communitarian literature. Local government law could help undermine the power of suburban consciousness by organizing interlocal negotiations to highlight these contradictory instincts. There are many different people who could bring these conflicts into regional negotiations, because there are a multitude of ways that the fight over closure and openness occurs within both suburbs and central cities. There are advocates of race consciousness and proponents of racial integration; residents who prefer stability and residents who prefer growth; property-owners who want to preserve the existing community and property-owners who want to profit from development or gentrification; people who fear the dangers of city life and people who love living in cities; parents who feel that the suburbs are "a great place to raise a family" and unmarried singles who consider the suburbs vacuous; women who feel trapped by living in the suburbs and women who feel protected by living there; activists who seek to rid their neighborhood of "undesirables" and the undesirables themselves. Local government law could also bring the conflicting instincts of inclusion and exclusion into the negotiations by ensuring the participation not only of each individual suburb but of central-city neighborhoods. The suburbs are often spoken of collectively as if they presented a uniform contrast to the central city, but the competition between them, their division along class lines, and their desire to distinguish themselves from each other prevent them from having a single unified interest. Differences among central-city neighborhoods—and between "the neighborhoods" and downtown—deny the central city a single identity as well.

Institutional innovations are indispensable to the structuring of intercity negotiations in terms of these conflicts. But the law of exclusionary zoning and condominium conversion must also be changed. The instincts for inclusion and exclusion both have to be embraced by local government law. The extent of inclusion and exclusion has to become the result of intercity bargaining, not the product of entitlements brought to the bargaining table. Those who want to move to a neighborhood should not face community-imposed obstacles to their doing so (the community should have no right to exclude them). But the ability to maintain a relatively homogeneous community should also not be forbidden (there should be no right to be included). If suburbs and central-city neighborhoods are denied a legal right to exclude, they will be sufficiently vulnerable that they are likely to be anxious to make a deal rather than to walk away. And if the formation of relatively homogeneous communities remains a possibility, people seeking inclusion will want to make a deal as well: they will want to find a way actually to move to the community, a prospect that, as the history of *Mt. Laurel* suggests, is by no means easy to achieve. Not only would the extent of acceptable exclusion become negotiable, but the negotiations could also face up to the kinds of questions local government law now doesn't even have on the agenda. Would the reallocation of resources from suburb to central city or neighborhood to neighborhood be preferable to changes in neighborhood character? Where will the excluded people go?

As Roberto Unger's work suggests, the transformation of America's metropolitan areas, and of the forms of personal identity that they nurture, will require more than the adoption of this republican strategy of changing the structure and rules of political dialogue about exclusion. Local government law intersects with the rest of the legal system in a multitude of ways. Transformative change requires a modification of the entitlements not only of localities but of the people who live within them. Restrictions on condominium conversion legislation, for example, give property-owners considerable leeway to gentrify, while lack of protection for suburban property-owners who want to develop low- and moderate-income housing gives the suburbs substantial power to exclude. Altering these legal rules could thus affect the outcome of negotiations over both urban and suburban exclusion. Similarly, the people displaced by condominium conversion and exclusionary zoning currently have little legal protection and therefore would not be taken seriously in a negotiation process. The postwar gentrification efforts known as urban renewal recognized these kinds of displacement costs, but reinforcement of that recognition could transform the negotiation process. So might changing the entitlements of other possible participants in the negotiations: city neighborhoods opposed to "downtown" interests, women who want to ameliorate the work-family conflict by living near their work, people who prefer race consciousness to racial integration, people others label "undesirables." It is not possible to list here the rule changes that would further the negotiation process; answers are likely to vary from locality to locality. And only experience will teach us how any particular modification works in any specific context. But, clearly, reform of exclusionary zoning and condominium conversion law is only one step in such an effort. The *Mt. Laurel* court was mistaken when it treated some local regulations as having "little, if any, outside impact." This statement perpetuates the pretense that local government law's embrace of centered subjectivity reflects a real inside/outside distinction, with exclusionary zoning simply an exception to this general rule. Fully confronting the impact of the current fragmentation of our metropolitan areas requires abandoning this pretense: it requires recognizing that every local decision—from schools to sanitation, from housing policy to transportation policy, from gun control to pollution control—affects outsiders. Localities need to recognize across the board that their identity, as Michael Sandel puts it, is "defined to some extent by the community of which they are a part."

The Institutional Implications of Situated Subjectivity

To build local government law on the notion of situated subjectivity, we need to organize local institutions, as well as legal doctrine, in terms of interlocal relationships. By allocating power principally to individual cities or the state, current local government law treats as irrelevant the fact that localities are situated within a region. Legal decision making therefore oscillates between increasing the centralized power of the state government and empowering localities in a way that affects their neighbors without the neighbors' participation in the decision-making process. It is time to create another option.

This new option has to do more than simply increase the power of the regional organizations that have already been established in America. Every state in the nation has created public authorities to deal with specific issues on a regional basis (such as transportation, natural resources, and parks), and, in a few parts of the country, regional governments have assumed a considerable share of local political power. But neither of these regional entities fosters interlocal relationships; each simply replaces the city's version of the centered subject with its own. Public authorities centralize power in a corporate-style bureaucracy structured more like businesses than like government: their managers are appointed, not elected; they are exempted from many limits placed on governmental entities; their authority is defended in terms of expertise; and they replace rather than involve local democratic decision-makers. Regional governments, by contrast, centralize power in yet another form of sovereignty. They are substate governments with qualities intermediate between those of the state and cities: like the state, they can exercise power across the region; like cities, they are subservient to state power. Although both of these entities decrease the authority of city governments, neither transforms the subjectivity of the region's localities in any way.

If a situated conception of local identity is to be fostered, new forms of regional organization have to be created. One possibility would be to shift the power to define the legal authority of a metropolitan region's cities from the state government to a regional legislature. The purpose of establishing such a regional legislature would not be to enable it to act as a regional government. The purpose instead would be to create a democratic version of the idea of regional planning embodied in federal legislation of the 1960s and 1970s.[15] These federal statutes sought to inject a regional voice into local decision making by requiring local decisions to be consistent with a regional plan. Congress hoped that such a requirement would overcome the selfish pursuit of local self-interest by forcing each locality to consider the impact of its actions on the region as a whole. But the effect of these federal statutes was limited. They made regional considerations relevant only in the context of federal grant allocation; they created as many different regional planning agencies as there were subject matters to plan for; they focused on requiring agencies to prepare a written plan rather than on an ongoing process of regional negotiations; and they relied on existing political boundaries in the organization of the regional planning process. Nevertheless, the germ of the idea was sound. The object was not to have regional bodies replace local decision making but to require localities, when making their decisions, to take the interests of other localities within the region into account.

As just mentioned, the task of the regional legislature would be to perform one specific function of the state legislature and the state courts: defining the power—specifying what lawyers call the legal entitlements— of local governments. An example of such a task is the articulation of standards, such as the *Mt. Laurel* standard, that describe the extent to which localities must accommodate the interest of others in the region when they decide their land-use policies. But there are also countless other entitlement issues facing local governments: What portion of the funds derived from the property tax can a locality use solely for its own schools? Can a locality exclude a facility the region needs (a waste dump)? What incentives can a locality offer a business in a neighboring jurisdiction to move across the border? Are stricter gun control laws more appropriate in one area of the region than elsewhere? We must recognize that these entitlement questions cannot be distinguished "in principle" from substantive local decision making. One could frame every local issue as an entitlement question and thereby eliminate city decision making altogether (and frame every local issue as suitable for local resolution and thereby eliminate regional decision making altogether). What, then, is the distinction that I am making between the entitlement allocation function of a regional legislature and a regional government?

The answer to this question cannot be found in an analytical distinction between entitlement allocation and governance. It must be found instead in the way the regional legislature is organized. The regional legislature, rather than the individual cities, must have the power to determine which questions it can decide. However, it should be structured to encourage its members not to exercise power themselves but to turn the legislature into a forum for interlocal negotiations about how to decentralize power. The best chance of doing so, in my view, lies in electing representatives from the geographical areas to which people feel most attached—central-city and suburban neighborhoods. If the legislature were organized on such a basis, its members would be sufficiently connected to their communities that they would be under constant pressure to decentralize power. Moreover, since the neighborhoods would be selected with current city lines in mind, the representatives from each city could work together to defend the city's interests. On the other hand, the fact that each of the region's cities would be represented by more than one person would also enable the divisions that now exist within these cities to become part of the decision-making process. Representatives could thus form alliances across city boundaries, thereby helping to undermine the current obsession with the distinction between the central city and its suburbs. Above all, the very act of empowering a regional legislature to determine city entitlements would transform the meaning of the decentralization of power. The objective could no longer be the advancement of a parochial definition of self-interest because no city could achieve its goals without convincing fellow legislators that its vision of decentralization was a good idea. Legislators would thus regularly experience the conflict between attachment to their neighborhood and the pull of the larger community, a conflict that parallels the struggle between the attachments to the self and to others embodied in the notion of the situated self. Indeed, the contradictory pulls of the situated self would structure decision making about the decentralization of power.

A blizzard of issues are raised by this proposal that need further work. Current interpretations of the Equal Protection Clause limit the ability to adopt neighborhood lines precisely. Neighborhood representation might be inadequate to generate an appropriate amount of conflict between the desire for decentralization and the need for coordination; it might be necessary to have a wider variety of people in the legislature. Perhaps each neighborhood should be represented by more than one individual (through the adoption of a form of proportional representation) so that different factions within the neighborhood can say what the neighborhood stands for. Institutional innovations might also be required to prevent legislators from becoming so enamored with their own power that they attempt to transform the regional legislature into a regional government.[16] Finally, careful attention needs to be given not only to the rules that structure the election of regional legislators but also to those that structure decision making within the legislature, since both are bound to affect the outcome of regional negotiations. My purpose at the moment is not to resolve all these issues but simply to persuade you that a regional legislature, if properly organized, could foster the situated identity of local governments: it could enable the rules under which localities operate to be decided collectively by the localities themselves. Once cities learn, through battles in the regional legislature, what the regional impact of their decisions are, they can begin to internalize this perspective. They can improve their own "capacity," to return to Frank Michelman's formulation, "for reflexively critical reconsideration . . . by reaching for the perspective of other and different persons." Considerable authority could then be delegated to cities and neighborhoods; the review (and potential review) by the regional legislature would help overcome the fear of the centered subject that has limited the possibility of decentralizing power in America. There surely would no longer be much reason to prefer state over local decision making. Regions are as diverse as states, and they therefore can serve the purpose of protection against parochialism usually advanced for state power. In fact, they can serve it better. Because many metropolitan regions in America cross state boundaries, state decision making often increases the fragmentation of metropolitan regions rather than reducing it. Moreover, little popular participation in the states' decision making is possible because of their size. Decentralizing power to cities and neighborhoods thus seems a far better alternative than state decision making, as long as regional needs are incorporated into the process.

Other mechanisms might also foster a situated identity for localities. Although a regional legislature can lay down rules about local entitlements, case-by-case applications of these rules are necessary as well. One could therefore create a citizen group of (say) one hundred people to serve for a stated period of time as public representatives to evaluate cities' performance of this task; the group could be chosen from the metropolitan area by lot, rather than by election or through interest-group representation, to ensure that its members were a microcosm of the region. Once constituted, the group could be authorized, for example, to judge disputed instances of exclusion (how many centers for the homeless are appropriate in this neighborhood?) or extraterritorial effects (what restrictions on pollution are necessary before an industrial development project is undertaken?). One way to understand this proposal is to see it as an expanded and modified form of the jury: as with jury service, citizens would be expected to devote a portion of their time to public policy decision making. Like jurors, these public representatives would listen to and evaluate expert testimony and would apply legal rules to the facts as they found them. And the regional legislature would retain the authority to ensure that they kept within this mandate. But, as Tocqueville emphasized, it is important to see juries as political institutions, not just as vehicles for deciding issues.

> Juries invest each citizen with a sort of magisterial office; they make all men feel that they have duties toward society and that they take a share in its government. By making men pay attention to things other than their own affairs, they combat that individual selfishness which is like rust in society.[17]

If so, the institution of the jury is too important to be limited to deciding questions raised by civil or criminal trials. The need to experience the opposite pulls of community and self can become a vehicle for involving ordinary citizens in the experience of local democratic decision making. The more rapid the turnover of this citizen group and the greater the number of issues decided by this process, the more widespread this learning experience would become.

A council of mayors from the region's cities might also be a helpful forum for a discussion of regional needs and priorities. Because the size of city populations varies considerably, it would be a mistake to give such a council decision-making power. Nevertheless, even as an advisory body, a council of mayors can inform individual localities about interlocal needs and thereby speed the process of internalizing these needs into city decision making. This experience of forming a city agenda in discussion with neighboring city leaders might also redirect a city's energy. If, for example, the mayors could agree on a plan of decentralization, they could be an effective lobbying force in the regional legislature. But in order to agree, they would have to confront their differences. Like the other institutional forms suggested here (and many others that might be proposed), the council of mayors is based on a strategy about how to build unity out of differences: a sense of situated identity is more likely to be formed by small groups living near each other than by the actions of a central government.

Beyond the Situated Subject

I think that local government law—and the chances for effective decentralization of power—would be vastly improved if localities were treated as situated subjects. Accomplishing such a change would take an extraordinary amount of political effort and doctrinal innovation—as much as, perhaps more than, it's sensible to expect. Yet the situated self is but one of the possibilities for basing local government law on a decentered subject, and it is one that, at least for me, has significant problems. Two interrelated difficulties seem worth mentioning here: romanticism and hedging.

Much of the literature of the situated self suffers from an overly romantic view of human connection. Somehow, it suggests, we will all recognize
our connection with each other. Last paragraphs of articles and books
written in this tradition are a place to look for this sentiment. Here's
Minow: "By taking difference into account, we can overcome our pre-
tended indifference to difference, and people our worlds with those who
can surprise and enrich one another." And Sandel: "When politics goes
well, we can know a good in common that we cannot know alone." And
Unger: "If someone were to ask us why we want to live in the present in
this way, we should answer: first, because this is the kind of being we really
are and, second, because by living in this fashion we empower ourselves
individually and collectively." These quotations are examples of romanticism not just in the popular sense of sentimentality but in the sense associated with premodernist nineteenth-century thought:

> Largely from the nineteenth century, we have inherited a *romanticist* view of
> the self, one that attributes to each person characteristics of personal depth:
> passion, soul, creativity, and moral fiber. This vocabulary is essential to the for-
> mation of deeply committed relations, dedicated friendships, and life purposes.

And, one might add, the same vocabulary is essential to optimism about
intercity negotiations as well.[18]

The hedging problem can be seen in the literature's use of qualifiers like
"partly" in the definition of the relationship between self and others. For
example, to return to quotations from the beginning of this chapter,
Charles Taylor says that "our identity is always *partly* defined in conversation with others. . . ." Sandel argues that "community . . . describe[s] not
just a feeling but a mode of self-understanding *partly* constitutive of the
agent's identity." And Michelman describes "a self whose identity and
freedom consists, *in part*, in its capacity for reflexively critical reconsideration. . . ." For me, this kind of hedging raises an irresistible question: how
much is partly? If the individual self is divided between a "real" self and
an other-created self, how much is allocated to each part? The connection
between the literature's answer to this question and its romanticism seems
clear. People writing in the tradition of the situated self think that a lot
of the self can be recognized as other-created; skeptics disagree.

These two problems exist not only in the writers I have just mentioned
but in my own work in this tradition as well, as exemplified by this chapter.
When I write in this tradition, it feels inescapable to be optimistic about
interpersonal or interlocal dialogue—why else would one be trying to further it? Hedging seems equally unavoidable. The extent of people's ability
to relate to each other is unknowable—it has to be worked out in practice.
It's not surprising, therefore, that much of the criticism of the concept of
the situated self is based on these two problems. Critics first attack the

romanticism of the situated self: people, they suggest, are more selfish than those who write in the tradition think. People are likely to have different values and to be willing to sacrifice the rights of others, particularly those of minorities. Besides, some add, no one wants to talk as much as would be necessary to engage in all that dialogue. The critics then seize on the hedging to redescribe human nature, reducing the degree of romanticism to whatever extent they see fit and substituting self-interest in its place. As a conclusion, many of these critics end up embracing some version of the centered self.

It bothers me that my criticism of the concept of the situated self shares as much as it does with that of these critics. Readers of this book could well find the criticism of romanticism and hedging so compelling that they would reject my entire discussion of the situated self in local government law and end up back where we started. My reaction to my own (and others') romanticism and hedging, however, is the opposite of that of the critics. While they attempt to recenter the self in something more "realistically" selfish, it seems to me that the preferable alternative is to decenter the self more than those who espouse the situated self, let alone their critics, propose. Romanticism and hedging stem from the fact that the situated self is only partly decentered. First of all, a portion of the self seems not to be constituted by others at all. This is the self-defining self that the critics seize upon and emphasize. Moreover, the situated self as a whole remains relatively identifiable, relatively centered. The world seems to be composed of the self and others, with the question being how the two should relate to each other. "Self" and "other" seem to have identifiable content both within the definition of the situated self and within the definition of a person's relationships with outsiders. After all, how else could one tell that the self was "in part" constituted by two different ingredients? And why else would the goal be both romantic (bringing the two ingredients together) and hedged (bringing them together to the extent possible)?

One way to reject simultaneously the romanticism and hedging of the situated self and the critics' retreat to the centered subject, then, would be to adopt a more fully decentered conception of self. This would involve moving beyond giving content to the self as other-directed, as selfish, or as partly both. In the local government context, it would mean a rejection of the organization of local government law in terms of suburb vs. city, us vs. them, inside vs. outside, self vs. other. It would, in short, require us to replace the relatively decentered position of the situated subject with a postmodern sense of self.

5

The Postmodern Subject

A Glimpse at the Literature

There is now an enormous literature that extends the critique of the centered subject beyond the notion of the situated self. Considerable differences exist within this literature among aspects labeled (for example) poststructuralist, postmodernist, feminist, and critical race theory. As in the previous chapter, I intend not to survey the work of even a single proponent of any of these strands. Moreover, here, as there, the writers I mention do not add up to a single school of thought; on the contrary, they often have different objectives and criticize each other's positions. Once again, I seek merely to suggest the kinds of ideas that those who write in these traditions advance, all of which could be a source of innovation in local government law, and only a few of which I have room to discuss below. In chapter 4, I described the situated subject in terms of a relationship between self and other; here my sketch of the postmodern subject will be presented in terms of a critique of both of these ingredients—a critique of both the "self" and "other."

Let's start with a look at the self. Exponents of the situated subject use the term "self" to refer to the individual taken as a whole, although the term could also be used to mean only that part of the situated subject that is self-defining rather than constituted in relationship with others. For the critics of the situated self (and perhaps some proponents as well), this self-defining aspect of the self is the "real" self—the core component that distinguishes an individual from outsiders. The postmodern subject has no such core component. On the contrary, the more one tries to nail down what this core is, the more one realizes that the core is empty, that what seems to be a core is an absence rather than the very center of the self.

This conception of the self has been articulated in many ways, including (among others) psychoanalytic, poststructuralist, and feminist approaches. One ingredient in the psychoanalytic literature, for example, focuses on the gap that exists, before the acquisition of language, between the fragmented and confused sensations that an infant experiences and a coherent sense of self. An infant desires the focus and coordination of a unified identity, but that is just what he or she lacks. The only way for the infant to forge a coherent self out of an experience of a swarm of objects, fantasies, and sensations is to identify with something—like an image in the mirror—other than the self. "If I *desire* to be (an) I, if I *desire* myself, it must, following elementary logic, be because I am not it. . . . [The] foundation of identity . . . does not exist within me: it is elsewhere, in this other." But achieving a feeling of oneness with this other—and thus filling this lack of self—can never be accomplished.

> The mirror can no more be assimilated than can any of those other privileged objects [that might fulfill the infant's desire], yet the subject defines itself entirely in relation to it. As a consequence of the irreducible distance which separates the subject from its ideal reflection, it entertains a profoundly ambivalent relationship to that reflection. It loves the coherent identity which the mirror provides. However, because the image remains external to it, it also hates that image.

Because the mirror image is a fiction that one can only misrecognize as (one)self—because one can never *be* such a self—narcissistic desire is permanent, unsatisfiable, abyssal.[1]

Poststructuralists, along with many who follow a psychoanalytic approach, add to this picture the acquisition of language. Indeed, "add" is the wrong word because the preverbal stage of life can be understood only through language, by which it is transformed. The personal pronoun "I," like the mirror image, holds out an unattainable promise of unity. "I" represents all that a person is. But, at the same time, "I" is a word that, like all words, comes from outside and is subject to a structure of language that the individual neither invents nor controls. Although people constitute themselves as subjects through use of such a word, their subjectivity "is defined not by the feeling which everyone experiences of being himself (this feeling, to the degree that it can be taken note of, is only a reflection) but as the psychic unity that transcends the totality of the actual experiences it assembles and that makes the permanence of the consciousness." This assembling of the totality of experience—this forming and transmitting of experience through the word "I"—is "the self." Yet this act of assembling, this unity represented by the word "I," itself relies on language. As each speaker uses the word "I" "to express himself[,] . . . the interior 'thing' he claims to 'translate' is itself no more than a ready-made lexicon, whose words can be explained only through other words, and this ad infinitum." Use of the word "I" to represent the self thus opens an unbridgeable gap between language and referent, symbol and reality, meaning and being—unbridgeable because the "referent," "reality," and "being" of subjectivity are available to us only through language.[2]

Judith Butler's brilliant book *Gender Trouble* extends this postmodern conception of the subject to gender, a fundamental aspect of identity (and the body). By understanding the "self" as a fantasy, Butler argues, one can recognize that the acts, gestures, and desires associated with gender do not express an already existing interior essence. People have no interior essence. Instead, these acts, gestures, and desires are attempts to act out—to inscribe on the surface of the body—an idealized, publicly created image of what gender is.

> In what sense . . . is gender an act? As in other ritual social dramas, the action of gender requires a performance that is *repeated*. This repetition is at once a reenactment and reexperiencing of a set of meanings already socially established; and it is the mundane and ritualized form of their legitimation. Although there are individual bodies that enact these significations by becoming stylized into gendered modes, this "action" is a public action. There are temporal and collective dimensions to these actions, and their public character is not inconsequential; indeed, the performance is effected with the strategic aim of maintaining gender within its binary frame—an aim that cannot be attributed to a subject, but, rather, must be understood to found and consolidate the subject.

Butler suggests that one can best understand the constructed nature of gender by examining such overt gender performances as drag and cross-dressing. Dissecting these performances allows us to recognize the performative nature of all gendered identities while, at the same time, exposing possibilities for reconfiguration, redeployment, and opposition to existing gender norms.[3]

Butler's invocation of the socially constructed nature of the gender system brings us to the second aspect of the postmodern subject, its critique not of "self" but of "other." The critique to which I am referring examines the "postmodern condition"—the experience of living in a world without a core sense of self. Situated subjects, as sketched above, long for interconnection with others: they seek the experience of collective unity no matter how difficult (even impossible) it is to achieve. Postmodern subjects, by contrast, deny themselves this solace, this hope of bringing the mysterious hidden core of the self to the surface and sharing it with others. For the postmodern subject, relationship with others—and with the world at large—is an experience not of consensus, totality, or oneness but of conflicting multiplicities. Here, for example, is Jean-François Lyotard's description of the postmodern condition:

> A *self* does not amount to much, but no self is an island; each exists in a fabric of relations that is now more complex and mobile than ever before. Young or old, man or woman, rich or poor, a person is always located at "nodal points" of specific communication circuits, however tiny these may be. Or better: one is always located at a post through which various kinds of messages pass. No one, not even the least privileged among us, is ever entirely powerless over the

messages that traverse and position him at the post of sender, addressee, or referent. One's mobility in relation to these language game effects (language games,
of course, are what this is all about) is tolerable, at least within certain limits
(and the limits are vague). . . . It may even be said that the system can and must
encourage such movement to the extent that it combats its own entropy; the
novelty of an unexpected "move," with its correlative displacement of a partner
or group of partners, can supply the system with that increased performativity
it forever demands and consumes.

This quotation from Lyotard provides a contrasting language to that associated with the situated subject: communication circuits rather than community, language games rather than intersubjectivity, moves in a system
rather than desire.[4]

There are dozens of attempts such as Lyotard's to characterize the postmodern experience. Some writers use the word "pastiche" to describe the
experience of recognizing the endless connotations and references invoked
by one's own activity. Everyone knows that his or her actions are under-
standable only because they can be compared to actions already taken by
others; postmodern subjects base their presentation of self on this recognition of intertextuality and quotation. In the postmodern world there are
no originals, only copies. (Umberto Eco's oft-quoted postmodern reading
of the phrase "I love you madly"—reproduced in the note—illustrates
this phenomenon.)[5] The term "schizophrenia" is also widely used in the
postmodern literature. For example, Jean Baudrillard says at the end of
"The Ecstasy of Communication":

With communication and information, with the immanent promiscuity of all
these networks, with their continual connections, we are now in a new form of
schizophrenia. . . . The schizo is bereft of every scheme, open to everything in
spite of himself, living in the greatest confusion. . . . What characterizes him is
less the loss of the real, the light years of estrangement from the real, the pathos
of distance and radical separations, as is commonly said: but, very much to the
contrary, the absolute proximity, the total instantaneity of things, the feeling of
no defense, no retreat. It is the end of interiority and intimacy, the overexposure
and transparence of the world which traverses him without obstacle. He can no
longer produce the limits of his own being, can no longer play nor state himself,
can no longer produce himself as mirror. He is now only a pure screen, a switching center for all the networks of influence.

Finally—to offer one last example—Brian McHale argues that living in a
postmodern world raises not the kind of epistemological questions that
might be asked by a situated subject ("How am I to interpret this world?
And what am I in it?") but ontological questions ("Which world is this?
What is to be done in it? Which of my selves is to do it? What happens when

different kinds of worlds are placed in confrontation, or when boundaries between worlds are violated?"). The appropriate literary genre for postmodern literature, he concludes, is not the mystery (as it might be for the situated subject) but science fiction.[6]

How can a person affect—intervene in—a world understood in terms of communication circuits, language games, moves in a system, pastiche, schizophrenia, science fiction? How can there be individual action without a "self"? From the perspective of a situated subject (like a centered subject), individual action is located in the self, and political effectiveness depends on winning others over. For a postmodern subject, by contrast, a situated subject's effort to build a community does not express an inner self but reenacts a performance, a game, a role in a publicly created system. The domain of politics, Michel Foucault argues, lies in examining and challenging the ways in which such a performance, game, or system creates the notion of the individual.

> The systematic dissociation of identity . . . is necessary because this rather weak identity, which we attempt to support and to unify under a mask, is in itself only a parody: it is plural; countless spirits dispute its possession; numerous systems intersect and compete. . . . [What is required] is to reveal the heterogeneous systems which, masked by the self, inhibit the formation of any form of identity.

There is no viewpoint that allows us to examine current forms of identity by stepping outside them; the power of the heterogeneous systems that form our identities is not an outside force that individuals might resist as an act of will. On the contrary, Foucault contends,

> one of the prime effects of power [is] that certain bodies, certain gestures, certain discourses, certain desires come to be identified and constituted as individuals. The individual . . . is not the *vis-à-vis* of power. . . . The individual is an effect of power, and at the same time, or precisely to the extent to which it is that effect, it is the element of its articulation.

Foucault argues that "we have to promote new forms of subjectivity through the refusal of the kind of individuality which has been imposed on us for several centuries." Yet such an effort always has the potential of backfiring: it might reproduce, rather than subvert, the kind of identity that one is seeking to contest. In Lyotard's words, "the system can and must encourage such movement . . . [to] increase [the] performativity it forever demands and consumes."[7]

Whether despite or because of these difficulties, many scholars, such as postmodern feminists and critical race theorists, are currently trying to subvert reigning notions of identity. Thus Angela Harris has argued that black women—not uniquely but in poignant and striking ways—have articulated a multiple consciousness, an experience not of "a single inner self (much less one that is essentially gendered), but many selves." "We are not born with a 'self,' " Harris says, "but rather are composed of a welter of partial, sometimes contradictory, and even antithetical selves." Harris relies on this sense of multiple identity to question dominant conceptions of the subject in feminist theory. Patricia Williams and bell hooks, among others, have used a related strategy to challenge the prevailing notions of race.[8] I now turn, in a similar fashion, to an attempt to subvert the centered subjectivity of local government law.

The Postmodern Subject as Local Government Law

A postmodern conception of local government law must start with a post-modern conception of localities. Chapter 4's version of local government law was based on the notion that cities and suburbs are interrelated rather than separate, independent entities, and it therefore treated those who live in one jurisdiction as constituted, in part, by actions taken by those who live in others. The postmodern version sketched here rejects both that chapter's emphasis on residency as the focal point of a person's relationship to the metropolitan area and the city/suburb distinction itself. Instead of envisioning people as located on one side or the other of a city/suburb line, it builds on the idea, to quote Lyotard again, that "young or old, man or woman, rich or poor, a person is always located at 'nodal points' of specific communication circuits" spread throughout the area.

The city/suburb distinction is often used to contrast two images: a congested, dangerous, deteriorating central city and a quiet, prosperous residential suburb. Such a picture misrepresents life in contemporary American metropolitan areas. Parts of America's central cities are certainly characterized by congestion, poverty, and urban decay, but so are many suburbs. Often, these suburbs are worse off than central cities because their property values are so low that they cannot afford even the limited social services that central cities offer their poorest residents. Moreover, if we think of a suburb as a homogeneous residential area dominated by well-kept single family houses set in yards, "almost all large cities," as Robert Fishman has noted, "have suburbs . . . within their borders."[9] These residential areas within central cities (Riverdale in New York, West Roxbury in Boston, Chestnut Hill in Philadelphia, Chevy Chase, D.C., in Washington, Sauganash in Chicago, Palmer Woods in Detroit, River Oaks in Houston, Sea Cliff in San Francisco) are indistinguishable from neighborhoods on the other side of the city line. And people of color live in both kinds of neighborhoods. One-third of African Americans live in middle-class suburbs; in some suburbs a majority of residents are African Americans, Chinese, or Latino. Although lines of race divide American metropolitan areas as sharply as the Berlin Wall formerly divided Berlin and the Green Line divided Beirut, these racial lines are more often found within central cities and between suburbs than along the city/suburb boundary (East Ninety-sixth Street and Howard Beach in New York, South Side and Bridgeport in Chicago, Roxbury and South Boston in Boston, South Central and the Westside in Los Angeles). Finally, it's not just the middle-class and the poor who live on both sides of the border: there are working-class suburbs just as there are working-class neighborhoods within central cities.

The other characteristic that has traditionally been associated with central cities—a central business district with offices and stores—also describes suburbs as well as central cities. "Most large metropolitan areas," Christopher Leinberger reports, "have ten to thirty urban cores, the downtown being just one of them." Two-thirds of American offices are currently located outside of city downtowns. Tyson's Corner, Virginia, has more office space than downtown Miami; Southfield, Michigan, has more office space than Detroit. "By 1980," Robert Fishman has found, "38 percent of the nation's workers commuted to their jobs from suburb-to-suburb, while only half as many made the stereotypical suburb to city trek." Shopping malls have similarly brought the density and feel of central-city commercial life to the suburbs. Suburban stores now outsell their central-city competitors, and some suburban malls are as big as central-city downtowns. (On Route 202 in King of Prussia [Pennsylvania], the sign reads, MALL NEXT FOUR LEFTS.) So powerfully has the aggregation of restaurants, entertainment, shopping, and pedestrian walkways in suburban shopping malls captured the image of America's commercial life that central cities have begun to restructure their own commercial areas by copying them (Quincy Market in Boston, the Inner Harbor in Baltimore, Watertower Place in Chicago, the Skyways in Minneapolis, Ghiradelli Square in San Francisco, pedestrian zones everywhere).[10]

In sum, in the words of urban historian James Vance, "today it is hard to draw a significant concrete distinction between a Clayton and a St. Louis."[11] Except, of course, that most of us have never heard of Clayton. The only difference between St. Louis and Clayton is a legal distinction— local government law treats these two parts of the same region as separate and independent sovereignties. During the course of my argument that the city/suburb distinction no longer describes American metropolitan areas, I have repeatedly invoked this legal distinction myself. I have used the words "city" and "suburb" to refer to one side or the other of the invisible line that marks the legally recognized boundary between them. My use of these terms has masked the plurality and heterogeneity on both sides of the line. The terms thus have had the characteristics of the term "I" in the creation of subjectivity: the unity that "city" or "suburb" has assembled has been a unity of (legal) language. As Foucault suggests, use of this language is the exercise of power: the current identities of central cities and suburbs are "an effect of power, and at the same time, or precisely to the extent which . . . [they are] that effect . . . [they are] the element of its articulation." To promote an alternative to this form of power, we must start by recognizing the arbitrariness of the city/suburb lines that now fracture America's metropolitan areas. We must look at our metropolitan areas anew, without focusing on the legally recognized borders between localities.

Most Americans who live in these areas already disregard jurisdictional boundaries. Instead of sharply dividing central city and suburb, residents create their own idea of the region in which they live by organizing it in terms of the places they know. They think nothing of crossing city lines for child care, work, shopping, recreation, entertainment, visiting friends, and the like. Their relevant space, as Robert Fishman has argued, "is defined by the locations they can conveniently reach in their cars." They often don't even know the name of the town where the mall they shop in is located; all they need to know is the name of the mall. Areas that do have names are commonly identified in a way that ignores local government boundaries: Route 128 in Massachusetts, Silicon Valley in northern California, King of Prussia in eastern Pennsylvania, the Galleria in Houston, Tyson's Corner in Virginia. Other areas both in the central city and in the suburbs—even some close by—are so unfamiliar that people get lost if they try to go there. The metropolitan area as a whole is a hodgepodge of elements—shopping/office/hotel complexes, strip shopping malls, industrial parks, office buildings, department stores, neighborhoods, subdivisions, condominium communities—that is "impossible to comprehend," "vertigo-inducing." For many Americans the symbol of this contemporary form of metropolis is Los Angeles. And, as Joel Garreau reports, "every single American city that is growing, is growing in the fashion of Los Angeles, with multiple urban cores."[12]

This reference to Los Angeles suggests more than simply the absence of a metropolitan center. Los Angeles symbolizes another feature of contemporary urban life as well: issues of ethnicity, race, and class crosscut America's metropolitan areas without stopping at jurisdictional borders. Los Angeles has aptly been labeled the capital of the Third World: immigrants from El Salvador, Guatemala, Mexico, the Philippines, Korea, Thailand, Vietnam, Iran, India, Pakistan, Armenia, Russia, and Israel (among other places) have formed communities in the area in both the central city and the suburbs.[13] Similar communities are being created across America. This influx of immigrants has not merely changed the character of the neighborhoods where the immigrants reside. As in Los Angeles, many immigrants do business in the region's poorest neighborhoods (Korean and

Latino stores in African American neighborhoods); others work in mini-mum-wage jobs in the area's shopping/office/hotel complexes; still oth-ers spend most of their time in the region's fanciest neighborhoods because they have come to serve as the indispensable maids and baby-sitters for the upper middle class. Los Angeles is also famous these days as the site of riots and of gang warfare in its South Central neighborhoods. Fears of this kind of urban unrest and gang violence have increased throughout the country, and the proximity between the neighborhoods where the civil unrest and violence have occurred (or threaten to occur) and other neighborhoods has increased with the extent of this fear. Neigh-borhoods close by were once virtually forgotten ("no one lives in Detroit," someone who lived in a nearby suburb once informed me); now, they seem all too close.

As early as 1923, Frank Lloyd Wright declared that "the big city is no longer modern." He was right: as Joel Garreau points out, "we have not built a single old-style downtown from raw dirt in seventy-five years." It's harder to realize—but it is also true—that the suburban era, the era of lawns and cul-de-sacs, has reached its end as well. Now, as Michael Sorkin argues, people live in "a wholly new kind of city, a city without a place attached to it," one that Sorkin calls the "ageographical city." Sorkin uses the term to describe the pastiche of highways, skyscrapers, malls, housing developments, and chain stores—the endless urban landscape of copies without an original—that constitute the place bites (the spatial equivalent of sound bites) of modern America. Metropolitan residents combine these place bites in countless ways, each of which makes equal sense, when they try to imagine what their metropolitan area looks like. The ageographical city, Sorkin suggests, is the urban form of the 800-number: the area code for no-place-in-particular. To frame local government law in terms of the postmodern subject, we must locate it in this ageographical city.[14]

Local government law, however, gives priority to a single place bite within the metropolitan area: the place where people live. Residency has always been at the center of local government law's conception of people's relationship to the space around them. Perhaps this emphasis on residency was justifiable when, once upon a time, home, work, family, friends, market, past, present, and future, were (so we imagine) linked together in one community. But these days some people don't even live at their place of residence: students who spend full-time out-of-state, people who are serving in the military, and businesspeople who are assigned abroad are all residents of the town they're never in. And those who do live in the area are not found solely at home. Most people spend most of their day in other parts of the region. If the neighborhood where people work deteriorates or their mall closes down, such a change would affect their lives just as much as an event three blocks away from their residence. In an era when people often don't even know the names of neighbors who live a block away, a person's territorial identity should not be reduced to his or her address.

By locating people in their houses or apartments, local government law romanticizes the home as a haven in a heartless world.[15] But in contemporary America, as Baudrillard says, one's place of residence provides "no defense, no retreat. . . . The overexposure and transparence of the world which traverses . . . [people] without obstacle" leaves only a weak sense of "home." The ageographical city is, in other words, the urban form not just of the 800-number but also of the 700-number—the telephone number that is yours regardless of where you live. The average American moves twelve times in a lifetime. I was born and went to school in Berkeley, California; I met and married my wife (who was from St. Joseph, Missouri) in Washington, D.C.; our son was born in New York City; our daughter was born in Philadelphia; most family vacations have been taken in the same house in Westport, Massachusetts; I now live in Cambridge, Massachusetts. Where am I from? Where are you from? Most people recognize that the millions of new immigrants in our metropolitan areas are fractured by attachments to their country of origin, their current neighborhood, the place where they work, and the place where they hope to move—feeling "at home" in none of these locations. But in the age of the jet plane, the Internet, the fax machine, satellite disks, and USA Today, it's not just recent immigrants who feel more linked to areas far away than to those close to home. Someone in the upper middle class in Boston is likely to be more connected to, and know more about, midtown Manhattan than Medford.

Of course, many people still feel an attachment to their neighborhood. Sometimes this attachment is linked with commonalities of race, ethnicity, or class; sometimes it is attributed to the fact that a family has lived in the same community for generations; sometimes it is expressed in terms of maintaining property values; sometimes it is expressed as a negative—residents feel trapped, by poverty and exclusion, in an area from which they cannot escape. But local government law has never given legal protection to neighborhoods. On the contrary, recent developments in local government law have presided over the destruction of many neighborhoods to which people have felt connected.[16] In the 1960s and 1970s, some reformers sought to resist this destruction by recentering local government law's sense of place from the city to the neighborhood. They wanted the neighborhood to play the role for territorial identity that biology has played for racial and gender identity—to be the common core that unites the group. But a postmodern reading suggests that, like the reliance on biology (and like the mirror image of the self), the concept of neighborhood provides no stable basis for either personal or group identity. The image of neighborhood conjures up the ideal of community, but it is a fantasy community—a (comm)unity that is never achievable. One can succeed in maintaining an inside/outside distinction that delimits a neighborhood only by failing to see people who are there but do not fit in. Property-owners who own property in the area but rent it to others, workers who spend more hours in the area than residents, residents whose violence or addiction threatens neighborhood stability, the homeless who live on the street, part-time residents who spend much of the year elsewhere, maids who "live in," undocumented aliens living with family members—which of these are included in the sense of "neighborhood"? Some local people are regularly treated as outside the definition of the neighborhood, while outsiders are often included as community members. Even the definition of a neighborhood is contestable: people who have lived in a neighborhood for years often disagree about its borders. Attachment to a neighborhood, like the maintenance of the gender system, is, in Judith Butler's words, a ritual social drama: "a performance that. . . . is at once a reenactment and reexperiencing of a set of meanings already socially established. . . . [a performance that] is effected with the strategic aim of maintaining . . . [the neighborhood] within its binary [inside/outside] frame." Such a performance is constantly jeopardized by aspects of the ageographical city that people in the area cannot avoid or that they even find attractive.

To replace our current legal conception of localities with one that embraces the ageographical city, we have to stop building local government law on residency and on the importance of local jurisdictional boundaries. We must treat people not as located solely in one jurisdiction but as "switching center[s] for all the networks of influence" within the region that affect their lives. Under current law, residency within city limits determines people's legal rights on issues ranging from voting to their entitlement to participate in government programs. And the location of property within city limits determines who pays for these government programs through the property tax, still the predominant source of local government revenue. To illustrate how embracing the postmodern subject would transform local government law, I turn to a discussion of two specific local government doctrines: one dealing with residency (eligibility for government services) and one with the property tax (school financing).

Many local services are now available only to the people inside specified jurisdictional borders. Students must live within a school district to attend its schools; police and fire protection stop at the city line; city hospitals exclude nonresidents. One justification offered for these policies analogizes local government services to property rights: only those who pay for services are entitled to receive them. But those who pay for local services are not the same people as those eligible to receive them. Nonresidents who are property-owners pay the property tax, but they cannot send their children to city schools or use city hospitals. On the other hand, residents who own no property and therefore do not pay property taxes (at least directly) can use city services. Moreover, many city services are supported by state and federal as well as locally generated revenue. Yet residency remains a qualification for services no matter where the funding comes from. The reason that services are allocated only to residents is not the source of financing but the equation of residency and decentralization: local control means control by residents. A local government law organized in terms of the postmodern subject, by contrast, would recognize that the maids who clean the residents' houses, the grocery store family who provide their milk, and the consumers who drive to the area to shop are also connected to a neighborhood. Even Justice Rehnquist, in *Holt Civic Club v. City of Tuscaloosa*, has acknowledged that decisions made by city residents have an impact on nonresidents whether or not the nonresidents enter the city.

> The granting of building permits for high rise apartments, industrial plants, and the like on the city's fringe unavoidably contributes to problems of traffic congestion, school districting, and law enforcement immediately outside the city. A rate change in the city's sales or ad valorem tax could well have a significant impact on retailers and property values in areas bordering the city. The condemnation of real property on the city's edge for construction of a municipal garbage dump or waste treatment plant would have obvious implications for neighboring nonresidents. Indeed, the indirect extraterritorial effects of many purely internal municipal actions could conceivably have a heavier impact on surrounding environs than . . . direct regulation. . . .

To be sure, Justice Rehnquist used this analysis to defend a residency requirement, not to attack it. "No one," he concluded, "would suggest that nonresidents likely to be affected by this sort of municipal action have a constitutional right to participate in the political processes bringing it about." Well, I'm suggesting something of this sort, albeit not on constitutional grounds. In the ageographical city, residency within invisible boundary lines should not determine who can use schools, hospitals, addiction treatment centers, or the like. Local services should be open to all local people. The problem is to decide who they are and how to do so; I discuss some possibilities below.[17]

Building local government law on a postmodern subjectivity would similarly transform local government financing. At present, only property located within jurisdictional boundaries is subject to tax, and only people who live within the same boundaries benefit from the tax. School financing provides the best-known example of the impact of this inside/outside distinction. The Supreme Court of Texas' description of the effect of juris-dictional wealth differences in that state is illustrative:

> Because of the disparities in district property wealth, spending per student varies
> widely, ranging from $2,112 to $19,333. Under the existing system, an average
> of $2,000 more per year is spent on each of the 150,000 students in the wealthi-
> est districts than is spent on the 150,000 students in the poorest districts. The
> lower expenditures in the property-poor districts are not the result of lack of
> tax effort. Generally, the property-rich districts can tax low and spend high while
> the property-poor districts must tax high merely to spend low. In 1985–86, local
> tax rates ranged from $.09 to $1.55 per $100 valuation. The 100 poorest dis-
> tricts had an average rate of 74.5 cents and spent an average of $2,978 per stu-
> dent. The 100 wealthiest districts had an average tax rate of 47 cents and spent
> an average of $7,233.[18]

In the celebrated case of *San Antonio Independent School District v. Ro-driguez*, the United States Supreme Court rejected an argument that dis-parities such as these violated the Constitution's Equal Protection Clause. Instead, the court upheld the current system on the grounds that it en-hanced local control—an idea it defined in classic centered-subject lan-guage. State supreme courts, by contrast, have been divided on the ques-tion of whether property-based school financing systems violated state constitutions. But even those state courts that have held school financing systems unconstitutional have continued to recognize the importance of local boundary lines. The Texas Supreme Court, for example, has made clear that its decision to invalidate the state's school financing system does not require localities to educate people who live outside their borders. And, the court indicated, once the state adds enough money to the system to ensure that there is an efficient system of public schools throughout the state, school districts will be able to supplement the education of their residents through locally raised property taxes. Other state courts have similarly permitted this kind of local supplementation, thereby perpetuat-ing the idea that the property located inside jurisdictional borders exists for the benefit of residents.[19] By defining the tax base in terms of the prop-erty found within a jurisdiction and by defining the beneficiaries of the tax base in terms of residency, local government law creates and intensifies inequality within the metropolitan area. It's no accident that the locations of major sources of tax revenue, such as large suburban malls and office complexes, are often at some distance from the locations where the reve-nue is most needed. Localities within the region compete for these sources of revenue, just as they compete for the ability to exclude those who need government services. But the imposition and the dispersion of the prop-erty tax need not be organized in terms of jurisdictional lines. Nor must taxes on sales or income—taxes often paid by people who are not resi-

dents—be treated as benefiting only residents. The current mismatch between the ability to raise revenue and the need for the money would be
alleviated by a local government law that embraced the postmodern subject. Again, the critical issue (discussed below) is determining how best to
do so.

It should be clear by now that building local government law on the
model of the postmodern subject would engender a profound transformation of current legal rules. Almost no local government law issue would
remain unaffected. To date only a few local government services—such as
beaches—have been required to be open to residents and nonresidents
alike, and property-based tax schemes have been invalidated only in the
area of school financing.[20] But it is no more justifiable, in my view, for the
quality of police protection, hospitals, or welfare programs to vary with
district wealth than the quality of the schools. Nor should the ability to
support social programs in innovative ways, or the power to raise taxes,
depend on where developers choose to put their office complexes. Currently, only some localities are able to condition zoning approvals for office
buildings on the developers' agreement to help support local services—a
practice known as "exactions"—because they can do so only if they can
attract the developer, and developers have an incentive to shop around for
a jurisdiction not interested in insisting on such a requirement. If, however, an exaction could be imposed for the benefit of the region's poor
wherever the development is located, more exactions would be possible,
and, as a result, more local services could be provided.

In the interest of preserving a national economy, courts have long invoked the Commerce Clause to prevent cities from enhancing their welfare by favoring their own residents over outsiders.[21] But court decisions
relying on the Commerce Clause have simply invalidated local ordinances;
they have not created a basis for a regional system of revenue sharing and
service entitlement. A local government law founded on the postmodern
subject has a chance of doing so. No doubt, as Justice Brennan suggested
in *Holt*, a refusal to build local government law on local boundary lines and
residency challenges our understanding of what it means to be a political
community. "At the heart of our basic conception of a 'political community,' " Justice Brennan said, "is the notion of a reciprocal relationship
between the process of government and those who subject themselves to
that process by choosing to live within the area of its authoritative application."[22] Indeed, the prospect of organizing local government law in terms
of the ageographical city raises fundamental questions about what decentralization means. To whom would power be decentralized if not to people
defined within local boundaries? And where would people participate in
the democratic process if not at their place of residence?

The Institutional Implications
of Postmodern Subjectivity

Many who write in the postmodernist tradition would consider it a very odd idea to try to build an institutional structure on postmodern subjectivity. The postmodern subject, as described above, is usually thought to resist legal and institutional forms. Instead, it is imagined as seeking to escape established structures through "subversive repetition," irony, and play. Nevertheless, given the account of contemporary American metropolitan areas just advanced, there are very practical reasons for our trying to figure out how localities can best be endowed with this kind of subjectivity. Many of America's giant shopping malls and office complexes are private businesses located in areas where few people live. What is the role of democracy in places like these? If we can't democratize Tyson's Corner or King of Prussia—when so many American downtowns have been superseded by developments of this kind—a vast amount of American life will never be subject to popular participation and control. Moreover, the current disjunction between the locations where America's commercial and business life is growing and the locations where job-seekers live is but one example of the urgent need to reconsider the mix of place bites that constitute America's urban areas. In countless ways, the current mix combines, yet separates, areas of crushing poverty and elaborate wealth. If increasing the power of America's poor suburbs and central cities to tax their own residents is unlikely to help them improve the lives of their citizens, and if the notion of the situated subject is too romantic or idealistic to affect the current city/suburb structure, perhaps postmodern theory is our most promising source of ideas for changing the present-day allocation of power in metropolitan areas.

One way postmodern subjectivity might be introduced into local government law is through a modification of the regional legislature proposed in chapter 4. There, the regional legislature was imagined in terms of the representation of neighborhoods, with each neighborhood defined by residency. If, however, as argued above, people have multiple attachments to the metropolitan area, including attachments to places where they shop or work, a different system of representation might be better. Consider a plan, for example, in which everyone gets five votes that they can cast in whatever local elections they feel affect their interest ("local" still being defined by traditional city boundaries). They can define their interests differently in different elections, and any form of connection that they think expresses an aspect of themselves at the moment will be treated as adequate. Under such an electoral system, mayors, city council members, and neighborhood representatives in the regional legislature would have a constituency made up not only of residents but of workers, shoppers, property-owners, the homeless, and so forth. People are unlikely to vote in a jurisdiction they don't care about, but there are a host of possible motives for voting (racial integration, racial solidarity, redistribution of wealth, desire for gentrification, etc.). There is also no reason to assume that the constituency would be limited solely to those who live in the region. These days, as I have already argued, people feel connected to areas far away as well as close to home. Puerto Ricans in New York, therefore, may want to vote not only in New York but in San Juan; of course, if they do, that would leave them one vote fewer for local elections in the New York region. On the other hand, the voting system might also mimic the idea of proportional representation, allowing someone to cast all five votes in one locality if that's where her or his attachments are felt to be.

What exactly would happen under such an electoral allocation is hard to say. Its unpredictability might be felt to reproduce the sense of "vertigo" that life in metropolitan areas is now said to induce. All we know for sure is that members of the regional legislature, elected in such a manner, would allocate entitlements (as proposed in the previous chapter) for decentralized decision making by officials elected in the same manner. It seems likely, however, that the property tax generated by giant shopping malls and office complexes will be allocated more broadly than simply to those who live within the borders where they are located. In fact, the rules adopted by the regional legislature for allocating all taxes might have a better chance of meeting the needs of people throughout the metropolitan area than would negotiations between the central city and its suburbs (defined in terms of residency). The attempt to limit services to those "inside" an area is also likely to be rethought and, perhaps, replaced with another form of allocation. Above all, such an electoral scheme would radically change the idea of what a neighborhood or city is—of who is included in a reference to such a locality. The "self" in the phrase "local self-interest" would become a gesture toward an unknown and unspecifiable multiplicity.

Still, the change would not be quite as radical as it might at first appear. The idea that Puerto Ricans who live outside of San Juan have an interest in being represented in its governance is not mine. Attempts have already been made to recognize their interests in the organization of San Juan's municipal government. Even the Supreme Court recognized, in *Kramer v. Union Free School District*, that those who vote in school board elections could not be limited to people who own or lease property in the area, their spouses, and the parents or guardians of the children who attend the schools. Many others, the Court reasoned, have a direct interest in school decisions: "senior citizens and others living with children or relatives; clergy, military personnel, and others who live on tax-exempt property;

boarders and lodgers; parents who neither own nor lease qualifying property and whose children are too young to attend school; parents who neither own nor lease property and whose children attend private schools."[23] But why stop there? Many more—including many nonresidents the Court did not consider—are just as interested: teachers and staff who work at the school; parents who would like to send their children to the school system if they weren't excluded by residency requirements; parents who are sending their children to schools with fewer resources; citizens who believe in school integration. Adding this group to the list of residents that the Court did include would no doubt make the school's constituency very uncertain and unstable. But school constituencies are already uncertain and unstable: residents are constantly moving in and out. In our mobile society, the notion of residency has provided an ever-shifting referent for the population of school districts, neighborhoods, and cities; in fact, reliance on residency has demonstrated that a fixed population is not a necessary element in the definition of a political constituency. Constituencies are defined tautologically: a locality includes whoever is delineated by its rules of inclusion. There is no reason to interpret the Constitution as requiring the rule of inclusion to be residency.

A local government law based on a postmodern subjectivity also need not respect the current territorial boundaries of cities and towns, as has so far been assumed. Even now the residents of America's metropolitan areas live in a multitude of legally defined jurisdictions with different borders: the areas defined by school districts, transportation districts, redevelopment authorities, park districts, and the like often differ not only from city borders but from each other. Currently, however, each of these governmental agencies reproduces the model of the centered subject adopted by cities: special districts and public authorities serve those defined by *their* borders. Thus the experience of the loss of boundaries that might have been produced by the multiple definitions of each citizen's location within the metropolitan area has been eclipsed by the reassuring sense that one's location is defined by the purpose of each territorial definition (the fact that you're in the same congressional district as someone else doesn't mean that your kids can go to her school). Endowing localities with a postmodern subjectivity would replace this comforting feeling with an intensified experience of geographic dissonance. Bringing just the current multiplicity of boundaries to consciousness can help undermine the boundary-fixation that characterizes so much of present-day local government law.

One form this consciousness-raising could take would be to increase the level of popular participation in the multitude of territorially defined governmental bodies that now exist within a metropolitan area. At present their bureaucratic structure renders the differences among their boundary definitions virtually invisible; only insiders pay much attention to how the area is divided up. If, however, members of the public worked together on education, parks, transportation, and similar issues, they would begin to recognize the uncertainties of defining who counts as part of their community. Moreover, this experience need not be confined to currently existing agencies. Often it would be better to set up a series of temporary task forces—ad hoc organizations—created to solve specific problems and disbanded after the task is completed. The temporary character of these task forces would make it easier for people to participate than would be possible in permanent organizations. And the task forces could divide up the region in new ways to examine aspects of metropolitan life now largely left untouched: the need for better working conditions in offices (a region of buildings), the need for health and retirement benefits for people who work in others' houses (a region of domestic workers), the need for child-care facilities (a region of kids), the need for consumer protection (a region of shoppers). These suggestions are simply examples of the many ways that a postmodern form of local government law might provoke in the minds of local residents the kind of questions Brian McHale has associated with the postmodern subject ("Which world is this? What is to be done in it? Which of my selves is to do it? What happens when different kinds of worlds are placed in confrontation, or when boundaries between worlds are violated?").[24]

Another form that postmodern subjectivity in local government law might take would question not whom the locality includes but the kinds of activities it undertakes. So far, the discussion of localities has referred only to the traditional tasks of municipal governments, such as zoning, condominium conversion, school financing, and the allocation of public services. But this limited view of the role of local government is by no means necessary. David Osborne and Ted Gaebler, for example, have sought to "reinvent government" on a model of entrepreneurial activity. Localities, they argue, should see themselves as profit-oriented market-innovators and entrepreneurs, not as regulators and lawmakers. They should serve as catalysts for economic development, foster community-run organizations, and organize their own activities to increase worker participation. Later in the book, I shall make proposals for other changes in the functions cities now perform. My ideas, like theirs, will work best if they are combined with the other proposals advanced in this section, spreading their risk and benefits across the region rather than having each locality undertake innovative activities as a separate entity (defined in terms of residency). But even if they are implemented city by city, proposals such as these illustrate one more way to destabilize the identity of localities: they challenge the justification for the public/private distinction that now determines what cities are permitted to do.[25]

Beyond the Postmodern Subject

Building a local government law on postmodern subjectivity would help
transform America's metropolitan areas (to return to Baudrillard's formulation) into "switching center[s] for all . . . [their] networks of influence."
Not only boundaries but the sense of community they engender would
disappear. For some people, such an "end of interiority and intimacy"
would be precisely the problem with these proposals. The last kind of future
they hope to promote is the world of the ageographical city. They therefore
would look, in many possible directions, for something beyond the postmodern subject. I would like to address here only one of the possible be-
yonds: beyond the postmodern subject might lie the situated subject.

I argued in the last chapter that the situated subject suffers from romanticism and hedging. The postmodern subject, by contrast, suffers from
a lack of romanticism and from relentlessness. Postmodernists and the
ageographical city seem to lack an ingredient many people find essential:
the feel of human connection. The postmodernists' relentless irony and
self-conscious, playful presentation of self often come across as inauthen-
tic; their concentration on appearances—their rejection of the modernist
search for a truth beneath the surface—undermines others' experience of
being in touch with who a person really is. The postmodern city feels
similarly cold and distant: the disbelief in neighborhood cohesion, let
alone that of the city and the suburb, renders not only intergroup but
intragroup relations hard to understand. Being connected everywhere
seems the equivalent of being connected nowhere (and to no one). Not
only "I" but "we" becomes a word with no particular meaning. Indeed,
viewed from the perspective of a situated subject, postmodern subjectivity
shares all too much with centered subjectivity. Centered subjects also seem
distant, cold, and lacking in human connection; their inability to relate
to others may be attributed to self-interest rather than lack of authenticity,
but the two positions may nevertheless be experienced as indistinguishable. Postmodern local government law might even be thought to offer
less of a sense of connection than current law: at least it allows for a group
cohesion *within* local boundary lines. The problem with current local
government law is that its view of community is too truncated; it divides
communities and people by creating too many boundaries. Postmodern
local government law divides communities and people by creating
too few boundaries. Both the centered and postmodern forms of subjectivity thus lack just what the situated subject wants most: the capacity to
nurture a sense of community. To promote the idea of community, then,
one needs to move beyond not only the centered subject but the postmodern subject as well.

Of course, a postmodernist response to this critique could easily link the situated subject's longing for community with the centered subject's longing for self: both hunger for the same thing—an (unachievable) sense of wholeness and togetherness. Postmodernists have a different idea of community, one more in tune with the feel of Los Angeles or Las Vegas or Disneyland than of small-town America or a commune. To a postmodernist, it is the situated subject who seems indistinguishable from the centered subject. Both are so earnest, so obsessively focused on fulfilling some personal mission. Neither could possibly understand (what some postmodernists might think of as) the real reason behind this chapter's proposed reform of local government law: neither would think it relevant, let alone decisive, that it would be so much *fun* to have an electoral system with everyone having five votes usable wherever one likes. The earnest, focused, serious form of politics of the situated subject, like that of the centered subject, demands a more inspired goal. And it requires more than can possibly be known in advance about the results of political activity. The postmodern subject might well prefer the devastating politics of laughter.

In this book, I seek to advance a third reading of the relationship among the three subjectivities: I have presented the situated subject and the postmodern subject as alternatives to the current reliance on the notion of the centered subject adopted by local government law. Both of these alternatives reject the centered subject's focus on boundary lines, an emphasis that so far has dominated thinking about local government organization. Both refuse to treat cities as if they are individual units that have a relationship only with the state; both seek instead to build a form of metropolitan life in which people across the region learn to recognize, and make policy on the basis of, their interactions with each other. At the same time, both are postintegration visions of America: integration remains possible, but it is no longer a master goal. Either version of regional negotiations allows people to form their own communities (defined by notions of race, ethnicity, class, sexual orientation, gender, or whatever); it's just that they cannot do so without dealing with people in other communities—as well as dissidents in their own communities—whose lives they affect. Above all, both alternatives reject the current social policy of local government law and the form of consciousness that it fosters, one that has fragmented our metropolitan areas into areas of privilege and want, us vs. them. No doubt the kind of metropolitan life that the two versions would foster would differ. But in both cases decentralization would mean not local autonomy but the ability to participate in the basic societal decisions that affect one's life. Decentralization would be designed to foster public freedom and community building rather than to mimic state or national power on the local level.

I will not—I cannot—resolve the choice between the situated and the postmodern subject in this book. One reason is that I am very attracted to both views. To me the two positions may be irreconcilable, but they both are indispensable. In the language of the situated subject, they replicate the contradictory experience of community: the desire for connection with others and the desire for the feel of the modern metropolis. In the language of the postmodern subject, they allow me to live out contradictory versions of (my)self. Besides, there is no need for me to make such a choice. On the contrary, it would be very odd, here at the end of a discussion of the decentered subject, for me to try to center myself in one or the other of these versions. After all, these two models of subjectivity don't *exist*: they are my own creations. It would be ridiculous to imagine being forced to make a choice between them—or to imagine that there aren't thousands of other choices as well. The purpose of these two chapters has not been to spell out a policy proposal that legislators might simply enact into law. The purpose instead has been to suggest the possibility that local government law can be based on something other than the model of the autonomous individual or the nation-state. The key question, of course, is whether pursuing an alternative to the current legal conception of cities is worth doing. That is the topic to which I now turn.

Part Three

THE GEOGRAPHY OF COMMUNITY

6

Community Building

Two Worlds of Strangers

Replacing local government law's reliance on the notion of the centered subject with a more decentered version of the self would dramatically change the nature of intercity relationships within America's metropolitan areas. And this, in turn, would transform the relationships among the more than 75 percent of Americans who live in these areas. As I describe in this chapter, every level of government has helped make city boundary lines a central ingredient in people's lives. These boundary lines not only determine which public resources are ours and which are theirs, but help to define who "we" and "they" are. Diminishing their importance would erode the privatized feel that now dominates the exercise of city power in America and, thereby, affect the life of every metropolitan resident. Clearly, the prospect of opening up the region as a whole to everyone who lives there generates images that are terrifying as well as liberating. For that reason, I suspect that many readers will have doubts about whether it would be a good idea. In the process of justifying such a change, I shall not emphasize here the point already made in chapter 3—that replacing the current legal definition of city power is an indispensable prerequisite to any genuine decentralization of power to American cities. Instead, I focus solely on its impact on city residents. There are three principal reasons, I suggest, for creating a more public version of cities and city life: to expand, and thereby enrich, the lives of the people who live in America's metropolitan areas; to reduce the tensions that now exist between them; and to enable them, at long last, to address a host of problems—ranging from the lack of affordable housing to the need for crime control and from traffic congestion to the caliber of public education—that now affect their quality of life.

In this book, I call efforts to achieve these objectives—as well as the task of forging intercity connections—"community building." I seek to avoid the romantic sense of togetherness often associated with the term "community" by offering a much more modest goal: the purpose of community building is to increase the capacity of metropolitan residents to live in a world composed of people different from themselves. Neither cities nor the individuals who live within them need to rely for their protection on fortifying the boundary lines that separate them from others in the region. But they also do not have to fuse with these others into a larger whole. Instead, they can develop the kind of relationship with each other that has historically characterized city life, one built on the ability to find an accommodation with those who inhabit the same geographic area, no matter how dissimilar they may be. As I noted in the introduction, Iris Young helps illuminate this alternative conception of community through her description of the ideal of city life—a version of human relationship that she defines as "the being together of strangers."[1] Standing by itself, however, the concept of "the being together of strangers" is ambiguous. These days American cities nurture two different kinds of relationships with strangers.

It has long been recognized that cities are a "world of strangers," a world very different from that of a village or small town where, it is often said, "everyone knows each other." "The city," as Lyn Lofland puts it, "is the locus of a peculiar social situation: the people to be found within its boundaries at any given moment know nothing personally about the vast majority of others with whom they share this space." In the United States, this definition of a city encompasses much more than our large central cities, such as Boston, Chicago, or San Francisco. Residents of their suburbs, such as Wellesley, Winnetka, and Orinda, also know nothing personally about the vast majority of those who live within their city boundaries. Virtually every suburban city in America is predominately populated by strangers. What distinguishes many suburbs from central cities is not the presence of strangers but the fact that the strangers who live in a suburb often think of themselves as constituting a coherent group. "The decision as to whether to leave the central city (and where precisely to settle in the suburbs)," Hadley Arkes says, "implied a judgment about the kind of people one wished to live with, and the conditions under which one expected to live." This picture of a suburb presents it as being like a voluntary association, such as a political organization, church, or country club. People join voluntary associations to be with people like themselves or to pursue a common interest; if big enough, voluntary associations, like suburbs, can also be populated by strangers.[2]

Residents of America's central cities lack this sense of a common identity. On the contrary, big cities are a prime location in America for the experience of otherness: they put people in contact, whether they like it or not, with men and women who have values, opinions, or desires that they find inexplicable, unsettling, even obnoxious. An encounter with strangers such as these does not generate what Richard Sennett calls "the 'we' feeling"—the sensation of similarity arising out of the desire to identify with other people, the desire to belong.[3] These are the people experienced not as one of "us" but as one of "them." The only way a resident of one of America's central cities can avoid this experience of otherness is to live in a neighborhood that, although often filled with strangers, can approximate "the 'we' feeling" of a homogeneous suburb. But central-city residents regularly leave their own neighborhood to work, shop, or go out. They thus encounter, often every day, the wider world of strangers that defines their city. Moreover, city neighborhoods themselves are fragile and subject to change. Residents come and go, and city power over land use can radically change the character of the neighborhood without the residents' consent. To be sure, individuals can choose which central city to live in, just as they choose to live in a suburb or to join a church or a political group. But no one has the power to control the nature of the other people who also choose to live in the same city.

The experience of otherness is obviously not limited to residents of central cities. Many of America's suburbs are not at all homogeneous; like central cities, they too are filled with ethnic, class, and cultural diversity. Even the residents of relatively homogeneous suburbs have the experience of otherness when they leave their suburb to work, shop, or have fun. In order to do so, however, they have to leave town—to travel to another suburb or, better still, to the central city itself. Thus community-building efforts could have a very different meaning in a homogeneous suburb than in a diverse suburb or the central city if they were restricted to city residents. They could reinforce the residents' sense of being a coherent social group rather than enhance their capacity to engage with disparate kinds of people. If so, they would further the definition of community that Iris Young sought to oppose by developing her conception of city life. Young identifies four normative values that she associates with city life, values she calls social differentiation without exclusion, variety, eroticism, and publicity. Social differentiation without exclusion means the formation of a multiplicity of group affinities—ethnic, gay and lesbian, religious, and so forth—in an atmosphere that promotes their intermingling. Variety adds to this mix a diversity of activities within each city neighborhood and a differentiation between neighborhoods, thereby producing a distinct sense of place when one travels from one location to another. Eroticism stresses the pleasure and excitement derived from the unusual, the strange, the surprising; it includes the stimulation not only of people watching but also of architectural and commercial variety. Publicity refers to the feelings generated when one enters a public space—a space that, because it is open to anyone whatsoever, provides exposure to opinions and cultures very different from one's own. A central city could devote its community-building efforts to promoting all four of these normative values. But they are not the values that characterize America's homogeneous suburbs.[4]

I propose that cities engage in community building in order to further the kinds of normative values Young associates with city life, not the type of "being together with strangers" that characterizes homogeneous suburbs. As I discuss below, I think that even homogeneous suburbs should foster their citizens' engagement with otherness. Such a transformation of city policy is usually not considered possible, however, unless a central government forces it on unwilling cities. The reason that centralization is treated as necessary is local selfishness: the cities that constitute a metropolitan area, it is thought, are too self-protective to open their borders in any meaningful way. Iris Young, for example, thinks that, in order to promote the normative ideal of city life, cities "should cease to have sovereign authority." Instead, she argues, "the lowest level of governmental power should be regional." She adopts this position because she assumes that decentralizing power to cities means ceding power to separate, autonomous, ministates. In order to restrict the exclusionary power of homogeneous suburbs, she therefore has to deny power to all cities, no matter how diverse. Although she tries to give neighborhoods some influence over regional decision making, she effectively abandons any meaningful effort to decentralize political power in America by transferring to regional governments, with millions of people within their jurisdiction, all of the conventional city functions—"powers of legislation, regulation, and taxation, significant control over land use and capital investment, and control over the design and administration of public services"—without significant change.[5] The previous two chapters were designed to suggest that this kind of centralization of power is not the only way to foster the goals that Young seeks to promote. My argument, like Young's, is based on values such as social differentiation without exclusion, variety, eroticism, and publicity. But I attempt to nurture these values by reconceiving the nature of city power rather than by centralizing power in a regional government. The reason to prefer this alternative is that decentralization itself has advantages, above all (as I described in chapter 1) the ability to nurture public freedom. If the equation of decentralization with local autonomy is rejected, the benefits of decentralized decision making and of city life can be fostered simultaneously.

Before turning to an examination of how cities could be organized to promote these goals, I must first explain why I think it would be desirable to cultivate in America a sense of community characterized not by a feeling of mutual connection but by an acceptance of difference, complexity, and strangeness. Why, one might ask, would anyone even want to live in such a world, let alone want to make it a city function to expand upon citizens' contacts with people unlike themselves? Isn't it human nature to avoid otherness and seek instead association with similar people? Isn't that why homogeneous suburbs were created in the first place? Questions such as these can be approached in a variety of different ways. I offer three responses: psychological, sociological, and political.

The Psychology of City Life

Richard Sennett's important book *The Uses of Disorder: Personal Identity and City Life* presents contrasting psychological pictures of homogeneous and heterogeneous communities. Sennett associates the desire to live in a homogeneous suburb or neighborhood—the desire for what he calls a "purified community"—with a psychological style developed in adolescence. Adolescents, he says, fear being overwhelmed by life's painful uncertainties and complexities. To overcome this fear, they attempt to create an orderly, coherent, and stable self-image by organizing their lives to preclude exposure to the unknown or the bewildering. For example, they decide on a career before they have any experience that might indicate what the alternatives would be like; they search for an ideal romantic relationship rather than confront the endless conflicts and mysteries of human intimacy; they seek to get "on top of things"—to assert control—in order to escape from the embarrassment and confusion of being uninformed or surprised about what's going on around them. These instincts to exclude, to purify, and to control, Sennett contends, generate in adults the efforts to foster the sense of solidarity and cohesion symbolized by homogeneous suburbs.

These purified communities reflect a desire for a collective form of identity, a collective defense against the unpredictable, the disorienting, or the painful. Often, people develop the aspiration for such a collective identity before moving to any particular location. The aspiration expresses a longing for a fantasy of a community, not the actual experience of interpersonal contact. On the contrary, the image of a purified community enables its residents to avoid dealing with each other. Residents of a purified community need not suffer the disruption and annoyance of actual engagement with the strangers who live nearby because the "we" feeling allows them to "imagine that they know all about each other, and their knowledge becomes a vision of how they must be the same." Although this common identity is a fabrication,

> the lie they have formed as their common image is a usable falsehood—a myth—for the group. Its use is that it makes a coherent image of the community as a whole: people draw a picture of who they are that binds them all together as one being, with a definite set of desires, dislikes, and goals. The image of the

community is purified of all that might convey a feeling of difference, let alone
conflict, in who "we" are.

Like the adolescents' purified sense of individual identity, this collective
self-image has concrete consequences. It produces efforts to create a stable
social order that can provide isolation from people considered unusual or
deviant. It leads people to protect themselves against the unfamiliar and
the surprising, not to mention the unpleasant. At times, the feeling of
vulnerability to otherness becomes so strong that acts of aggression
against outsiders, even violence, can appear life-preserving; the very survival of the community seems to depend on the exclusion of difference,
on the control of disorder.[6]

Sennett's work is a sustained critique of this psychological and social
phenomenon.[7] He finds it manifested not only in the defense of homogeneous suburbs but also in the revolutionary's (and the reactionary's) intolerance for dissent, the history of city planning, the increasing intensity of
family life, and the aesthetics of the modernist city. The more widespread
the phenomenon, however, the more insistent the question becomes:
what's wrong with these purified forms of identity? Sennett's response is
that they create "a state of absolute bondage to the status quo" and, as a
result, limit people's lives. A reliance on stability, coherence, and order
inhibits openness to experience: it undermines one's ability even to ab-
sorb, let alone profit from, the flux and variety the world has to offer.
In advancing this criticism, Sennett adopts two quite different tones.
Sometimes he suggests that a purified identity is bad for you—indeed,
self-destructive; at these moments, his text becomes evangelical, urging
self-improvement. But he also highlights a psychological state that often
accompanies a reliance on a purified identity—namely, boredom. Thus he
entices people to have more fun as well.

In his evangelical mood, Sennett argues that walling off dissonance and
disorder in the effort to protect oneself from vulnerability paradoxically
increases vulnerability to these very aspects of life. The reason is that the
barriers are designed to exclude what cannot be excluded: uncertainty,
instability, change, pain, and disorder are inevitable. This inevitability is
not attributable simply to the actions of others; a purified identity is an
attempt to escape from the self. Otherness, confusion, and complexity are
part of every human experience; they threaten to enter consciousness at
any moment. To prevent their doing so requires relentless patrolling of
one's borders, both internal and external—a vigilance that heightens the
sense of anxiety because reliance on exclusion robs people of the experience needed to develop a capacity to deal with problems as they occur.
There is, however, an alternative strategy of self-protection, Sennett suggests, one that can provide more security. The alternative requires giving

up the idea that the world can be purified or controlled, and nurturing instead what he calls "ego strength." By this, he means a sense of resilience, an ability to cope with whatever surprises and conflicts one encounters, a confidence that one won't be overwhelmed by complexity or disorder, a feeling that one can live with, even learn to enjoy, otherness. Ego strength enables "the acceptance of *chance* in life," as well as the acceptance of change, of growth, of disappointment. This capacity goes by many names in the psychological literature, such as "human plasticity," "the protean self," and "the dialogic self"; sometimes, as a contrast to adolescence, it is simply called "maturity."[8]

The reason for incorporating the experience of surprise, disorder, and difference in one's life is not simply to learn how to tolerate the pain they cause. Openness to these experiences makes life more fun. Building a world on the security derived from the familiar and the predictable causes people to feel bored, feel stuck, feel that they have "given up." This, one should recall, is a standard critique of the 1950s-style suburban bedroom communities: there, "there is nothing to do." Thus one psychological consequence of living in a purified community—other than resignation or a redoubled dedication to its defense—is a desire for a more interesting, fuller life. Lack of stimulation produces a longing for variety, surprise, mystery, excitement, adventure. For people so moved, it triggers an ambition to escape from the secure place to which they (or their parents) have escaped. But fulfilling this ambition requires openness to the unexpected, the disorienting, the new—a frightening prospect, perhaps, but a thrilling one as well.

It would be a mistake to read Sennett's contrast between a purified identity and ego strength as presenting two mutually exclusive psychological styles. Neither exists in pure form. We all have an impulse to withdraw from strangers and dissonance, and we all also have an impulse to open ourselves up to new experiences. But these two desires are in conflict with each other: new experiences weaken the boundaries protecting a purified identity, while a defense of these boundaries prevents people from having new experiences. Sennett argues that too many Americans have nurtured the purified side of their identity at the expense of building their ego strength. He seeks to redress this imbalance without romanticizing what it would mean to be more open to strangers and strangeness. Thus he focuses both on facing the painful and on having more fun. By doing so, he captures the familiar psychological experience of openness to others as a source of both vulnerability and pleasure.

Sennett's contrast between a purified identity and ego strength parallels the traditional comparison between living in a homogeneous community and living in a central city: the city is often seen as seducing people from a world of security and predictability into a more exciting, albeit more dangerous, existence. Roland Barthes' image of Paris can be generalized to cities at large:

> [T]he city center is always felt as the space where subversive forces, forces of rupture, ludic forces act and meet. Play is a subject very often emphasized in the surveys on the center; there is in France a series of surveys concerning the appeal of Paris for the suburbs, and it has been observed through these surveys that Paris as a center was always experienced semantically by the periphery as the privileged place where the other is and where we ourselves are other, as the place where we play the other. In contrast, all that is not the center is precisely that which is not ludic space, everything which is not otherness: family, residence, identity.[9]

It is important that we examine this picture because embedded within it lies an important sociological issue: how has the city's association with otherness fostered both an attraction to cities and a desire for purified communities?

The Sociology of City Life

The equivocal nature of city life is often lost in the literature about the city. Some writers overemphasize the pleasures cities offer. Iris Young, for example, sometimes slips into a romanticism about cities. She describes cities as "heterogeneous, plural, and playful, a place where people witness and appreciate diverse cultural expressions that they do not share and do not fully understand," and imagines city residents "celebrating . . . distinctive characteristics and cultures." Far more common, however, is an overemphasis on cities' negative aspects. From colonial times to the present day, a long and powerful tradition of antiurbanism has been articulated by a wide variety of Americans: the founding fathers (Jefferson, Franklin), major novelists (Hawthorne, Henry James), philosophers (Emerson, Dewey), architects (Frank Lloyd Wright), even the authors of classic works of urban sociology. In the summary words of Morton and Lucia White

> the American city has been thought by American intellectuals to be: too big, too noisy, too dusky, too dirty, too smelly, too commercial, too crowded, too full of immigrants, too full of Jews, too full of Irishmen, Italians, Poles, too industrial, too pushing, too mobile, too fast, too artificial, destructive of conversation, destructive of communication, too greedy, too capitalistic, too full of automobiles, too full of smog, too full of dust, too heartless, too intellectual, too scientific, insufficiently poetic, too lacking in manners, destructive of family, tribal and patriotic feeling.

This catalog of complaints can be reduced to two basic grievances: the city's physical conditions (too big, too noisy, etc.) and the kind of people who live there (too full of Irishmen, too intellectual, etc.). These two grievances have had such a powerful impact on the American imagination that, before I turn to the sociological argument for city life, I must first respond to these arguments against it.[10]

Cities and Nature

The objection to the physical conditions of central cities need not detain us long. The Whites' list—noisy, dirty, smelly, crowded—is simply a restatement of the familiar American romanticization of the countryside, a position Leo Marx has labeled sentimental pastoralism. Suburbs have endlessly associated themselves with this idealization of nature ("Forest Hills," "Golden Valley," "Meadowlane Drive"), and their success in doing so has helped inspire the exodus from central cities. But the suburbs have benefited from an urban image as well: far from being backward rural areas populated by peasants, suburbs are seen as even more modern and civilized than central cities. Thus, to sustain the symbolic link between the pleasures of the suburban yard and life in the suburbs, one has to edit out a lot of daily experience: the freeway, the mall, the office complex, the carpools, the noise coming from the neighbors. The dramatic transformation of the suburbs in the last twenty-five years has converted many of them into what Joel Garreau calls "edge cities." As a result, the credibility of the equation of the suburbs with the countryside has been significantly undermined. Moreover, like the suburbs, central cities have themselves created a "middle landscape" between the urban and the rural. They have incorporated nature into the fabric of urban planning—not only through the construction of parks but through zoning requirements for residential neighborhoods and downtown skyscrapers. Consequently, the city/suburb line does not separate noise from quiet, dirt from cleanliness, smells from fresh air, crowds from isolation. Many central-city neighborhoods are as free of these problems—if they are problems—as are suburban communities; in fact, many American central cities as a whole (Phoenix, Houston, San Diego) look more like classic suburbs than like Manhattan. At the same time, many suburban areas are characterized by noise (airports), dirt (smog), smells (industry), and crowds (traffic jams). Surely there is at least a touch of irony—given the amount of natural beauty destroyed by the suburbanization of America—in the attempt to associate the suburbs with a love of nature.[11]

Sentimental pastoralism, whether embodied in the suburbs or in city planning, also undervalues the desirable features of city life. In her justly celebrated *The Death and Life of Great American Cities*, Jane Jacobs offers a book-length response to the Whites' list of charges by describing the positive aspects of city congestion. She defends the richness, vibrancy, stimulation, spontaneity, energy, and commotion of city streets against urban planners' portrayal of these streets—and of the city neighborhoods in which they are located—as slums. Jacobs' picture of the life of the street reflects her embrace of the values of difference, variety, eroticism, and publicity advanced by Iris Young. Like Young, Jacobs can be accused of overlooking the cost of these values, such as noise and dirt. But these costs can themselves be reinterpreted as benefits. Consider Richard Wright's description of the Chicago in which he placed Bigger in *Native Son*:

> Then there was the fabulous city in which Bigger lived, an indescribable city, huge, roaring, dirty, noisy, raw, stark, brutal; a city of extremes: torrid summers, and sub-zero winters, white people and black people, the English language and strange tongues, foreign born and native born, scrabby poverty and gaudy luxury, high idealism and hard cynicism!

The "fabulous"—and the exclamation mark—transvalue the complaints about the physical conditions of the central city into virtues. Such a transvaluation helps put city life into proper perspective. Spending time in the countryside obviously enriches one's life. But cities too have their pleasures. As Elizabeth Wilson contends, "we will never solve the problems of cities unless we *like* the urban-ness of urban life." Cities, she says, aren't villages; they are "spaces for face to face contact of amazing variety and richness. They are spectacle—and what is wrong with that?"[12]

The Metropolitan Type of Individual

These days, the answer to this question is most often articulated in the language of the Whites' second category of complaints about cities: the kind of people who live there. Here, we reach the central sociological criticism of life in America's central cities: the classic works of urban sociology have argued that city conditions produce undesirable changes in human behavior—that they produce or, at the minimum, attract the wrong kind of people. But who are these people? The Whites' list offers two quite different pictures of them. On the one hand, they are commercial, pushy, artificial, heartless, intellectual, unpoetic, and lacking in family, tribal, and patriotic feelings. On the other hand, they are immigrants, Jews, Irishmen, Italians, Poles—to which, these days, many would add African Americans, Latinos, Asians, poor people, the homeless.

The classic literature of urban sociology focused primarily on the first of these two pictures. The three writers who dominate this literature— Georg Simmel, Robert Ezra Park, and Louis Wirth—built their critique of cities on the sociological contrast between the face-to-face, closely knit personal interaction of a small town or village (*Gemeinschaft*) and the kind of impersonal human relationships that characterize modern society (*Gesellschaft*).[13] They claimed that cities have eroded *Gemeinschaft* relations and have replaced them with an emphasis on the division of labor, the market economy, and the power of the mass media. By doing so, they argued, cities have created a new type of person. Simmel's seminal essay, "The Metropolis and Mental Life," lists a series of qualities of this new character type: a heightened intellectuality, that is, a preference for head over heart; an indifference to the individuality of people or things that levels the world into "an evenly flat and gray tone"; a calculating, precise, punctual exactness; a blasé attitude, leading to the "incapacity . . . to react to new sensations with the appropriate energy"; "a slight aversion, a mutual strangeness and repulsion" in interpersonal encounters; loneliness and a sense of being lost; a life so dominated by impersonal contacts and experience that a person has to exaggerate his own uniqueness "in order to remain audible even to himself."

Park and Wirth argued that specific features of city life forged this new species of individuality. But empirical research has failed to substantiate their claim that central-city characteristics, such as size and density, have caused the psychological stress and feelings of alienation they describe.[14] Read today, Simmel, Park, and Wirth seem instead to be critics of the world of strangers as a whole, a world that characterizes both central cities and their suburbs. The contrast between central city and suburb is not between a face-to-face community and modern society: *Gemeinschaft* does not exist in the metropolitan area. No one can seriously contend that the artificial, the heartless, the capitalistic, the scientific, the mobile, the commercial, the intellectual, the unpoetic—in short, *Gesellschaft*—characterizes the central city more than the suburbs. To be sure, the longing for *Gemeinschaft*, which is thought to have spurred suburbanization, still exists; indeed, it inspires residents of central-city neighborhoods as well. But everywhere in the metropolitan area, it is felt to be disappearing— or gone altogether. Simmel himself, it should be noted, did not seek to distinguish central city from suburb but the metropolis from a small town or a rural community. He called his character type the "metropolitan type of individual."

City Heterogeneity

Park and Wirth, however, populated cities with more than the metropolitan type of individual. At the end of a discussion of the breakdown of family values that he associated with the temptations of city life, for example, Park suddenly changes tone:

What lends special importance to the segregation of the poor, the vicious, the criminal, and exceptional persons generally, which is so characteristic a feature of city life, is the fact that social contagion tends to stimulate in divergent types the common temperamental differences, and to suppress characters which unite them with the normal types around them. . . . In the great city, the poor, the vicious and the delinquent, crushed together in an unhealthful and contagious intimacy, breed in and in, soul and body . . . a persistent and distressing uniformity of vice, crime and poverty . . . peculiarly fit for the environment in which they are condemned to exist.

Similarly, Wirth described cities as "the melting-pot of races, people, and cultures, and a most favorable breeding-ground of new biological and cultural hybrids." He discussed, albeit quite briefly, the presence of immigrants, Negroes, and ethnic minorities in cities, as well as the age and gender differences between those who live in the cities and the countryside. He then concluded:

[A] major characteristic of the urban-dweller is his dissimilarity from his fellows. Never before have such large masses of people of diverse traits as we find in our cities been thrown together into such close physical contact as in the great cities of America. Cities generally, and American cities in particular, comprise a motley of peoples and cultures of highly differentiated modes of life between which there often is only the faintest communication, the greatest indifference, the broadest tolerance, occasionally bitter strife, but always the sharpest contrast.

So important did Wirth consider the presence of this heterogeneity in city life that he built it into his classic definition of a city: "a city," he said, "may be defined as a relatively large, dense, and permanent settlement of socially heterogeneous individuals."[15]

We come, then, to the most important contemporary distinction between central cities and at least some of their suburbs: heterogeneity. From Wirth to the present day, sociologists have found that cities not only attract but foster the multiplication of social groups. Cities produce subcultures (to use examples from Claude Fischer's work) of bluegrass-music fans, college students, Chinese Americans, "singles," Jews, gays and lesbians, missionaries of new religious sects, professional criminals, and Palestinian grocery store owners. Park and Wirth saw this heterogeneity as a cause both of the alienation and anomie that characterize the metropolitan type of individual and of the vice and crime that they associated with city life. More recently, Herbert Gans has argued that a markedly heterogeneous community is likely to become the site of bickering and unsettled feuds because community members cannot understand each other. Gans considered heterogeneity undesirable, however, only on the block level, not for the city as a whole. He sought to find a middle way between heterogeneity and homogeneity: "Extreme heterogeneity is likely to inhibit communication and to encourage mutual resentment, whereas moderate heterogeneity provides enough compatibility of interests and skills to enable communication—and therefore learning—to take place."[16]

Other sociologists have responded to Wirth and Park by articulating positive aspects of living in a heterogeneous community. They have emphasized two contrasts with life in a homogeneous community, contrasts that parallel Richard Sennett's psychological analysis, discussed above, of the difference between diverse and purified communities. First, they say, heterogeneous communities promote tolerance for social and cultural diversity. Thomas Wilson's study, for example, found that residents of heterogeneous communities were more willing than residents of homogeneous communities to allow all of the following to speak or teach in school: a person who is against all churches and religions; a person who believes that blacks are genetically inferior; a man who admits he is a Communist; a person who advocates doing away with elections and letting the military run the country; a man who is openly gay. Tolerance of people such as these does not entail acceptance or approval. It suggests instead a capacity to put up with people who seem undesirable, unpleasant, even repugnant. This live-and-let-live attitude takes many forms. Some kinds of behavior are recognized as an ineradicable, albeit disagreeable, part of life; others are ignored; still others are found acceptable only if located in the neighborhoods where such behavior "belongs." At times, people adopt a stance that Erving Goffman calls "civil inattention": "[o]ne gives another enough visual notice to demonstrate that one appreciates that the other is present (and that one admits openly to having seen him), while at the next moment withdrawing one's attention from him so as to express that he does not constitute a target of special curiosity and design." The exact manner in which tolerance is manifested is not, however, the critical point. All of them are examples of what Sennett calls "ego strength": all of them illustrate how people learn to stomach a larger range of differences if they are repeatedly exposed to a variety of cultural and social practices.[17]

Of course, there are limits. City residents continue to find many of their fellow citizens intolerable; there would be no need for a city function of community building if cities automatically produced unlimited tolerance. What happens in cities is a shift in the location of the symbolic boundary that bifurcates otherness into the tolerable and the intolerable. Living in a heterogeneous community increases the kinds of otherness found to be bearable. By contrast, M. P. Baumgartner's analysis of suburban life suggests that that kind of environment promotes a shift in the opposite direction: almost any stranger not seen as "one of us" is experienced as upsetting, even frightening. So much time is spent in cars or at home, so little public space exists, that deviance of even a minor sort is hard to stand.

Merely walking along a residential street is viewed as "suspicious." "Simply having to deal with socially distant persons—however civil the interchanges—makes . . . [suburban residents] uncomfortable." Feelings of this sort help generate what Baumgartner calls "the moral order of a suburb": a culture of avoidance of contact with strangers and a strategy of withdrawal from confrontations and conflict.[18]

The second impact of living in a heterogeneous city is that it provides people with a broader range of life experiences. By this I mean not simply having more fun (as my discussion of Sennett emphasized). Cities offer stimulation for learning, creativity, experimentation, and growth. The classic literature of urban sociology itself stressed this aspect of city life. Simmel, for example, associated the city with "freedom," as compared to the pettiness and prejudices of a small town, and Wirth observed that the city "has not only tolerated but has rewarded individual differences." But for Simmel, Park, and Wirth, the freedom the city bestowed was a decidedly mixed blessing. Park, for example, portrayed the temptation of city life as a dangerous seduction, "like the attraction of the flame for the moth." In Park's words, "[t]he small community often tolerates eccentricity. The city, on the contrary, rewards it. Neither the criminal, the defective, nor the genius has the same opportunity to develop his innate disposition in a small town that he invariably finds in a great city." Park's linking together of the criminal, the defective, and the genius no doubt undercuts the force of his compliment about the city's capacity to nurture the freedom of the individual. Nevertheless, it allowed him to endorse Spengler's observation that "all great cultures are city-born."[19]

More recent sociologists have focused on how heterogeneous cities cultivate not simply individual eccentricity but the formation of groups that help expand the ways in which one can shape a life. Cities' intensification and multiplication of subcultures is not simply a phenomenon to be tolerated; these subcultures provide a basis for the development of what are popularly called "alternative life-styles." It's not surprising, just to take one example, that gay and lesbian culture thrives in America's central cities. But as this example can be used to illustrate—and as Simmel, Park, and Wirth emphasize—there is a dark side to the promotion of this kind of freedom. It can be understood as undermining morality: hence the classic image of cities as centers of vice and corruption. Moreover, the structure of city life threatens to spread this immorality—or, to put a positive spin on the same phenomenon, it expands the ability to develop one's life in a multitude of ways. Everyday encounters with strangers— at the bus stop, in the laundromat, in the bar—make people aware of a wide variety of subcultures. This interaction allows people to learn from strangers, even without speaking to them. "A good city-street neighborhood," Jane Jacobs says, "achieves a marvel of balance between its people's determination to have essential privacy and their simultaneous wishes for differing degrees of contact, enjoyment or help from the people around."[20]

The Threat of City Life

Still, a major objection to city life remains to be discussed because the kind of heterogeneity described by its advocates tends to understate the diversity of America's central cities. The term "heterogeneity" covers such a wide range of dissimilarities that we might usefully distinguish two different kinds of people considered "other": the unfamiliar (those who are from different cultures or generations, those whose habits or opinions are weird, funny, puzzling, interesting, off-putting) and the terrifying (those seen as physically violent or psychologically threatening). Those who defend the values of tolerance and freedom usually portray heterogeneity in terms of the unfamiliar. To many people, however, the central city is identified, above all, with the terrifying: the violent, the degenerate, the diseased (Park, quoted above, referred to the "criminal," the "vicious," and "contagion"). Indeed, for thousands of years, cities have been seen as populated by "the mob" or "the rabble," a conception that reached a fever pitch in the late eighteenth and nineteenth centuries. Those so identified have usually been located in the urbanized spaces populated by the poor, and they have been portrayed as harboring an impulsive and uncontrollable antagonism against people who are better off. In the eighteenth century, "the thieving shops, the stews and the rookeries, the fetid cellars and the dangerous tenements" of the city of London were perceived as the kind of chaotic places that threatened visitors with unpredictable violence. In nineteenth-century America, the scene changed—it became the overrun tenements of poor immigrant neighborhoods—but the fear did not. In the 1990s, some people see the homeless as the epitome of the modern rabble. One legal scholar, for example, has sketched two individuals as representing the kind of people who ought to be zoned out of better neighborhoods: "a panhandler, by assumption a mild-mannered one, who repeatedly stations himself on a sidewalk in front of a particular restaurant . . . [and] a mentally ill bench squatter who, morning after morning, wheels a shopping cart full of belongings to a bench in a downtown plaza, stretches out a sleeping bag on the bench, and dozes there intermittently until dark."[21]

The identity of those who have been labeled "the mob" has thus changed dramatically over the centuries, although they have always been poor and been associated with crime. These days, however, the people most often seen as part of "the mob" can all too easily be specified. It is, in my view, the single most shameful fact in American life that poor African Americans are so widely identified in the United States as the terrifying other. Of course, additional people are sometimes included in this category: Puerto Ricans, Chicanos, recent immigrants from Asia, gays (hence gay bashing), whites (because of group violence against African Americans and others on the list), and middle-class African Americans (because all African Americans are treated as indistinguishable). But, above all, fear of what is euphemistically called "the inner city"—a fear that has fueled the migration to the suburbs—has been a reference to the black poor. Moreover, the term "inner city" is itself important: it symbolizes the linkage that so commonly connects central cities, poor blacks, and violence.

One reason that this linkage is so shameful lies in the role that violence and discrimination by whites has played—and continues to play—in the creation and perpetuation of the ghettos that now house nearly half of the poor African Americans who live in metropolitan areas. Douglas Massey and Nancy Denton, in their provocative book, *American Apartheid: Segregation and the Making of the Underclass*, offer a useful summary of how these ghettos, now found in virtually every major American city, came into existence. In 1900, Massey and Denton emphasize, no such ghettos existed: urbanized African Americans lived in neighborhoods that, on average, were close to 90 percent white. By 1930, however, a combination of an upsurge of racial violence, antiblack actions by organized "neighborhood improvement associations," zoning restrictions, discrimination by real estate agents, and the invention and use of racially restrictive covenants established the beginnings of the black ghetto. From 1940 to 1970, with the dramatic increase in the number of (mostly poor) African Americans moving to cities, the size of these ghettos grew as black demand for housing overcame white resistance. Since threats of violence, racial discrimination, and practices of real estate agents continued to close off most areas of the city to new black residents, this growth was largely block-by-block. Neighborhoods "could be classified by their state in the transition process: all white, invasion, succession, consolidation, or all black." Meanwhile, the rapid growth of the suburbs, fostered, as we shall see, by government programs, provided a secure place to which whites could flee. As a result, African Americans are segregated today in a manner that no other minority in the United States is now or has ever been segregated— not ethnic Europeans, not Hispanics, not Asians. Eighty percent of African Americans in major American cities would have to move to produce an evenly integrated metropolitan area. And this "hypersegregation," to use Massey and Denton's term, is not simply a central-city phenomenon: black suburbs—and there are many—are as segregated as "inner cities."[22]

Like many before them, Massey and Denton describe the conditions of these poor black neighborhoods: a concentration of poverty and unemployment, combined with business disinvestment; deterioration and abandonment of residential and commercial buildings; a widespread fear of crime, leading people to avoid going out and thereby creating an environment that facilitates yet more crime; a stark isolation from outsiders, dramatically limiting the residents' social and economic world; the creation of a culture in opposition to standard American values, including black street speech, family dissolution, a drug culture, and disengagement from political life. These days the reason for this "concentration of effects" is a hotly debated issue. Massey and Denton attribute the cause to segregation itself, while others suggest it lies in the structure of job creation in American metropolitan areas, in a "culture of poverty," or in racism. Still others stress, as Massey and Denton do not, the diversity of the population in these black neighborhoods and the resilience and creativity that characterize so many who live there—positive aspects of the culture from which outsiders have a lot to learn. I do not intend to enter these debates here. Suffice it to say, as Massey and Denton point out, that hypersegregation itself has contributed to the undermining of the social and economic well-being of America's black ghetto residents. Moreover, poverty, discrimination, and the conditions of life in these ghettos—whether singly or in combination—have dramatically restricted their opportunity, historically available for residents of other urban ghettos in America, to move elsewhere if they want to do so. And, Massey and Denton insist, the evidence "suggests that the high degree of segregation blacks experience in urban America is not voluntary."[23]

Another reason that the identification of poor African Americans as the violent "other" is shameful is that this image is so often invoked by residents of relatively prosperous suburbs to legitimate their fear of the city. But these are the very people who, by moving to jurisdictions that are treated by the legal system as distinct from the central city, have been able to escape paying the city taxes that are designed to improve the quality of life in poor African American neighborhoods. One way to demonstrate the stark contrast between the relative comfort of outsiders who fear the black poor and the conditions in which residents of black ghettos themselves live is to focus on the issue of violence that the outsiders so often raise. It bears emphasis that the people most victimized by this violence are the residents of the black ghettos themselves. In 80 percent of all violent crimes, the race of both the defendant and the victim is the same. This is true even for the most serious crime: more than 80 percent of those who commit murder, black or white, have victims of the same race. Black residents, both inner-city and suburban, are also more likely than whites to be victims of household crime, such as burglary or household larceny. Even for robbery, 63 percent of cases involve victims and offenders of the same race, compared to 31 percent with white victims and black offenders.[24]

A fundamental issue is raised by the existence of America's poor African American neighborhoods—and, I should hasten to add, by the all-too-similar neighborhoods, both within the central city and in suburbs, that house Puerto Ricans, Chicanos, and other Hispanics. What should we, as Americans, do about these ghettos and the attendant fear that they generate both for those who live within them and outside of them? A response to this question requires more than a psychological or sociological analysis, although both of these disciplines can certainly contribute to the search for an answer. The question presents a central, perhaps the central, issue of American politics.

The Politics of City Life

As Massey and Denton demonstrate, for most of the twentieth century the overwhelming response to America's poor African American neighborhoods has been to isolate them by creating and defending the racially marked boundaries that separate them from the rest of the metropolitan area. Yet Massey and Denton's focus on black neighborhoods tells only part of the story, because a policy of isolation has affected the lives of many other people as well. Neighborhood boundaries, city/suburb boundaries, and the boundaries between suburbs have also divided residents of metropolitan areas along class and ethnic lines. And central-city and suburban zoning laws have separated residential areas from business districts, commercial uses from industrial uses, high-income shopping from low-income shopping. The overall impact of American urban policy in the twentieth century has thus been to disperse and divide the people who live in America's metropolitan areas, and, as a result, to reduce the number of places where people encounter men and women different from themselves.

Every level of government has played a role in formulating and implementing this urban policy. The major contribution of the federal government has taken the form of massive financial support for suburbanization. The suburban boom could not have occurred without the funding, provided by the Federal-Aid Highway Act of 1956, for the highways and beltways that now link suburbs with central cities and with each other. Nor would it have been sustainable without the existence of federally insured mortgages, a program created in the 1930s, expanded in later decades, and administered well into the 1960s in an overtly anti–central city and antiblack manner. By 1986 the federal government backed two-thirds of the one-family mortgages in the United States, and the interest on these mortgages—like local property taxes and unlike rent—is deductible for federal income tax purposes. Many other federal programs have also fostered suburban growth. One especially worth noting, given the amount of money involved, is the allocation of the federal budget for national defense. Defense spending has consistently favored suburban over central-city locations, fueling the growth of places like Silicon Valley in California, the Dallas–Fort Worth Metroplex in Texas, and the Cape Canaveral–Kennedy Center–Patrick Air Force Base complex in Florida.[25]

But the federal government has done more than simply fund suburban growth. From the late 1930s to the 1960s, it also furthered the isolation of African Americans through a series of programs designed for central cities. In fact, the influence of all levels of government in the expansion and consolidation of America's black ghettos was so significant during these years that Arnold Hirsch has distinguished this period of segregation from earlier eras by labeling it the "making of the second ghetto." The three important federal statutes that helped build this second ghetto—the Housing Acts of 1937, 1949, and 1954—provided federal funding for public housing and urban renewal, while decentralizing to local officials the authority to make critical decisions on matters such as site selection. These federal statutes were designed to improve the living conditions of city slum dwellers, including African Americans, and to revitalize central-city business districts. But in order to build a business center that was consistent with the then prevailing notions of urban planning, local officials had to destroy nearby residential neighborhoods—neighborhoods populated by African Americans or by working-class or lower-middle-class whites. Residents of these neighborhoods unsuccessfully fought the efforts, led by the business community, to rebuild city downtowns at their expense. In response, the cities' political leaders insisted both on downtown revitalization and on building public housing. At the same time, in an ineffective attempt to assuage the anger against urban renewal expressed by white working-class and lower-middle-class city residents, they decided to locate black-occupied public housing only in the black ghetto or in "transitional" neighborhoods (and white-occupied public housing only in white neighborhoods). As a result, the blacks evicted by urban renewal moved either to existing housing in the black ghetto or to newly constructed public housing in the same neighborhood; many whites moved to the suburbs. Moreover, city spending of federal funds allocated for highway construction had a similar effect. Again, cities condemned black and white working-class and lower-middle-class neighborhoods; again, the evicted blacks moved to the black ghetto while many whites moved to the suburbs. Often, new highways were designed in a way that divided the city along racial or ethnic lines.[26]

In the 1960s, at the height of the civil rights movement, the federal government sought to alter the urban policy I've just described and to promote instead the integration of the nation's housing through the enactment of the Fair Housing Act and the revitalization of inner-city neighborhoods through the Model Cities program. It also encouraged regional decision making on matters such as health care and the environment in an effort to reduce the importance of the city/suburb boundary. But none of these programs has had a lasting impact on desegregating the metropolitan area or undercutting suburban autonomy. Beginning in the 1970s, a combination of the rise of conservative national governments, court decisions holding race-conscious siting of public housing unconstitutional, and increasing opposition from neighborhoods led to the reduction and, ultimately, the elimination of federal efforts to build public housing and to stimulate urban renewal. Federal support of suburbanization, however, has continued.

Yet, important as it has been, the federal government is not the public entity that is most responsible for the kind of suburbanization that has spread across America. As Richard Ford has persuasively argued, state law has been an even more significant contributor to the division of America's metropolitan region into a multitude of cities that can all too easily be distinguished from each other through a description of their residents' racial, ethnic, or class status. This feature of suburban life is not simply a product of suburban growth. To achieve any significant level of homogeneity, suburbs need state-granted autonomy: the right to incorporate as a separate municipality; immunity from annexation by the central city; the privilege of engaging in exclusionary zoning; the ability to legislate and provide services solely in their own self-interest; the authority not only to tax the real property located within municipal boundaries but to spend the revenue collected solely on local residents. State legislatures and courts have been the source of these suburban powers through their formulation of local government law. Every state in the nation has given suburbs at least some of these powers, and many states have given suburbs all of them. But the very fact that there are suburbs in America that lack some of these powers demonstrates that the idea of suburban autonomy cannot be deduced from the nature of a suburb. A state has to decide to confer it. That they have largely done so has defined the meaning and importance of city/suburb and suburb/suburb boundaries throughout the country. One reason that state decision making on these issues has been so influential is that the United States Supreme Court has upheld the constitutionality of every one of these aspects of suburban autonomy.[27]

State law also enabled the central cities to adopt the theory of urban planning that required the separation of business from residential neighborhoods, and to condemn inner-city residential neighborhoods to make way for progress as that theory defined it. The decision to allow central cities to embrace this version of urban planning was not only discretionary but controversial, as powerful criticisms of the policy, by Jane Jacobs and many others, suggest. Moreover, states did not simply follow the federal lead when it allowed cities to pursue these zoning, urban renewal, and housing policies; sometimes states authorized these activities even before the federal government's programs began. Yet, at the same time, state law has denied many central cities the power to enact legislation that might have helped increase the diversity, or at least alter the decline, of city neighborhoods—for example, the power to tax commuters, to impose rent control, and to prohibit racial discrimination.[28]

It would be a mistake, however, to think that the states' urban policy, any more than that of the federal government, always pointed in the same direction. On occasion, states have pursued urban strategies that conflict with the one just described. They have curtailed the incorporation of new suburbs, allowed annexation of suburbs without their residents' consent, redistributed locally generated funds to more needy school districts, or limited exclusionary zoning. In addition, some states have given central cities the very powers mentioned above—to tax commuters, to impose rent control, and to ban racial discrimination. States plainly have the power to adopt this opposite urban policy if they want to do so: the United States Supreme Court has made clear that it too is constitutional. But this alternative urban policy has not been the general practice. Overall, states have promoted suburban autonomy and limited city power, and they have done so not just through the formulation of local government law but through state funding decisions as well.[29]

Cities themselves, however, have played the central role in the dispersal and separation of the many different kinds of people who populate America's metropolitan areas. Neither federal money nor state grants of authority would have accomplished this result if cities had not adopted programs that put this urban policy into effect. Suburbs had to enact zoning ordinances that excluded people considered different or deviant; to isolate their residents from such people effectively, they also had to allocate their revenue, and provide services, solely to residents. Suburbs across the nation have not only adopted strategies such as these but have fought efforts by states or the federal government to alter them. Similarly, the political leaders of central cities, more than anyone else, made the crucial decisions about urban renewal, public housing, zoning, and urban transportation that led to the "making of the second ghetto." In implementing their vision of urban planning, central cities reinforced the homogeneity of some city neighborhoods even as they destroyed others. Once again, there are exceptions: some central cities and suburbs have, from time to time, fostered diversity. Nevertheless, one does not have to read this book to recognize that this contrary policy is unusual. One simply has to travel to America's metropolitan areas to notice the astonishing replication, from coast to coast, of upper-middle-class suburbs, working-class suburbs, central business districts isolated from residential housing, comfortable central-city residential areas, upscale shopping areas, strip malls, and ghettos that house the black poor.

Politicians of all kinds—Democrats and Republicans, liberals and conservatives, centralists and decentralists—have helped produce this design for America's metropolitan areas. But for most of the century this urban policy has been the work of liberal Democrats. It was they who sponsored New Deal programs like public housing and urban renewal (many conservatives considered public housing to be "socialism"). Most big city mayors in this century have been Democrats, and Democratic state and federal leaders have been no less generous to the suburbs than Republicans have been. Over the last thirty years, however, the Republican party has developed a style of political argument that has built upon and reinforced this long-standing effort. In *Chain Reaction: The Impact of Race, Rights, and Taxes on American Politics*, Thomas and Mary Edsall trace the development of this style of argument from Goldwater, through Nixon, Wallace, and Agnew, to Reagan and beyond. The Edsalls have boiled the argument down to a few essential points: the link between race and taxes (taxes are for them, not for us); the threat to traditional moral values of family, work, church, school, and neighborhood (a threat posed not only by poor African Americans but by feminists, gays and lesbians, immigrants, and others seeking protection of their "rights"); fear of crime (another reference to race); and, finally, the identification of a liberal elite as the source of the current favoritism that "big government" affords blacks and other special interests. As the Edsalls see it, this argument has been crafted to appeal, in particular, to the fear of poor African Americans—and of others considered deviant—felt by working-class and lower-middle-class whites. But, they conclude, now that a majority of America's voting population lives in the suburbs, the overt nature of this appeal can gradually be eliminated. Metropolitan segregation can itself organize people politically. After all, most of those considered "other" live in the central city or in their own suburbs.[30]

In my view, the urban policy that I've just described has had enormously destructive consequences for American life. One of these consequences, emphasized in the previous paragraphs, has been the simultaneous creation of poor African American neighborhoods and of privileged, mostly white, suburbs. This spatial segregation has impoverished a significant percentage of African Americans and, at the same time, enriched America's upper middle class. Another consequence has been a diminution of the opportunity, even in central cities, to experience the city's traditional way of being with strangers. Many residents of poor African American neighborhoods virtually never leave their own neighborhood, and many suburban residents rarely go anywhere that might make them feel uncomfortable. Of course, there are still areas in cities across the country—from Greenwich Village to Telegraph Avenue—where one can feel the stimulation and hesitation associated with encountering people considered "other." But there are also neighborhoods in the same cities where people recognize they don't belong, and still other neighborhoods that are so unfamiliar they exist only as blank spaces on residents' mental map of the metropolis. Robert Park's famous observation about cities is thus truer today than it was in 1916, when he made it: "[t]he processes of segregation," he said, "establish moral distances which make the city a mosaic of little worlds which touch but do not interpenetrate."[31] Whether understood in terms of Iris Young's normative values of social differentiation without exclusion, variety, eroticism, and publicity or through my earlier discussion of ego strength, tolerance, and individual freedom taken from the psychological and sociological literature, this reduction of space for "city life" is a significant loss.

But America's dominant urban policy has had an even more insidious consequence. The division of metropolitan areas along racial lines and the erosion of the opportunity for "city life" have intensified metropolitan residents' feelings of suspicion and fear when they confront strangers. As a result, the Kerner Commission's infamous vision of America as two separate, hostile, and unequal nations now appears to be an understatement.[32] Metropolitan areas are not simply divided between black and white and rich and poor. Suburb after suburb and neighborhood after neighborhood are organized in terms of a multitude of "we" feelings, each of which defines itself in opposition to outsiders. This increased aversion to strangers has diminished the prospects for a political solution to the problems posed by America's impoverished, or declining, suburban and central-city neighborhoods. Decentralization of power to the dozens of cities into which metropolitan regions have been divided is likely to exacerbate their separation and inequality, given their current powers and policies. Only a central government seems capable of bringing together the disparate groups that have grown so remote from each other. Yet even this solution now appears improbable. As we have seen, the states and the federal government have themselves adopted policies that have promoted metropolitan fragmentation, reinforcing rather than overcoming the economic and social distance that separates the area's residents.

The suspicion and fear that infest our metropolitan areas threaten to generate a self-reinforcing cycle of alienation: the more people withdraw from each other, the higher the percentage of strangers that cause them anxiety, thereby producing further withdrawal. As the number of people experienced as "other" expands, it is likely to produce a comparable increase in the desire to build more walls separating one portion of the population from another. And I literally mean walls—physical structures made of bricks, stone, or wood. Walls of this kind now surround condominiums and housing developments in every metropolitan area in the country. Cities too are now building them—or considering building them. When constructed, they separate neighborhoods from each other by blocking public streets and are justified as crime-prevention measures. Many more such structures might become desirable or necessary if the current fear of strangers intensifies. In many other countries—El Salvador and South Africa, for example—walls now surround private houses in order to keep out the frightening others who live nearby. These kinds of walls are not yet common in America. But, as is well known, American central cities are becoming increasingly populated by the rich and the poor as the middle class has been forced—and has chosen—to move to the suburbs. And the suburbs have themselves become divided in a similar way.

A City Function of Community Building

Much of the support for this urban policy comes from the kind of people that the policy itself has nurtured: people who acknowledge that living in a world of strangers is unavoidable in an urbanized area, but who feel comfortable only with strangers who seem to be like them. Those who adopt this stance can be understood as one possible version of the "metropolitan type of individual," to return to the term used in the urban sociological literature. These people are often associated with the suburbs: Sennett described them as living in purified communities, and Baumgartner analyzed them when he described the "moral order of the suburb." Driving from their neighborhood to work and back home, they try to encounter as little disorder, surprise, strangeness, or otherness as possible. This requires withdrawing into a circle of family and friends, into their neighborhood, into voluntary associations, and into their workplace, and then fortifying the boundaries that define, for each of these places of refuge, "who fits in." But it is a mistake to think of this version of the metropolitan type of individual as living only in the suburbs. They now can be found everywhere in the metropolitan area. To give but one additional example, many who live in poor African American neighborhoods also feel comfortable only with people like themselves. They too devise methods, albeit different methods from those adopted in the suburbs, to exclude outsiders. As in the suburbs, policing the boundaries of the black neighborhood—and of voluntary associations, and, in some areas, of city

blocks—helps residents reassure themselves that the people they encounter will conform to the fictional unity often associated with the word
"community."

There is, however, another version of the metropolitan type of individual: the people whom Richard Sennett and other urban sociologists have
described as sustained by life in a heterogeneous community. They too
live in a world of strangers, but they have learned to tolerate the presence
of some of the unfamiliar strangers who populate their city and to enjoy
the presence of others. Richard Sennett's *Fall of Public Man* offers a brilliant historical account of this form of life and of the role of cities in fostering it. But his account is one of decline. Sennett ends his book by saying
that the city ought to revive this way of life by teaching people how to live
it. The city, he says, ought to be

> the forum in which it becomes meaningful to join with other persons without
> the compulsion to know them as persons. I don't think this is an idle dream;
> the city has served as a focus for active social life, for the conflict and play of
> interests, for the experience of human possibility, during most of the history of
> civilized man. But just that civilized possibility is today dormant.[33]

In fact, the possibility is worse than dormant. As we have seen, every level
of American government has adopted policies that reduce the amount of
public space in metropolitan areas and, with it, the opportunity for the
kind of experience Sennett describes. Moreover, this form of life is simultaneously being eroded by nongovernmental forces that collectively might
be called the trend toward privatization: the withdrawal into family life,
condominiums, office complexes, and shopping malls, as well as into the
cars that allow people to travel in seclusion from one of these private places
to another.

Despite the power and pervasiveness of this support for the privatized
version of the metropolitan type of individual, there is no countervailing
effort in American society designed to cultivate the alternative version, the
one Sennett associates with city life. Where could such an effort take place?
Certainly not in the private sector. Whether defined in terms of family or
in terms of work, this area of life has not characteristically been open to
engagement with otherness. Nor do the state and federal governments
seem much more promising. These levels of government can have a major
impact on character development, as their support of suburbanization
demonstrates. But they operate largely by passing laws and funding programs and thus are too remote from the kind of daily contact that the
effort demands. Other than someone delivering the mail, one comes
across a federal or state employee on official business no more than once
a month. In *The Uses of Disorder*, Sennett proposed a third possible way
to foster city life: anarchy. He suggested eliminating government's role

not only in urban planning but also in ordinary police work. Without government to turn to, he argued, city residents would have to deal with each other regardless of their differences. Sennett's proposal has a '60s feel to it (the book was published in 1970), and it has the value of making clear, in yet another way, how powerfully the government is now involved in the separation and division of different kinds of people in America's cities. But I don't think that many Americans these days, perhaps not even Sennett himself, consider it much of an answer.

The answer instead, I suggest, is located in the city itself. A primary city function—*the* primary city function—ought to be the cultivation and reproduction of the city's traditional form of human association. Cities— and I mean all cities, including suburbs—ought to teach people how to interact with unfamiliar strangers, how to deal with their terror of the black poor or of whomever else they imagine as "the mob," how (in Sennett's words) "to join with other persons without the compulsion to know them as persons." I have offered three reasons that cities should perform such a function. The first is based on the contribution that a more open way of life offers for human development and growth—the values of ego strength, tolerance, stimulation, creativity, experiment, eroticism, and play discussed above. The second, also discussed above, stems from the problems created by the current level of estrangement between metropolitan residents, let alone an intensification of it. The present degree of suspicion and fear that characterizes American metropolitan areas is an unacceptable basis for American life. There should be no neighborhood in America that outsiders can't visit because they feel—legitimately feel— they don't belong. But I suspect that many will think that it is utopian for me to say so.

The final justification for a city function of community building lies in its potential for reinvigorating the possibility of a political solution to the divisions that now characterize American metropolitan areas. For far too long, policy-makers have conceptualized relationships with strangers in terms of a polar choice between separation, on the one hand, and a romanticized sense of togetherness, on the other. The only way they thought they could avoid reinforcing the area's differences was to disregard neighborhood and suburban boundaries altogether, thereby adopting the opposite urban policy to the one that is currently predominant. This alternative policy has taken many forms, such as regional government, government-mandated racial integration of housing and schools, and neighborhood condemnation and dispersal. But opposition to these proposals has been intense, and not just from those who have been enriched by metropolitan fragmentation. The prospect of being absorbed into—or invaded by—a world of hostile strangers makes many people feel vulnerable. African Americans, Latinos, and Asian Americans often don't want to be assimilated into the white suburbs; many other groups, defined in terms ranging from ethnicity to class to sexual orientation, like having their own neighborhood. If the only alternative to accepting the differentiation of the region's population is to eliminate it, many have felt, the price is too high. Given this determined opposition, the alternative urban policy has been used only exceptionally, while more and more forms of estrangement between people at the local level have taken hold: pro-life and pro-choice, gay and homophobic, welfare recipient and investment banker, Cuban American and African American.

In my view, making togetherness the only alternative to separation has set the standard for relationships with others too high. Togetherness eliminates strangeness from strangers by requiring them to fit into a "we" feeling that banishes dissonance or discomfort. Such a standard is so hard to achieve that it tends to produce more separation than connection. For those who have perceived themselves as outside of the "we" feeling, the demands of togetherness have required assimilation to norms—white norms, or suburban norms, or upper-middle-class norms—with which they disagreed. And for those who have learned to identify with these norms, it has closed off the enrichment, and the challenge, of dealing with otherness. Above all, the demand for togetherness has suppressed the possibility that one might not feel comfortable with someone yet still be able to deal with him. Historically, cities have created just such a relationship with strangers. City life has not demanded a feeling of solidarity or affection or acceptance. It has held out no promise of commonality, no sense that persuasion can bring those with opposed views together. What it has suggested instead is that one needs to learn how to live with people—and to work with people—who are not like oneself. Moreover, we must not overstate the amount of contact with such strangers that city life has entailed. No one who lives in cities spends full time with unfamiliar strangers. Like Jane Jacobs' description of a city street, city life is a compromise between withdrawal from strangers and engagement with them. The exact nature of this compromise constantly has to be negotiated and renegotiated. It is this process of negotiation that represents the characteristic city alternative to the idea that the proper solution to one's problems or to the problems of society is to escape from them.

As the previous discussion has emphasized, we must not romanticize this form of human relationship. Dealing with unassimilated strangers often makes people feel uneasy or frightened. But it is equally important that we avoid romanticizing the alternatives—including the contemporary metropolitan design that has required so much effort, and so many billions of government dollars, to create. As I suggest in the next chapter, a wide variety of people would benefit from a change in current urban policy, and there is some reason to believe that political support for such a change could be generated. Yet even the most optimistic booster of the city-identified version of the metropolitan type of individual has to accept the fact that, given its current political power, the preeminence of the privatized metropolitan type of individual will remain a decisive ingredient in urban America for a long time to come. What I propose is that cities adopt a strategy to counter the overwhelming public and private support now fostering the dispersal and division of metropolitan residents. Cities in the future will continue to incorporate, as central cities and diverse suburbs do now, both interaction with unfamiliar strangers and withdrawal from them, public spaces as well as private spaces. The challenge is to alter the mix.

A city function of community building would be designed not only to lower the overall level of estrangement in America's metropolitan areas but also to begin the process of local negotiations designed to address the area's problems. It would obviously be foolish to be too optimistic these days about the prospects for these negotiations, given how successful America's urban policy in the twentieth century has been. Metropolitan residents are so foreign to each other that any proposal for a negotiated political solution to the current level of suspicion and inequality between (say) upper-middle-class whites and poor African Americans is bound to seem naive. Even so, I don't think that there can be a solution to the divisions fracturing America's metropolitan areas that fails to confront them. Moreover, the history of the twentieth century offers little hope that there can be a federal or a state solution to the estrangement of people living in our metropolitan areas if they themselves can find no way of dealing with each other. After all, federal and state officials are responsible to, and elected by, those who live in these divided communities. If the fear of outsiders that now pervades our metropolitan areas is to be overcome, everyone in the area, no matter where he or she lives, needs to be given a stake in eliminating the conditions that have brought this fear into existence. As I argued in the previous two chapters, an essential ingredient in the achievement of this objective is to change the current autonomy-centered conception of what cities are, thereby enabling them to become vehicles for community-building efforts. Yet implementing a city function of community building need not be postponed until the changes in local government law that I have proposed have been adopted. Many diverse cities already exist within America's metropolitan areas, and these cities could begin the task of community building right away. Even the most homogeneous suburb can take steps to confront the current differences not only between its residents and outsiders but also among its own residents. A good place to begin would be a revision of the legal structure that now governs city land use.

7

City Land Use

Zoning and Redevelopment History

City control over land use has contributed more to the dispersal and separation of metropolitan residents than any other city activity. This control has been exercised principally through cities' zoning power and through a combination of other city powers, such as condemnation, financial incentives, and municipal borrowing, mobilized to promote urban redevelopment. The decision to allow every city in a metropolitan area to adopt its own zoning and development policies was made by the states; cities can engage in these activities only because state law has authorized them. But the federal government has also been instrumental in framing cities' zoning and redevelopment authority. After New York City adopted the nation's first comprehensive zoning law in 1916, Herbert Hoover, then secretary of commerce, helped spread the idea of locally controlled zoning throughout the nation by authorizing the drafting and widespread circulation of a Standard State Zoning Enabling Act in 1923. By the mid-1920s, more than half the states had adopted a zoning law based on the federal model; today, every American central city other than Houston, and virtually every American suburb, has zoning authority. Like zoning, city development efforts originated before the federal government became involved in the issue. But the Housing Act of 1949, along with subsequent federal statutes, not only funded urban redevelopment but helped nationalize and standardize how it was done.

Zoning

Support for local zoning policies has often been articulated in the antiurban language of sentimental pastoralism: a bedroom community of detached, owner-occupied, single-family houses, located in a natural setting, is often said to be "the best place to raise a family." As Justice Douglas put it in *Village of Belle Terre v. Boraas*, a "quiet place where yards are wide, people few, and motor vehicles restricted are legitimate guidelines in a land-use project addressed to family needs." In such a place, he went on, "family values, youth values, and the blessing of quiet seclusion and clean air make the area a sanctuary for people." Similarly, Justice Sutherland, in upholding the constitutionality of zoning in *Village of Euclid v. Ambler Realty*, stressed that residential districts protected the health and safety of children against "fire, contagion, and disorder which in greater or less degree attach to the location of stores, shops, and factories." Even apartment houses, he continued, bring with them "disturbing noises incident to increased traffic and business, and the occupation, by means of moving and parked automobiles, of larger portions of the streets, thus depriving children of the privilege of quiet and open spaces for play, enjoyed by those in more favored localities."[1]

This sentimental pastoral version of residential zoning omits what by now has become obvious to everyone: noise, traffic congestion, contagion, and disorder are associated not just with apartment houses and commerce but with "the wrong kind of people"—those who have to be excluded to make a residential neighborhood seem desirable. The tight connection between exclusion and zoning is not news. Zoning began in America in the 1880s as an effort to curb the spread of Chinese laundries in Modesto and San Francisco, and New York City's ordinance was a response to Fifth Avenue merchants' fears of being overrun by immigrant garment workers. District Judge Westenhaver, whose opinion declaring zoning laws unconstitutional was overturned by the Supreme Court in *Village of Euclid v. Ambler Realty*, noted that the result of zoning "is to classify the population and segregate them according to their income or situation in life." Ever since *Euclid* was decided, critics of zoning have written countless books and articles decrying its role in fostering suburban homogeneity. In the summary words of one analyst:

> The basic purpose of suburban zoning was to keep Them where They belonged—Out. If They had already gotten In, then its purpose was to confine Them to limited areas. The exact identity of Them varied a bit around the country. Blacks, Latinos, and poor people always qualified. Catholics, Jews, and Orientals were targets in many places. The elderly also qualified, if they were candidates for public housing.

Although the quotation refers to suburban zoning, the same zoning effects characterize some central-city neighborhoods as well.[2]

This exclusionary impact of local zoning, however, is widely accepted as legitimate. Most states leave it unregulated, and the Supreme Court has found "little . . . that would spark suspicion" in suburban homogeneity without proof that intentional racial discrimination was the decisive ingredient in zoning decision making. In *Everything in Its Place*, Constance Perin offers an insightful anthropological account of this widespread defense of exclusion. Home ownership in a "nice" neighborhood, she says, is often seen as the top rung in the long climb up the ladder of life. Such an achievement can easily be threatened if neighborhood standards decline, and this decline is likely to be produced, people feel, by neighborhood diversity—in particular, by the presence in the neighborhood either of renters or of homeowners who cannot afford houses like one's own (whatever the price). This lower class of people is associated with multiple character defects, such as instability, disinterest in property maintenance, and propensity toward crime. Having such people in the neighborhood therefore threatens not only to lower neighborhood residents' social status but to make them feel uncomfortable in their own home. Race, of course, plays an important role in this portrayal of the kind of neighbor that produces these undesirable effects. But even if America had no racism, zoning would still serve one of its purposes: protecting people from their fear of otherness.[3]

It also protects them from their fear of a decline in property values. Given the felt connection between diversity and neighborhood deterioration, it is not surprising that people often associate "the wrong kind of people" with the undermining of what, for many, is the biggest financial investment of their lives. Thus although zoning is often described (and attacked) as a government restriction on the rights of property-owners, it is just as readily understood as a governmental effort to protect these rights. While zoning limits property-owners' ability to do what they want with their own property, it also assures them that their investment in a home will not be undermined by the actions of their neighbors. Like developers, homeowners have to think about the resale value of their property, and, like developers, they want to protect themselves against the risk of economic loss. And they are not alone. Zoning not only defines the nature of residential neighborhoods but separates out commercial from residential uses and controls the way business grows in those areas of the city in which it is allowed. Many suburbs rely on zoning to establish their business climate. City officials work with commercial developers to ensure that prime land is occupied by its "highest and best use," thereby promoting the city's economic growth. Suburbs also count on the exclusionary nature of zoning to promote their economy. Exclusion of "the wrong kind of people" can help them demonstrate that they are an attractive place for investment.

Redevelopment

Exclusion has been a central ingredient not only in zoning policy but also in central cities' efforts to use their redevelopment powers to entice businesses to move to town. As noted in the previous chapter, America's central cities spent the money they received from the federal government's urban renewal program primarily on rebuilding their business districts: approximately two-thirds of the $13.5 billion that the program awarded central cities from 1949 to 1974 went for projects in or near city downtowns. From 1974 to 1988, they spent the money they derived from the major federal programs that succeeded urban renewal—Community Development Block Grants and Urban Development Action Grants—on additional commercial projects. The impact of these federal programs on central cities has been profound. Government-sponsored support for downtown office development helped construct 1,325 office buildings, thereby transforming the economies of American central cities in a manner that provided jobs for many city residents and commuters. But in the process of constructing these office buildings, their designers acted like homeowners thinking of their property values: they sought to eliminate housing conditions that would scare away the kind of people they wanted to attract. As a result, these massive construction projects eliminated more than 400,000 nearby low-income dwellings—an act of destruction that separated and divided the residents of central cities in a manner similar to the use of exclusionary zoning in the suburbs.[4]

This "slum clearance" program has a benign reading—one articulated, as was the case for zoning, by Justice Douglas. Writing for a unanimous court in *Berman v. Parker*, he observed that miserable housing conditions can

> make living an almost insufferable burden. They may also be an ugly sore, a blight on the community which robs it of its charm, which makes it a place from which men turn. The misery of housing may despoil a community as an open sewer may ruin a river.

With this vision in mind, it is not surprising that he had no trouble upholding the District of Columbia's destruction of a neighborhood in southwest Washington, 97.5 percent black, along with the department store at issue in the case. "The entire area needed redesigning," he said, "so that a balanced, integrated plan could be developed for the region, including not only new homes but also schools, churches, parks, streets, and shopping centers. In this way it was hoped that the cycle of decay of the area could be controlled and the birth of future slums prevented."[5]

There is no doubt that housing conditions in many American neighborhoods were—and are—appalling (in the neighborhood at issue in *Berman*, 57.8 percent had outside toilets and 83.8 percent lacked central heating). Yet there is also no doubt that many of the neighborhoods that stood in the way of urban renewal were not slums, and that the money spent for new housing largely went for buildings too expensive for those displaced to afford. Most of the estimated one million people displaced by urban renewal, more than half of whom were black, were forced to move outside of the renewal area. "High-cost housing," in Lawrence Friedman's words, "eliminated blight and slum conditions just as efficiently as low-cost housing, and perhaps a good deal more so." In implementing urban renewal, central cities also condemned more than one hundred thousand small businesses, and the office buildings that replaced them provided more jobs for commuters than for the inner-city poor. Indeed, the unemployment rate for the central cities that had the greatest commitment to urban renewal increased rather than declined after 1970. Even the design of the new office buildings had a segregating effect on central cities. As Bernard Frieden and Lynne Sagalyn point out, three features of the modernist downtown office developments "cut them off from the rest of the city: they were very large, built to serve just a single function, and laid out in ways that emphasized their separation from the surrounding area." Since only certain kinds of people use these office complexes—and even they are there only a portion of the day—downtown office construction reduced "the likelihood of different kinds of people sharing the same space." Instead, it has had the opposite effect: those who work in these buildings often feel closer to people who work in similar buildings in a distant city than to people who live in a poor neighborhood nearby.[6]

In the 1970s and 1980s, the wholesale condemnation of central-city neighborhoods largely ceased, and government-supported redevelopment shifted from a focus on downtown office buildings to the construction of shopping centers designed to increase central cities' attraction to middle-class metropolitan residents—even if they lived in the suburbs. City financial support helped build more than three-quarters of the roughly one hundred new central-city retail centers opened in America between 1970 and 1988—places like Faneuil Hall Marketplace and Copley Place in Boston, Harborplace in Baltimore, Riverwalk in New Orleans, Water Tower Place and 900 Michigan Avenue in Chicago, and Horton Plaza in San Diego. Trump Tower in New York City alone received $100 million in tax abatements. Unlike office buildings, these shopping centers seek to attract a wide variety of people. But they too are private property and thus do not promote the kind of city life associated with the public street. Their owners not only seek to attract upscale customers but are entitled to have their property policed by private security guards to control who can enter and for what purposes. Moreover, in many central cities, new shopping malls sparked office development and gentrification in nearby neighborhoods—the very effect the cities hoped for. Thus these commercial developments have also contributed to the relocation of poor city residents to other parts of the metropolitan area.[7]

Although direct federal aid is now largely unavailable, central-city redevelopment efforts—fueled by the need to compete with the suburbs for business investment—have continued. These days, central cities normally finance redevelopment by issuing tax-exempt municipal bonds to pay for condemning land and making site improvements, with the bonds paid for by what is commonly called tax increment financing (the additional property-tax revenues gained from the project are pledged to pay off the bonds). This scheme has cost the federal government a lot of lost tax revenue: twice as much, in the mid-1980s, as the $520 million it annually spent during the twenty-five-year history of urban renewal.[8] And it costs central cities a lot of money too: not only do they use city property tax revenue to pay off their bonds (rather than provide city services) but they regularly sell the condemned land to developers below cost and, when necessary, offer tax abatements.

City policy-makers consider these expenditures well worthwhile because, as a wide range of scholars have found, a desire for economic growth dominates their consciousness. In his influential book, *City Limits*, Paul Peterson treats this desire as uncontroversial. Every citizen's life, he contends, is improved when the vitality of the city's economy is enhanced; thus the "consensual politics of development" is the most legitimate goal that a city can adopt. Stephen Elkin, by contrast, considers development policy a prime example of systematic bias in local political decision making. Elkin argues that cities routinely make decisions that benefit the interests of landowners and developers because cities depend on them to stimulate the local economy. Yet, he says, these decisions not only impose substantial costs, such as displacement, on others in the population but are hard for those adversely affected to overturn. Even though community action can occasionally derail a development project, the momentum is on the side of growth: so much time, organizing, and energy is required to stop any particular project that most of them succeed. Moreover, both the victories and defeats in these land disputes have cumulative effects on the relevant populations; thus, Elkin concludes, "growth strategies themselves contribute to inequality." John Logan and Harvey Molotch take Elkin's argument one step further. City competition to attract business is so intense, they say, that the media, unions, universities, arts groups, small retailers—among many others—join with the business elite and city officials to demonstrate that their city has a good business climate. This political alliance, they claim, transforms the city into a "growth machine," a machine that has power to overrun virtually any neighborhood, small business, or individual standing in its way. A similar "iron law of upgrading" exists in poor city neighborhoods: like central cities and suburbs as a whole, residents yearn for outside investment and want to rid their neighborhood of those ("the winos, the homeless, and the hoodlums") who threaten to scare investors away.[9]

Local zoning and redevelopment policies have, in sum, been dominated for decades by a connection between the same two images: "nice" neighborhoods, property values, and economic growth, on the one hand, and the exclusion of "undesirables," on the other. To break this powerful link, the fear of diversity felt by both homeowners and developers needs to be confronted head-on. Heterogeneity and prosperity have to be shown to be compatible goals, and heterogeneous neighborhoods have to be reunderstood as a "good place to raise a family." These objectives cannot be accomplished through the repeal of cities' zoning and redevelopment authority. As Houston's experience demonstrates, private real-estate covenants, policed by community associations and the city government, can have just as segregative an impact on a metropolitan area as zoning.[10] Moreover, a cessation of central-city redevelopment activity would most likely accelerate the efforts already under way to transfer America's office and retail life to the suburbs. Cities' power to zone and engage in redevelopment ought not to be eliminated; instead, these powers need to be reconceived in a way that promotes community building rather than the dispersal and separation of metropolitan residents. Such a re-conception requires addressing two questions: what kind of land use should cities cultivate through the exercise of their zoning and redevelopment powers? And how can cities accomplish a radical change in their land-use policies, given the current fragmentation of American metropolitan areas?

The New Urbanism

In *The Death and Life of Great American Cities*, Jane Jacobs urged America's cities to replace "zoning for conformity" with "zoning for diversity." By this she meant using zoning laws to ensure that no one kind of structure could dominate a city neighborhood. To accomplish this goal, she suggested that cities offer tax incentives to undermine the current pressure on property-owners to maximize the short-term profit potential of every piece of land. The way to raise a city's tax base, she argued, is not to develop each individual piece of land to its fullest; the better route "is to expand the city's territorial quantity of successful areas." Jacobs also urged cities to engage in "planning for vitality"—that is, planning that would attract the greatest possible variety of people into every district in the city, that would promote a continuous network of local streets capable of "handling strangers so they are an asset rather than a menace," and that aimed at "unslumming the slums" by encouraging city residents, whoever they were, to stay put by choice. In a similar vein, Vincent Scully, in his *American Architecture and Urbanism*, denounced the two predominant architectural forms that have characterized American city building in the post–World War II period—suburban sprawl and "super-blocks" of high-rise towers. Although these two architectural forms superficially look different, he argued, both share the same essential antiurban stance. Both destroy the diverse, pedestrian-centered feel of city streets, replace multiuse neighborhoods with geographically defined areas devoted to a single function, and promote the limitless extension of a decentralized metropolis accessible only by car. Scully called for an end to these forms of destruction of the urban environment: "we can hardly flee our neighbors along the ringing high-road forever," he said.[11]

Maybe not. But Jacobs and Scully made their proposals in the 1960s, a time when it would have been easier to implement them than it is today, and little has changed. More than half of California's man-made landscape has been built in the last thirty years, and most of it consists of the kind of urban environment that Jacobs and Scully denounced: single-income residential developments, high-rise business districts, and large-scale shopping malls surrounded by parking lots. The same "post-1965 city," to adopt Daniel Solomon's term, has similarly transformed vast areas in every other state in the nation. Recently, however, a number of architects and urban planners have begun exploring ideas like those advanced by Jacobs and Scully. Peter Calthorpe has criticized America's current form of city building for producing a host of regional problems: "serious environmental stress, intractable traffic congestion, a dearth of affordable housing, loss of irreplaceable open spaces, and lifestyles which burden working families and isolate the elderly." And Andres Duany and Elizabeth Plater-Zyberk have charged that it is also responsible (at least in part) for impoverishing central cities and for cutting off "a whole generation of Americans . . . from direct contact with people from other social classes." The resulting "mutual incomprehension and fear," Duany and Plater-Zyberk say, "accounts for no small share of the tensions in our national political life."[12]

Spurred by such concerns, these architects and urban planners have, at long last, begun sketching what a post-suburban-sprawl, post-superblock metropolis would look like. Their work, collectively labeled "the new urbanism," encompasses a wide variety of different, sometimes conflicting, views. Nevertheless, some common themes seem to be emerging. New urbanists want to transform the current mix of residential neighborhoods, office complexes, strip malls, shopping centers, and underused city land that now dominates America's metropolitan landscape into "neighborhoods of housing, parks, and schools placed within walking distance of shops, civic services, jobs, and transit." In the effort to accomplish this goal, they have focused on six aspects of urban design: creating multiuse environments, constructing grid systems for public streets, giving priority to the needs of pedestrians, facilitating reliance on public transportation, highlighting the importance of centrally located public space, and establishing focal points and boundaries for urban space. More specifically:

Multiuse Environments. New urbanists want to replace current zoning laws— virtually all of which now mandate the separation of different areas by function—with laws that require the reintegration of commercial, work, and home life. And they want to incorporate schools, parks, public squares, and public buildings into these multiuse neighborhoods as well. They also reject zoning requirements that define residential neighborhoods by income (minimum lot sizes, exclusion of apartment houses, and the like) and favor instead requiring the accommodation of different housing types—small and large, multifamily and single-family, rental and owner-occupied, units above stores and detached houses—within a single neighborhood.

Grid Systems. New urbanists restructure old neighborhoods, and build new ones, in a grid pattern—a web of interconnected public streets. They thus have repudiated the traditional suburban pattern of cul-de-sacs intersecting with collector streets that, in turn, connect at specific points to arterials and, finally, to highways. A grid system, they argue, facilitates intraneighborhood connections, creates redundant ways of going from one place to another, and, thereby, relieves congestion on collector and arterial streets.

The Needs of Pedestrians. New urbanists design neighborhoods to give priority to the desires of pedestrians over the convenience of car drivers. This involves, first of all, changing zoning laws and street design in the manner suggested above, so that people have destinations they want to walk to and streets on which to walk. It also involves designing streets so that people will feel comfortable walking along them. Car-oriented streets are built for speed: they have few intersections, soft curves, and large, easily accessible parking areas. Pedestrian-oriented streets, by contrast, limit the speed of passing cars, lead to nearby places, and are lined with trees and parked cars to protect pedestrians from traffic. As Peter Calthorpe puts it, pedestrians "want narrow streets lined with entries and porches leading to local shops, schools, and parks—not curving streets lined by garage doors leading to six-lane arterials."

Public Transportation. New urbanists promote public transit, as well as walking, in an effort to reduce the current level of reliance on transportation by car. They seek not to eliminate cars but to rebalance the three forms of transportation. (Eighty-six percent of all trips taken by Americans are by car, compared with 30–48 percent of trips taken by Europeans, and the number of car trips that Americans take daily is increasing four times faster than the population.) Public transportation and walking, they say, reinforce each other. Public transportation is most useful if one can easily walk to and from the station, and walking is encouraged if the streets are lined with stores and houses rather than parking lots and garages (these they place behind the stores and houses, not on the street). Among the new urbanists, Peter Calthorpe is most insistent on the importance of public transportation: his compact, walkable, multiuse neighborhoods are built around transit stops.

Public Space. New urbanists make public space—not just public streets but also squares, parks, and buildings—the focal points of neighborhood life. Public squares and parks, along with multiuse zoning, interconnected street design, and pedestrian-focused neighborhoods, help create an urban feel for city life. Post offices, meeting halls, day care centers, and other public buildings can perform this function too, particularly if they are located on the squares and parks. All of these forms of public space are important because they are the traditional place where one encounters strangers as well as neighbors—a phenomenon new urbanists seek to encourage. In Daniel Solomon's words, public space generates a form of intelligence known as "street smart"; "there is," he adds, "no comparable form of suburban wisdom . . . [such] as 'cul-de-sac' smart."

Centers and Edges. New urbanists want to define centers and boundaries for neighborhoods, cities, and the region as a whole. They think that neighborhoods need edges because walkable neighborhoods are best kept small, and that neighborhoods should have a center (preferably, public buildings located in public spaces such as parks and squares) that creates an urban feel. City centers and edges, in turn, create a comprehensible map for the multiplicity of neighborhoods linked together by interconnecting streets. They also facilitate the formation of specialized city neighborhoods, such as university areas, theater districts, and tourist districts, that allow residential, commercial, and work life to be combined in different ways. This form of specialization creates a diverse city yet avoids the rigid separation of functions that now characterizes office parks, shopping centers, and housing subdivisions. Finally, regional centers and edges allow neighborhoods and special districts to fit into a scheme for the metropolis as a whole. And regional edges define a limit for suburban sprawl.[13]

This brief summary of new urbanists' ideas does not begin to capture the vividness and complexity represented in their current projects and designs for a variety of urban contexts (building new neighborhoods, redeveloping inner cities, reconfiguring current suburban land use, establishing regional plans). But even the summary suggests the simultaneously nostalgic and radical nature of their proposed revisions of city zoning and redevelopment policy. New urbanists replace suburban nostalgia for the seclusion of life in the countryside with an urban nostalgia for city vitality. They reject the radicalism of more (and more and more) of the same and embrace instead a radicalism that integrates different types of people into a less car-centered environment. By combining classic urban forms (multiuse buildings built to the street without a setback) and contemporary commercial phenomena (anchor stores in malls), they offer one possible version of a postmodernist metropolitan area. As the new urbanists themselves emphasize, however, virtually everything they want to do is now illegal. To promote the new urbanist version of urban design, cities would have to revise municipal zoning laws and development policy from top to bottom. They would have to replace functional zoning with its opposite, establish a different street network, support public transportation, and build public space. They would have to use their redevelopment powers to foster the building of neighborhoods rather than concentrating on office buildings and shopping malls. And they would have to end their imposition of design requirements that segregate America's residential areas along income lines. New urbanists insist that the lack of affordable housing in America is due more to existing public policy than to economics. "We choose to subsidize highways rather than transit," Peter Calthorpe says, "we choose to zone mixed-use neighborhoods out of existence, and we choose to standardize and isolate housing types into two large categories: low-density unaffordable or high-density undesirable." Low-cost housing could be built over stores, in outbuildings placed in back of larger houses, and in buffer strips in suburban developments all across America, say Andres Duany and Elizabeth Plater-Zyberk, if local zoning laws that now forbid these housing types were changed to permit them.[14]

These efforts to provide affordable housing, reestablish pedestrian-focused environments, and make public space an integral part of neighborhoods have the potential of contributing significantly to community building in America's cities. New urbanists make clear that this is one of their goals. Peter Calthorpe, for example, has argued that withdrawal represents a self-fulfilling prophecy: "the more isolated people become and the less they share with others unlike themselves, the more they *do* have to fear." For this reason, he seeks to replace a landscape built to accommodate driving from the garage to the office parking lot and back with one that encourages walking on public streets, being in public squares, and living in integrated neighborhoods. These new designs, he hopes, will stimulate the opposite self-fulfilling prophecy: "the more diverse and open a community is, the less people come to fear one another." Like other new urbanists, Calthorpe does not claim that city design alone can undo the current level of suspicion and fear in America. He simply considers it a necessary step.[15]

One need look no further than to *Newsweek*'s cover story on the new urbanists, however, to see how easily their ideas can be defanged. *Newsweek* presents a suburban reading of new urbanism, reducing it to plans for building cutesy towns for the upper middle class ("the alternative to sprawl . . . must not evoke 'the city,' an alien place where by definition middle-class Americans refuse to live"). Although, as I have suggested, this reading is contrary to the new urbanists' own intentions, they share some responsibility for this suburbanized interpretation of their work. References to the notion of community embraced in new urbanist writing too often invoke the romantic associations with that word. No doubt, as Andres Duany and Elizabeth Plater-Zyberk succinctly put it, " 'community' sells" these days. But it sells most easily when issues such as racial conflict are not introduced into the discussion. And references to race—and to social conflict generally—are conspicuously absent in new urbanist writing. As a result, much of what the new urbanists envision building could be located—some of it has already been located—in areas of the country in which the degree of engagement with otherness is minimized. To promote genuinely diverse and open communities, a city function of community building will have to link new urbanism with a determination to overcome the racial, ethnic, social, and economic divisions that have fortified city and neighborhood boundaries across the country.[16]

Prospects for Change

This will not be easy to do. On the contrary, it is often said that current zoning and redevelopment policies reflect what people want. People like living in exclusionary suburbs and neighborhoods, the argument runs, and they like working and shopping in safe, comfortable office complexes and shopping malls. In short, *Newsweek* is right: people don't want to live or work in heterogeneous communities.

It would be foolish to underestimate the force of this argument. Government policy and individual choice have together built a remarkable appetite in America for withdrawal and isolation. No one thinks that this trend can be reversed overnight. The question is whether enough support can be generated to build alternatives. Some support for heterogeneous communities can come from those who already like living in them—those who find that the stimulation and fun produced by city life outweigh its unsettling effects. But the effort to build an unromanticized sense of community in America will also need to attract converts from those who now live in neighborhoods that define themselves in terms of opposition to outsiders. These converts could come from a variety of places, but four (overlapping) groups seem especially worth mentioning: women, residents of the declining working-class and middle-class suburbs, the elderly, and African Americans.

Women

The appeal of suburban isolation was built upon, and still depends on, specific ideas about the role of women in American society. As mentioned earlier, after World War II thousands of bedroom suburbs were constructed—and the houses within them were designed—as physical expressions of what has been called the "cult of domesticity." Zoning laws, developers, advertisers of home-related products, women's magazines, the

Federal Housing Authority, and bank officials sought to make the sharpest possible contrast between the private, comfortable, soft, and protected environment of the suburbs and the open, competitive, dangerous, and seductive world of the central city. Relying on this contrast, two-parent families with children moved to the suburbs, where the wife was expected to be a full-time homemaker and the husband a commuter. Since the husband was out of town most of the day, ensuring physical security for the women and children left behind was crucial. One way to do so lay in the design of detached, single-family houses and cul-de-sacs; another relied on the creation of homogeneous, and therefore "safe," communities. The origin of this suburban vision has been attributed, alternatively, to patriarchy, to capitalism, to commercial greed (of car manufacturers, real estate developers, or consumer product retailers), and to the residents' own desire for a good life for themselves and their families. Whatever its genesis, this "prescriptive architecture of gender" was embraced for decades by millions of (mostly white) women and their husbands.[17]

No doubt many women are still attracted to this way of life. But the vision of the family on which these residential communities were founded is now exceptional. By the late 1980s, the "traditional family"—a married couple with children, with the wife as a full-time homemaker—constituted only 10.8 percent of all households. One reason that this percentage is so low is that more women are working outside the home. Another is that two-parent families are declining (26 percent of all households in 1990, down from 40 percent in 1970), while single-parent families are on the rise (now 15 percent of households, 86 percent of which are headed by women).[18] Both trends have caused an increasing number of women to encounter a host of difficulties with combining work and family in a car-centered suburban residential development: the strain of commuting; the unavailability or inadequacy of child care; lack of time and energy to keep up the appearance of the house; too many errands. In America these are women's problems, notwithstanding feminist efforts to the contrary. Women remain largely responsible for child care, housework, and errands; women who work outside the home have found that their career is just one more "add-on."

Although many women experience these problems as their own individual predicament, in recent years feminist urban theorists have begun to document the role of urban design in creating them. A fragmented, car-centered culture, they say, is especially hard on women. It lengthens the time it takes them to commute to work, to shop, and to do household errands; it makes children dependent on having a chauffeur in order to go anywhere; it increases the likelihood that those hired to help with child care or household responsibilities live far away; it isolates families so that the nineteenth-century feminist alternative to hiring outside help—coordinating cooking, child care, and housekeeping tasks with neighbors—

becomes inconceivable. New urbanists have similarly criticized suburban design for its impact on women's lives. Their effort to reintegrate residential, commercial, and work life and to accommodate affordable housing is designed in large part to confront the problems that feminist urban theorists have identified. To be sure, this account of the effect of traditional suburbs on women sidesteps the issue of security. But no one thinks that women (or men) should live in a community filled with crime. The point instead is that isolation seems an especially undesirable way of providing security for women, given the substantial burdens that such a strategy imposes on them. Indeed, feminist urban theorists object not only to the practical problems that this isolation has created but also, more fundamentally, to the privatized, sheltered idea of women's lives embodied in suburban design. These theorists seek to enable women, like men, to enjoy the vitality—and the seduction—of city life. Women, like children, are isolated in the suburbs not only because these groups are considered vulnerable but also because of the city's attractions: traditionally only men have been thought able to withstand, and only men have been licensed to enjoy, the dangers and pleasures that central cities offer.[19]

Thus when people say (as they do over and over again) that the suburbs "are a good place to raise a family," one might well respond: what image of the family do they have in mind? For whom is it a good place: women? men? children? What is the definition of a "good" place? Andres Duany and Elizabeth Plater-Zyberk argue that, together with the elderly, children are the great victims of the current form of suburbanization.

> Fresh air and open spaces are good for . . . [children]. Suburban sprawl is not. Children in the postwar suburbs are kept in an unnaturally extended state of isolation and dependence because they live in places designed for cars rather than people. . . . Imagine how the lives of children would change if the suburban house and yard were assembled in the form of a traditional neighborhood so that kids could visit friends, go out for a hamburger, or walk to a library on their own.[20]

Imagine as well, one might add, the difference in their education and preparation for living in a diverse society if contact with otherness were routine rather than forbidden.

Residents of the Inner Suburbs

Another problem posed by the current design of American metropolitan areas lies in its contribution to the decline in the living standards of middle-class and lower-middle-class residents of America's inner suburbs. In metropolitan regions across the country, those who can afford to do so are moving out of the suburbs close to the central cities as well as out of the central cities themselves. And out means further out: to areas more and more remote from the central city. The people who are moving increase their housing costs: "moving up" is a prime reason for the move. They also endure (and pay the cost of) longer commutes and the intensification of the stress on women's lives described above. But the greatest cost of this migration is being imposed on those who remain behind in the inner suburbs and central cities because they cannot afford, or do not want, to move. The outward exodus of wealthier residents has helped cause—and has been stimulated by—the simultaneous relocation of shopping centers and office parks to the outer suburbs, a relocation that, in the last thirty years, has transformed many of them into edge cities. This shift in business and commercial life has reduced the number of jobs available to residents of the inner suburbs because the new jobs are inaccessible to those who cannot afford to maintain a car for every worker in the family. (Even those with both a car and a job are forced to pay higher commuting costs and, thereby, are rendered unable to afford better housing.) The urbanization of the outer suburbs has also diminished the tax base of the inner suburbs and, with it, these suburbs' ability to support schools and other local services. And, at the very time that their resources are decreasing, the economic decline of the inner suburbs has produced social problems and thus has increased the demand for city services. In short, America's inner suburbs are now beginning to undergo the kind of downward spiral that for decades has plagued many of America's central cities.[21]

The most careful study of this decline, by Thomas Bier, is for Cleveland. Bier found that in recent years more than 70 percent of those who moved from either the central city or the inner suburbs moved further out and that those who did so bought houses at least 50 percent more expensive. This migration, Bier argues, has imposed substantial costs not only on those who moved and those who stayed behind but also on the government. The growth of the outer suburbs has depended on government support through the provision of roads, highways, sewers, water, and utilities. It has also been spurred by federal tax code provisions that encourage buyers' spending more, but not less, for a new home. The fact that the more expensive houses are, by and large, located in the outer suburbs is itself attributable, at least in part, to government policy: government's financial support for these suburbs, when coupled with its failure to use the money instead to maintain and redevelop housing in the inner suburbs and the central city, has furthered the segregation of America's regional areas along the lines of class. And, as argued above, zoning and redevelopment policy has had the same effect.[22]

Bier's findings for Cleveland are echoed across the country. Myron Orfield, a state legislator from Minneapolis, describes the impact on his region:

> [F]or 20 years, the southern and western outer-ring suburbs have gotten all of the new freeways and sewer systems—billions of dollars of improvements—and therefore virtually all of the region's new tax base. The central cities, inner suburbs, and northern suburbs have paid for these improvements, but received no commensurate increase in [their] tax base. Hence, the central cities, inner suburbs, and northern suburbs have the highest comparable taxes and worst service levels, while the southern suburbs have the lowest comparable tax rates and the highest services.

With appropriate modifications of the geographic directions, the same paragraph could be used to describe much of the country. Those who live in the jurisdictions left behind realize that their quality of life is on the decline—and that housing prices freeze them out of escaping this decline. But, as is the case for many women, these residents do not attribute this decline to urban design. There are, however, some initial signs that a central-city–inner-suburb coalition can be created to reform regional land-use policy if it is made an explicit political focus. Orfield proposed, and convinced the state legislature to adopt, metropolitan-wide restrictions on the subsidization of the growth of the outer suburbs in order to reverse the trend toward intercity inequality described above.[23]

The Elderly

A third group of people disserved by America's current regional landscape is the elderly. Most people over sixty-five would prefer to stay in their own neighborhoods as long as they can, but a single-family house and a car-centered environment makes it hard for them to do so. The cost of maintaining such a house is a burden—especially for women living alone—and the prospect of becoming too old to drive raises the specter of becoming either dependent or isolated. Yet zoning laws that require single-family residences prohibit many plausible alternatives: sharing the house with non–family members; reconstructing the house to install a separate apartment for the elderly resident and then selling or renting the rest of it; building an elder cottage behind the single-family house and transferring the house itself to friends or relatives. Thus many elderly residents of traditionally designed suburbs feel they have no choice but to move elsewhere. At the same time, those who live in walkable, more affordable neighborhoods in central cities or inner suburbs often feel compelled to move for other reasons. Some of these neighborhoods have been subjected to the economic decline just described; many elderly people are driven out of the neighborhood by discomfort with neighborhood change or fear of crime. Other neighborhoods have been subject to gentrification, itself a generator of the displacement of the elderly. These difficulties—and the dramatic rise projected for the over-sixty-five population in the near future—suggest that those who want to "age in place" could become a powerful political force for opening up more options for housing and community design.

So could those over sixty-five who want to move. A central issue in framing options for this subgroup of elderly people will be determining the appropriate role of age-segregated residential communities. Proponents of these communities suggest that they offer many advantages: the company of like-minded people, appropriate activities, and the assurance of security. They also offer relief from the annoyance, tension, and misunderstanding that multigenerational interaction can produce. But, like other forms of engagement with otherness, multigenerational dissonance simultaneously has benefits. As Lewis Mumford argued in a classic essay:

> [J]ust as the young proceed with their growth through multiplying their contact with the environment and enlarging their encounters with people other than their families, so the aged may slow down the process of deterioration, overcoming their loneliness and their sense of not being wanted, by finding within their neighborhood a fresh field for their activities.

Maintaining the integration of the elderly into society at large has advantages for others too: a community that is integrated in terms of age provides a source of help and (often discounted) guidance to working parents and their children. But the issue for urban policy is not whether large-scale age-segregated communities should be made illegal. The issue instead is whether local government law can be redesigned to permit alternatives. For example, new urbanists' designs can accommodate the desire both for aged-based segregation and for integration. Walkable neighborhoods can be built to provide a variety of housing types that would serve the needs of the elderly, with some of this housing constructed on blocks that provide seclusion for elderly people while still being located within walking distance of commercial life and younger neighbors. There is no reason that housing for the elderly has to fill a whole community. Making age-segregated residential communities smaller can also minimize their discriminatory impact on families with children. And, unlike exclusive leisure-oriented retirement communities, new urbanist neighborhoods can provide housing that the poor and near-poor can afford, as well as less isolated institutional accommodations for the frail and the infirm. Yet these options are not available under the zoning laws now adopted by most American suburbs.[24]

African Americans

One final group that would benefit from a change in land-use policy is African Americans. This group includes, first of all, residents of the poor African American neighborhoods described in the previous chapter. As Paul Jargowsky's analysis of the 1990 census data demonstrates, one of every five black Americans now lives in one of these ghettos—up 36 percent since 1980.[25] And the percentage of ghetto residents who are poor is increasing even more rapidly: those who can afford to do so are leaving these neighborhoods faster than are the poor, while it is largely the poor who are moving in. The physical size of these neighborhoods is also increasing at a rapid rate—even in cities in which the number of poor ghetto residents is relatively stable. This growth of America's poor African American neighborhoods in terms of both population and geography is generating a powerful centrifugal force in central cities across the country. Fear and prejudice are fueling the expansion of the outer suburbs and, as a consequence, the difficulties described above now confronting women, middle-class and working-class suburban residents, and the elderly. At the same time, the growth of the outer suburbs is, in turn, contributing significantly to the decline in living standards of the residents of poor African American neighborhoods. Whether one focuses on the loss of employment opportunities or on the ways in which isolation has intensified social problems, suburban growth has been a major cause, as well as an effect, of the impoverishment of the black poor. Yet at present there is no genuine prospect that the states or the federal government will provide funding— for enterprise zones or anything comparable—that could begin to compensate for the overwhelming financial and legal support that they currently provide the outer suburbs. As long as an urban policy of separation and division is maintained, the exodus of middle-class black residents from these neighborhoods, like the exodus of wealthy residents and commercial life from other parts of the central city and the inner suburbs, will continue, perhaps even accelerate. And the people who are left behind in America's poor African American neighborhoods will continue to be subjected to the magnified version of the downward spiral that, as we have seen, has now spread to the suburbs, both black and white. These are the people who are paying the highest cost for America's romance with suburbanization: workers employed in low-wage industries along with the chronically unemployed; elderly people as well as the young; individuals struggling against crime together with those engaged in it; those who would leave if they could afford to do so and those who would like to stay.

Still, two-thirds of African Americans live in metropolitan neighborhoods outside of these poor districts. These neighborhoods cover quite a spectrum—ranging from those almost as poor as the most impoverished neighborhoods to those populated by the substantial number of African Americans (almost one-third) now in the middle class. But the current metropolitan design poses problems for residents of all of them, even for the black middle class. African Americans who want, and can afford, to live in integrated neighborhoods continue to face considerable barriers of discrimination by real estate brokers, mortgage lenders, homeowners, and landlords. The attitude expressed by these groups is not unique: opinion surveys suggest that a majority of white Americans object to having more than a token number of blacks living in their neighborhood. It's thus not surprising that, although open housing laws have been on the books for thirty years, most African Americans at every income level live in segregated neighborhoods. Although to some extent this racial isolation reflects a desire to live in a black community, the kinds of choices that members of the black middle class are now making are a consequence of a limited number of options. On the one hand, discrimination, exclusion, harassment, and white flight inhibit the possibility of blacks' living with whites even though opinion surveys suggest that most blacks—unlike most whites—would prefer to live in neighborhoods roughly equally balanced in terms of race. On the other hand, since middle-class black Americans are becoming more prosperous at the very time that the living standards of poor African Americans are declining, the increasing class disparity has made it more difficult for the black middle class to remain in poor neighborhoods. This simultaneous segregation of middle-class African Americans from whites and other blacks has increased their distance from, and has heightened their tension with, both groups. Their isolation from white neighborhoods has generated many practical problems (such as diminished employment opportunities and inferior city services), while their separation from other black neighborhoods has produced, in Charles Banner-Haley's words, "political confusion, a dilemma of identity, and alienation from the larger black community." Throughout the twentieth century, he says, "African Americans of the middle class [have] sought a way not only to be included in American society but also to retain a distinct racial identity." If so, the current form of racially identified neighborhoods serves neither purpose very well.[26]

The Need for Community Building

Those included in the four categories just canvassed—women, residents of declining inner suburbs, the elderly, and African Americans—constitute a majority of the people who live in America's metropolitan areas. When combined with others who might be equally concerned with the current urban landscape—environmentalists, Latinos, singles, residents of declining central cities, people who detest commuting, gays and lesbians—they make up a vast majority of the urban population. There is, in short, a potential for a considerable coalition that might support a change in American land-use policy. Why, then, does the status quo seem to reflect "what people want"? The answer, I suggest, lies in the fear of otherness. American politics is dominated by tensions between members of the four groups I've just discussed (despite the fact that one person could belong to all four groups simultaneously). As I have argued above, these tensions both contribute to, and result from, current land-use policy. Moreover, they effectively prevent people from recognizing, let alone remedying, the costs that the fragmentation of the metropolitan area is imposing on all of them. An alteration of the status quo thus requires confronting the fears and suspicions that underlie and reinforce this fragmentation. It requires, in short, community building.

New urbanists recognize the importance of community building in the creation and implementation of their neighborhood designs. They routinely organize lengthy negotiation sessions—called charrettes—that bring together diverse interests, such as developers, neighborhood residents, bankers, and city officials. In part, these charrettes are designed to enable residents, developers, and bankers to provide concrete feedback that the architects can use to modify their development projects. But they serve a second purpose as well: they educate people about the costs of current zoning and development policies and the advantages of change. For example, neighborhood residents, developers, and bankers who fear that race and class integration will lower property values can learn that "price is sociological": just as fear of integration can generate lower property values, a recognition of the desirability of new urbanist neighborhoods can generate higher property values.[27] In fact, new urbanists have found the second phenomenon to be a significant problem: housing prices in some of their developments has exceeded expectations, and, as a result, the planned "low-cost" housing has become very expensive.

These site-specific meetings are important, but they are no substitute for a more broadly based discussion about the aversion to strangers that now dominates American land-use policy. Such a discussion requires that city land-use policy itself be put on the table and, with it, the structure of local government law. By enabling each city in the metropolitan area to engage its own zoning and redevelopment policy, state law has created and continues to perpetuate the current metropolitan design. In chapter 4, I proposed that these state-granted entitlements be eliminated and that, to replace them, a regional legislature be created to establish new city entitlements. The regional legislature, I argued, should be organized in a way that avoids the current obsession with the boundary between the central city and its suburbs and fosters instead alliances across local boundaries among, for example, women, middle-class residents of inner suburbs and central-city neighborhoods, elderly people, and African Americans. Negotiation over zoning and redevelopment policy is precisely the kind of task I had in mind for such a regional legislature. Such an interlocal negotiation about zoning and redevelopment is most likely to be successful, however, if failure to agree would leave cities without any power over land use. In other words, unless an entitlement to do so results from intercity negotiation, no city should have the right to zone in a way that excludes "undesirables," or to foster development favoring its residents over outsiders.

It doesn't follow from the establishment of this starting point that city residents would be unable to preserve existing neighborhood character through negotiation. On the contrary, given the widespread desire—in the black community as well as the white—to live in neighborhoods that generate a "we" feeling, it is unlikely that any negotiation would result in a uniform distribution across the region of people classified by race, ethnicity, or class. Like Richard Ford's conception of "desegregated spaces," such a negotiation

> is different from the classic model of integration in two important respects. First, it does not impose a particular pattern of integration, but rather removes the impediments to a more fluid movement of persons and groups within and between political spaces. Second, this model does not accept the current manifestation of political space and simply attempt to "shuffle the demographic deck" to produce statistical integration, but instead challenges the mechanism by which political spaces are created and maintained, and by extension, challenges one of the mechanisms by which racial and cultural hierarchies are maintained.[28]

The negotiation could thus open up alternatives to the stark dichotomies—integration/segregation, togetherness/separateness, sameness/difference—that now dominate both public policy and the popular imagination. The choice facing the negotiators is not simply between preserving homogeneous neighborhoods and eliminating them: there have always been neighborhoods that have a particular character (Italian neighborhoods, Korean neighborhoods) even though they include many different types of people. And, as I suggested earlier when discussing the elderly, integration and segregation can coexist: differences can be block-by-block. In sum, an expansion of opportunities for new urbanist neighborhoods has the potential of combining aspects of integration and segregation in a multitude of ways in the process of promoting the ideal of city life.

Interlocal negotiation over commercial and business development is equally unlikely to produce a uniform pattern throughout the region. There is too much concern in many neighborhoods about the ill effects of uncontrolled economic growth, just as there is concern in other neighbor-hoods about the lack of job opportunities. Instead of establishing unifor-mity, chances are that a regional negotiation about commercial develop-ment will focus on the regional allocation of costs and benefits of decision making about the location of office complexes and shopping malls. One central issue will be the proper allocation of tax revenues generated by development wherever it is located; another will be the comparative value of commercial development and the rebuilding of neighborhoods (the expansion of "the territorial quantity of successful areas," to return to Jane Jacobs' phrase). The results of these negotiations are not only unpredict-able but likely to differ from region to region. But the negotiations them-selves would be valuable even if they failed to achieve substantial changes in metropolitan design. There is little doubt that the retention of existing state-granted entitlements without the establishment of a regional negoti-ation process will produce more and more fragmentation and dispersal, spurred by continued financial and legal support from the federal and state governments. Negotiations, by contrast, open up a dialogue among the groups who populate the same metropolitan region, and, if they begin to make progress, could take a variety of directions. They could, for example, build on the fact that the negotiators represent the entire range of Ameri-can society in order to mount political pressure to reverse the pro-frag-mentation policies, described above, now adopted by the federal and state governments. They could also begin to focus on more than land use. In fact, if the negotiations begin to make progress, other basic urban prob-lems are bound to be put on the agenda. No one thinks that a revision of local land-use ordinances could, by itself, promote community building across the boundaries that now divide America's metropolitan areas. Changes are equally necessary in other city functions, above all in the organization of the public schools, in crime prevention efforts, and in a vast array of similar city services.

Part Four

CITY SERVICES

8

Alternative Conceptions of City Services

LOCAL government law now organizes the provision of public services, like decisions about land use, in a way that fosters metropolitan fragmentation. It does so by allowing each individual city to generate its own revenue, provide its own services, and limit the availability of its services to city residents. Because of this method of allocating city services, moving across a city line has become a mechanism for effectuating a dramatic change in one's quality of life. City services are better in some jurisdictions than others, and the taxes one has to pay for them could well be lower. One problem that many people experience with this way of organizing city services is that the housing prices in the most favored jurisdictions are high. Thus the kind of services one can receive tends to be tied to the amount of money one has. But the divisive effect of this structure is not limited to the fact that it generates inequality, although that itself is important. It also promotes a consumer-oriented understanding of city services and, as a result, undermines the public nature of public services. These days, the difference between public and private services usually refers to nothing more than the fact that the government, rather than a nonprofit organization or private corporation, provides them. But even if the government is the provider, one still evaluates them, in the manner one adopts when shopping for a pair of socks, by determining where one can get the most bang for the buck. Before I describe how community building provides an alternative to this way of understanding and organizing city services, it is important that I specify the problems with this what's-in-it-for-me model of city services, not only its popular version but its academic counterpart, commonly called the theory of public goods.

The Theory of Public Goods

The current academic literature predominately discusses city services in the language of economics: whether a city should provide any particular service is thought to turn on analysis of the concept of "public goods." Public goods, according to the standard definition, are either the kind of goods that one person can consume without diminishing anyone else's ability to do so (they are "nonrival"), or the kind that cannot easily be allocated solely to those who pay for them (they are "nonexcludable").[1] The examples of public goods regularly referred to in the literature are national defense and lighthouses. People can benefit from services such as these no matter how many other people are also doing so. Moreover, it would be unreasonably expensive to try to stop anyone from taking advantage of them. Thus they are services that the market cannot properly apportion, and, consequently, that government can legitimately offer. As the proponents of the theory of public goods recognize, however, American cities do not protect the national defense or build lighthouses. Instead, they provide services—like police, fire, sanitation, and education—that not only can be allocated to some people at the expense of others but often are. As a result, the theory of public goods, when applied to local governments, largely consists of arguments about whether, and to what extent, it is efficient for cities to supply these kinds of "mixed" or "impure" public goods.

Those engaged in this argument usually take Charles Tiebout's influential article "A Pure Theory of Local Expenditures" as a starting point. Tiebout sought to let the market determine the kinds of services cities should offer. He therefore set himself the task of imagining how an efficient market for city services could be created: is there a mechanism comparable to conventional market competition for private goods, he asked, that could allocate local public goods efficiently? The mechanism he identified was mobility. Metropolitan residents, he contended, decide to live in a particular city because it provides the mix of public goods that they are looking for, and cities compete for residents by offering packages of public goods that they think will be attractive. Tiebout's picture of people choosing cities by voting with their feet had immediate intuitive appeal. His article was written in 1956—a time when the suburbanization of America was intensifying—and the idea of mobility fit comfortably with a widespread belief in freedom of choice ("I have a right to live wherever I want"). But to make the argument work for *his* purposes—that is, to create a mechanism that generated an efficient allocation of public goods—Tiebout had to rely on "a set of assumptions so patently unrealistic as to verge on the outrageous." These included assuming that people were fully mobile (he put aside restrictions imposed by jobs by assuming that everyone lived on dividend income), that citizens had full knowledge of the differences between cities, and that the packages of public goods that cities offered imposed no adverse (or benign) impact on neighboring communities.[2] For forty years, Tiebout's successors have devoted themselves to refining his model so that it could be applied to a more realistic version of the world in which we live. Abandoning Tiebout's assumptions, however, has had a significant cost: it has sacrificed the model's intuitive appeal.

Two examples of post-Tiebout scholarship illustrate this phenomenon. In Tiebout's vision, everyone is fully mobile, and everyone can live wherever he or she wants. In other words, nothing in Tiebout's model envisions what is now called "fiscal zoning"—zoning adopted by property-rich communities designed to prevent poor people from moving to town and, once there, voting to support public services that the rich don't need. To those concerned about an influx of poor people into prosperous communities, Tiebout's model, as Bruce Hamilton puts it, is "a formula for musical suburbs, with the poor following the rich in a never-ending quest for a tax base." Like many others, Hamilton therefore modified Tiebout's model by assuming that localities would engage in exclusionary zoning. This modification, however, replaced Tiebout's assumption that people are free to move wherever they like with an explicit bias in favor of the rich, one that rationalizes the creation in America of separate and unequal communities for the rich and for the poor. James Buchanan has taken Hamilton one step further. Unlike many writers in the public goods tradition, Buchanan recognized that a decision by the wealthy to move to an exclusive suburb has a negative impact on the quality of public services available to the middle- and low-income people left behind. In other words, Buchanan did not simply abandon Tiebout's assumption that a city's decision making about public goods has no impact on outsiders, but asserted the opposite proposition: mobility itself, if unequally allocated, imposes negative consequences on one's neighbors. Because of this negative impact, Buchanan argued, it is in the interest of everyone who lives in a diverse city to make a deal designed to keep the rich from moving out of town. Such a deal, he suggested, might include offering them better schools, parks, and police protection than are available to others in town in exchange for their agreement to stay. Buchanan acknowledged that these "bribes," as Clayton Gillette calls them, "may seem to violate traditional equity norms." Nevertheless, under his version of the Tiebout model, poor and middle-class residents have an interest in offering them.[3]

I do not rely on the theory of public goods in this book—and not simply because I find the homogeneous neighborhoods and bribes for the rich found in Hamilton's and Buchanan's more "realistic" versions of Tiebout's model an unacceptable foundation for public policy. The literature as a whole, Tiebout's original article included, is based on two assumptions that I reject—one about the nature of city services and one about the nature of cities. The first is the assumption that city services can be understood simply as objects of consumption. Tiebout portrays people shopping for a city in which to live just as they shop for any other consumer good: they choose a city by determining whether the package of services it provides is worth the price charged for it in taxes. The only difference from private market transactions that Tiebout allows is that consumers make their choice not by handing over a credit card but by moving to the location where they get the best deal. Along with others who work within the public goods tradition, Tiebout also assumes that a city is similar to a voluntary association, such as a political organization, church, or chat group. People are seen as choosing a city in which to live in the way they choose a country club: what attracts them is the fact that they share interests in common with others making the same choice. This homogeneity is even said to promote efficiency: since the rich and poor tend to want different levels of services, both groups are thought to be better off if they move to homogeneous cities. By picturing cities as locations where people share interests or values in common, public goods theorists thus embrace a suburban image of what cities are like.

As I suggested earlier, this conception of cities and their services is by no means simply an academic construct. Residents of America's metropolitan areas themselves often evaluate city services by deciding whether they are getting what they pay for; if they think they aren't, they vote for a more businesslike mayor or move to a city that is doing better. Many of them—particularly those who reside in America's most prosperous suburbs—also act as if the cities in which they live are like voluntary associations. They decide where to buy a house by picking a community filled with the kind of people they want to associate with. Once there, they support rules of exclusionary zoning that allow the city's residents to keep "undesirable" people from moving to town. To support city services, they pay taxes with the same expectations they have when they pay dues to be a member of a club: taxes are seen as the collective property of city residents, just as a club's dues are the collective property of club members. As a result, they think it obvious that the city's tax revenues should be spent only on city residents, and that only they should be entitled to use city services.

The popularity of this conception of cities and of the services they offer explains why the current debate over city services largely focuses on the issue of privatization—that is, on the question of whether any particular service, such as schools or sanitation, should be run not by the city but by a private corporation. Once one adopts a consumer-oriented definition of city services and a voluntary association image of cities, transferring public services to the private sector seems easy and uncontroversial. After all, don't private companies offer most consumer goods already? In fact, once one adopts this understanding, privatization has already largely occurred even if no transfer of city functions to the private sector is made. By this I mean that the current feel of a prosperous suburban high school more closely resembles that of a private school than that of a central-city high school. Its "exclusive" quality is simply maintained through zoning rather than an admissions office. Similarly, many suburban police forces perform work more like that of security guards than like that of a major city's police department, and the parks found in homogeneous suburbs—if any can be found at all—remind one more of open space in a condominium complex than of Central Park. Admittedly, these schools, police departments, and parks are run by the government. That's why privatization (as the word is usually defined) is the issue being debated. But the debate over privatization is able to concentrate on technical points about how to deliver consumer goods to city residents efficiently because it assumes, as a starting point, a privatized version of what the public sector is and what it can accomplish.

This consumer-oriented vision of city services has significant undesirable consequences. First of all—by definition—it abandons for public services the notion of equality traditionally associated with the public sector, replacing the one-person, one-vote principle associated with democracy with the one-dollar, one-vote rule of the marketplace. It thus has a built-in bias in favor of the rich. Everyone knows that those with more money not only can afford more consumer goods than those with less money but are considered entitled to them. It is because of this inherent bias that market-based allocations are commonly rejected for the public sphere. It is considered unacceptable, for example, to treat voting rights, jury duty, and military service as commodities available for sale, just as it is considered unfair to allocate many city services, such as admission to public schools or public parks, according to the ability to pay. Indeed, it is a crime to pay a police officer to protect oneself rather than someone too poor to make such a payment.

The consumer-oriented vision of city services, again by definition, also equates the concept of freedom of choice with that of freedom of consumer choice. By doing so, it perpetuates a pervasive, but false, justification for the radical differences that now exist in the quality of city services available in different parts of America's metropolitan regions. The public goods literature is filled with rhetoric about how public services in America are allocated in accordance with differences in people's "preferences" or "tastes." And many suburbanites say that they moved to their particular suburb because they (unlike others?) cared about the quality of education for their children. Yet it seems odd to suggest that the division of America's metropolitan areas into areas with good schools and safe neighborhoods and areas with deteriorating schools and high crime rates is explicable in terms of people's differing "tastes." People who live in unsafe neighborhoods or send their children to inadequate schools don't do so because they have a taste for them. They do so because they feel they have no other choice. If they had a choice (and I am not using the word to mean "consumer choice"), they would prefer better schools and less crime.

These two defects can be understood simply as illustrations of a third, more fundamental, problem with the consumer-oriented vision of city services. Once again by definition, it radically limits the aspect of the self considered relevant in the design and implementation of public services. Consumption is an individual activity: spurred by their own economic interest, people buy consumer goods one by one (or family by family) with little concern about the impact of their purchase on those living nearby. As a result, values commonly associated with democracy—notions of equality, of the importance of collective deliberation and compromise, of the existence of a public interest not reducible to personal economic concerns—are of secondary concern, or no concern at all, to consumers. Yet it is widely recognized, in political theory as well as daily life, that reducing human experience to the act of consumption falsifies it. It is commonly said, for example, that human beings see themselves not simply as consumers but also as citizens—and that they think differently in these two different roles. As Mark Sagoff puts it,

> Last year, I fixed a couple of tickets and was happy to do so since I saved fifty dollars. Yet, at election time, I helped to vote the corrupt judge out of office. I speed on the highway; yet I want the police to enforce laws against speeding. . . . I love my car; I hate the bus. Yet I vote for candidates who promise to tax gasoline to pay for public transportation.[4]

The consumer-oriented understanding of city services makes this distinction disappear by collapsing citizens into what Tiebout calls "consumer-voters." The impact of this disappearance is not simply on the outcome of government decision making, important as that is. It affects the evolution of American society itself and, thereby, the forces that shape and nurture consumer preferences. The consumer-oriented vision of public services strengthens the consumptive aspect of the self over alternatives: consumer preferences help generate a social world that, in turn, shapes consumer preferences. By doing so, it narrows the aspects of human nature that city services have the potential of fostering.

The public goods theory's definition of a city has equally undesirable consequences—indeed, it has the same undesirable consequences as the adoption of the consumer-oriented understanding of city services. By picturing cities as voluntary associations, public goods theory imagines them as collective versions of the self, and it presents these collective selves as acting, like classically defined autonomous individuals, in a way that maximizes their own self-interest regardless of the impact on their neighbors. The public goods conception of cities, in other words, is modeled on the image of the centered subject. Public goods theorists simply assume that the metropolitan area is fragmented into a multiplicity of separate cities, each of which is empowered to defend its borders through autonomy-enhancing local government law rules, such as exclusionary zoning, protections against annexation, and the allocation of property tax revenues solely to those who live within the city borders. Actually, they do more than just assume this kind of fragmentation. They offer arguments in its defense, and they do so in the language of consumer choice. Only a fragmented metropolitan area, they contend, can offer consumers a range of choices about packages of public goods from which they might want to select. In fact, the more fragmented the area is, the better their range of choices. Public goods theory thus overlooks, or understates, the powerful, negative impact of fragmentation on urban policy that I described in the last two chapters. By undervaluing the impact that cities within a single metropolitan area have on each other, as well as the links that metropolitan residents have to cities other than their place of residence, it fosters for cities, along with their inhabitants, one version of the self at the expense of alternatives.

In this book, I offer community building as a substitute for the public goods conception of city services. Before turning to an exploration of this substitute, I want to emphasize a central feature of both the technical and the popular version of public goods theory that is well worth preserving. As most articulately presented by Robert Nozick, the public goods model appeals to a desire for human freedom.[5] Freedom of choice and freedom to move wherever one likes are important aspects of liberty, and critics have far too often responded to them in the language of coercion. As a result, segregation, separation, and suburbanization have become associated with "what people want," while integration, diversity, and city life have been thought possible only if forced on an unwilling populace by government action, most often in the form of a court order. As I hope to demonstrate below, a rejection of the public goods model does not entail a limitation on human freedom. Quite the contrary. It expands freedom of choice for most Americans by refusing to define choice solely in terms of consumption. And it supplements the freedom to move with the freedom to stay put—a freedom possible only if fear of violence and concern about bad schools no longer compel people to move, if they can, whether they want to or not. What I envision, in short, is not the replacement of Tiebout's version of freedom with coercion but the substitution of an alternative definition of freedom for the one that he and other public goods theorists have adopted.

Community Building

As I argued in chapter 6, no one thinks of America's central cities as being like country clubs, political action committees, or other voluntary associations. They are characterized not by the similarities among the people who live in them but by the wide variety of different kinds of people they include: gay and straight, cosmopolitan and streetwise, elderly and recent college grad, Latino and Anglo, office employee and service worker. Rather than being like a voluntary association, they thus are an example of what I shall call a fortuitous association—a group of people in which individuals simply find themselves, one that demands an ability to get along with the other members of the group no matter how different they are. In this chapter, I embrace this fortuitous association version of cities rather than the voluntary association model assumed by public goods theorists. In chapter 6, I described the ways in which fortuitous associations contribute to human freedom and growth. No doubt voluntary associations make an important contribution to these values too. But there are a multitude of entities that foster the benefits offered by voluntary associations: political parties, interest groups, organized religion, clubs of all kinds. The advantages of fortuitous associations as diverse as heterogeneous cities, by contrast, are much harder to come by. Clearly, these advantages come at a cost—ranging from the annoyance that unfamiliar people often generate to the stark fear that they sometimes cause. Costs such as these are imposed by every form of association, including the most important fortuitous association in American life—the family. One does not choose who one's parents or children (or in-laws or siblings) are, and their ability to provoke both joy and pain is quite different from that of chosen friends in a voluntary association. Of course, the disparate strangers that constitute a big city are nothing like one's family. But that is the point. Heterogeneous cities offer a form of human association, other than the family and voluntary associations, that can help shape who we are. They offer us an opportunity to expand our capacity to cope with, and, hopefully, learn to appreciate, the variety of people who live in America's metropolitan areas.

Like the benefits provided by voluntary associations, the benefits offered by fortuitous associations can be obtained only with conscious effort and nurturing. That is the reason that cities need to engage in community building. The consumer-oriented vision not only inhibits such an effort but strengthens the opposite phenomenon: the separation and division of the people who live in America's metropolitan areas into unequal, even antagonistic, groups. The flight of wealthy Americans to prosperous suburbs in the hopes of establishing a "you-get-what-you-pay-for" environment for city services is only one aspect of this phenomenon. Many of the people they have left behind in the older, declining suburbs have tried to defend themselves against the resulting reduction in the quality of their schools and the safety of their streets by fortifying the city borders that separate them from those who are worse off, thereby intensifying the level of suspicion and distrust on both sides of the line. Even America's central cities have become less diverse as more and more middle-class people, African American as well as white, think they have no choice, given the quality of the schools and the crime rate, other than to move to the suburbs. Those who leave don't always object to diversity. On the contrary, they often fear that, whether or not they stay, the central city will become not diverse but simply the home of the poor. There is, in fact, a widespread feeling of hopelessness when people confront their choice about where to live in a metropolitan area. Sending one's child to the central city's public school or living in a dangerous neighborhood, people worry, threatens to jeopardize the welfare of their family. Moreover, an individual cannot affect the dynamic that is enriching some parts of the region and impoverishing others simply by deciding as a consumer, acting alone, to stay in town. Yet moving out of one's neighborhood means leaving friends and family, lengthening commutes, and substituting isolation for the stimulation of city life. When people decide to move, therefore, it is partly an expression of choice (they don't have to move) and partly an expression of the absence of choice (social forces are larger than they are). If, on the other hand, they stay, they will be required to pay costs that those who leave can avoid. Either way, the consumer-oriented model of city services creates a dynamic that makes it increasingly difficult for anyone who can afford to leave to remain in America's diverse cities. As a result, it becomes increasingly difficult to have diverse cities at all.

But the reason to transform city services into vehicles for community building is not just to reverse this negative impact. Community building requires the widespread support of metropolitan residents, and these days this support is unlikely to be generated simply by an evangelical appeal to the values of diversity and tolerance. Its chances of success are better if community building is seen as a mechanism for solving the kinds of problems that metropolitan residents have in common. And many of these problems involve city services. Concerns about the quality of public schools and violent crime cross city boundary lines throughout America's metropolitan regions, as do concerns about commuting and the environmental damage caused by suburban growth. These concerns have the potential of uniting different kinds of people rather than dividing them if metropolitan residents come to realize that the ever-increasing centrifugal dynamic that now affects metropolitan regions throughout the country aggravates urban problems for a majority of Americans, not just the residents of central cities. This does not mean that cities have to abandon totally the consumer-oriented focus adopted by public goods theorists. But it does mean that the conception of city services that stresses self-protection and fragmentation has to be replaced with one that builds on the notion that the ability to live in a diverse society is inextricably dependent on the welfare of others.

Such a basis for city services is not a new idea. As I envision it, community building is a contemporary version of the reason that city services were organized in the first place. It is important that we consider for a moment the extraordinary idea, developed in America in the nineteenth century, that cities should provide a wide range of services. Until that time, there were (for example) no city police officers, no city fire departments, no public schools, no city parks, and no forms of public transportation in American cities. Why did nineteenth-century thinkers and activists consider it a good idea to create these public services—thereby inventing what Eric Monkkonen calls the "service city"? The answer to this question is too complex to permit a neat summary here. But there is little in the historical account to suggest that city services were designed to fragment American cities into separate, homogenous components, each of which would supply consumer goods on a fee-for-service basis. On the contrary, one important reason for the creation of city services was the recognition by educated, enlightened elites that it was in their own self-interest to improve the circumstances of the immigrants and other poor people who were increasingly populating America's cities. This attitude is perhaps least surprising when one considers the creation of city police. Police historians emphasize that control of the "dangerous" classes—the imposition of a "middle-class sense of order on its citizens"—was an important objective in the creation of city-run police departments. Historians of American education have similarly found that the proponents of public education saw public schools as a way to instill moral values in, and impose order on, the children of the poor. Worried about crime, vice, poverty, disease, and class conflict, advocates considered public education "the most humane form of social control and the safest method of social renewal." Even city parks were seen, in Frederick Law Olmsted's words, as vehicles for elevating the poor "to [the] refinement and taste and the mental & moral capital of gentlemen." The intermingling of the different classes in the common space of parks, it was thought, would help cultivated people demonstrate to the rest of society the kinds of behavior necessary to life in a diverse city.[6]

No doubt this nineteenth-century vision of city services is based on a patrician condescension toward the poor and on a belief in assimilation to universal, middle-class values that are offensive to (at least many) modern readers. But if one strips it of its hierarchical overtones, it offers valuable lessons for the contemporary world. The founders' vision and community building share in common the idea that city services should be open to everyone and supported by everyone. Both agree that a consumer's understanding of "what's-in-it-for-me" fails to capture the ways in which city services can promote not just the public interest but individual self-interest as well. And, in both cases, the justification for these positions lies in the recognition that the behaviors of different groups of people in our society have an impact on each other, whether one likes it or not. To be sure, a community-building perspective replaces the founders' emphasis on assimilation and the imposition of a common set of values with one that stresses not merely the acceptance of cultural differences but the importance of increasing everyone's level of comfort when differences are encountered. Moreover, it now seems clear that those who live in prosperous suburbs have more to learn from the rest of society about how to live with different kinds of people than the other way around. Nevertheless, the central idea remains: like the nineteenth-century thinkers who created America's public services, community building offers an alternative to the privatized conception of what city services are.

At this point, those who adopt the consumer-oriented version of city services might object that it is not appropriate for cities to prefer community building over a voluntary association model as the basis for civic life. Individuals, they might say, should have a choice about whether they want to live in cities organized as voluntary associations or as fortuitous associations. Why not let the market decide what kind of association people want rather than have cities organized to prefer one value over another? The answer is that there is no such thing as a free market in the selection of cities. Markets for cities, like other markets, are structured by legal rules, and currently, as I argued in chapter 3, these rules promote the voluntary association conception of cities. Local government law now fosters the separation and autonomy of individual cities within the same region through its rules of incorporation, voting rights, exclusionary zoning, and annexation. And it advances the voluntary association conception of city life and the consumer orientation toward city services by empowering these autonomous cities to generate their own revenue, to provide their own services, and to limit the availability of these services to city residents. It is this emphasis on locally generated taxes and resident-only services that has encouraged some cities to increase their tax revenue while excluding those who require the most services, thereby generating for other cities a high demand for services along with insufficient revenue to deliver what their citizens need. The national scandal of unequal school funding is only the best-known example of the government-generated inequality that has resulted from this legal regime. The task, then, is not to make the law neutral as to the choice between the voluntary and fortuitous association conceptions of cities—that is not possible—but to reverse the current emphasis, substituting community building for fragmentation as the basis of service delivery.

This requires breaking the current link between metropolitan fragmentation and the privatized conception of city services. Despite the widespread agreement that public schools and police protection should not be allocated according to the ability to pay, they are often now allocated on just that basis because separate, autonomous cities are allowed to offer them only to city residents. One of the reasons people move to a prosperous suburb is that the act of moving eliminates the obligation to pay for city services across the border either directly (through taxes) or indirectly (by admitting outsiders to their municipality's facilities). Of course, the services provided by these suburbs remain public in the sense that residents have to pay taxes that support the other people in town, not just themselves. Nevertheless, city borders, once zoned to segregate people by income level, function like the boundaries of private property: a suggestion that one should pay for services for nonresidents is experienced as a demand for the reallocation of wealth. This understanding of city services is by no means limited to the prosperous suburbs. Residents of retirement communities think that they should not have to pay for schools; people in safe neighborhoods think that they should not have to pay for crime prevention; people who live in gated communities think that their monthly assessment fees for garbage pickup should be deductible from city taxes raised to pay for sanitation services. This fee-for-service mentality nurtures the idea that defects in the services across the border are of no concern to outsiders, notwithstanding the fact that the people voicing this idea expect police protection, fire protection, and emergency health care whenever they cross the city line. Given this privatized vision of public services, it is not surprising that one public goods theorist has called for research on the question of "why the revenue of municipal corporations is viewed as a tax at all."[7] Aren't people simply paying for the city services that they themselves have chosen to have?

A vast array of innovations in the way local government law now organizes cities could undermine this conception of city services. As suggested in the previous chapter, one could modify the zoning and redevelopment policies that currently foster the segregation of metropolitan regions by income level. Alternatively, one could create regional entities empowered to provide specific city services. Many city services, such as transportation and water supply, are already delivered by regional authorities in cities across America. Although these regional authorities are rarely organized democratically, they could be reorganized and transformed into vehicles capable of promoting community building. In the discussion that follows, in short, I explore only one possible modification of the autonomy model. I shall retain the idea that individual cities supply city services one by one in order to describe how even this fractured model of metropolitan organization can be modified to promote community building. Moreover, I concentrate solely on altering two key ingredients of city autonomy: the manner in which the services are funded and the identity of the people who are entitled to use them. Current law usually allows individual cities to add resources derived from (state-authorized) local property-based taxes to their share of state and federal funding of local services. I shall assume below that this system has been replaced by a new institutional mechanism—such as the regional legislature described in chapter 4—that ensures that all decisions about the funding of city services within the region are made through a negotiation process in which every city in the region participates. I shall also assume that all inhabitants of the region, no matter where they are located, have become eligible to obtain the benefits of city services, wherever provided. What this opening of city services to nonresidents will mean in practice will differ depending on the service involved; examples are discussed below. The principle, however, remains the same: it stems from my rejection of the voluntary association conception of cities. That conception assumes that a city's citizens are entitled to exclude others from their services because they pay for them. Even now this idea overlooks state and federal funding of local services—as well as the fact that nonresident property-owners pay taxes to support city services that they are not entitled to use. Given my change in the method for funding city services, the supposed tie between payment and entitlement to use will simply become weaker still.

As readers will no doubt recognize, these two changes undermine city autonomy. That is their objective. Other modifications might accomplish the same purpose better, and I invite readers to consider what they could be. The central task, in my view, is not to pinpoint the specific institutional form that a revision of the autonomy model should take. The central task is to ensure that community building becomes the basis both of the relationships among the people who live in the metropolitan region and of the connections among the cities themselves. If this goal is met, city services could be organized in countless ways and, in the best tradition of the decentralization of power, thereby foster local experimentation and innovation.

I concentrate in the next two chapters on the two aspects of city life that are most responsible for the current fragmentation of America's metropolitan areas: the desire for good schools and the fear of crime. By discussing in some detail how education and police services could be organized as instruments for community building, I hope to demonstrate how such a conception can give meaning to what "public" services are and what they offer city residents.

9

Education

The "Public" Aspect of Education

"Education," the Supreme Court declared in *Brown v. Board of Education*, "is perhaps the most important function of state and local governments," but these days many people find it hard to understand why. The reason is that education is also perhaps the most important consumer good that people ever acquire, not only for themselves but also for their children. Education is considered the road to advancement, for the poor as well as the rich: the better the education, the better the job and, as a result, the better the quality of life. Parents thus think it essential for their children to go to a school that offers "academic excellence." Many parents shop for such a school by deciding where to live on the basis of the quality of the public schools. Others want to go further, arguing that there is no justification for making local governments the primary vehicles for running the schools. Instead, they say, everyone should have access to academic excellence wherever it is found, whether in public or private schools, paid for with vouchers or in some other way. This search for a high quality education is not surprising given the widespread anxiety about the kind of competitive world today's children are destined to enter. The problem with it is not the demand for excellence—itself a worthy goal—but the fact that it includes no vision of the public nature of education. Education simply becomes a product everyone acquires individually, with each family trying to obtain the very best product it can get.[1]

From its inception, however, public education has not merely been a market commodity parents provide their children. It has also had a social function. In school, as John Dewey put it, "each individual gets an opportunity to escape from the limitations of the social group in which he was born, and to come into living contact with a broader environment." It is there, Dewey continued, that individuals are introduced to a perspective broad enough to encompass the "different races, differing religions, and unlike customs" that constitute American life. This educational experience affects more than the ways that individuals think about the world. It is a primary vehicle for the reproduction of American society itself. Schools, the founders of American public education recognized, are the "public's agencies for creating and re-creating publics." Parents obviously have, and should have, a major influence on their children's education. But everyone else in the community has a stake in the educational process as well.[2]

The idea that education is, in part, a process of socialization by the state has always been controversial. It therefore has traditionally been defended by an appeal to values thought to be above controversy. A common republicanism, a common Protestantism, assimilation to American norms, universal ideas of merit and excellence, consensus values, the need to prepare citizens to engage in democratic decision making—ideas like these have justified, or sought to justify, public education for more than 150 years. These days, however, no rationale for government-sponsored socialization seems uncontroversial. The meaning of the term "public," when used as a modifier to describe the nation's schools, has thus become hard to decipher.[3]

Community building—the justification I offer for public schools—is controversial as well. Its usefulness lies not in its universal acceptance but in its focus on a central issue: one way or another, the nation's schools prepare children for living in our diverse society. What is controversial is how we should prepare them to do so. As I describe below, the American education system now largely responds to diversity by creating boundaries, intellectual and social as well as geographic, that separate children along lines of race, class, and ethnicity. By relying on school district lines to define school populations and on the tracked curriculum to organize individual schools, it helps divide Americans into groups that are increasingly incomprehensible to each other. Many—although by no means all—school choice proposals would simply intensify this process. A public school system organized to promote community building, by contrast, could have the opposite effect by giving a particular content both to the word "public" and to the word "education." From my perspective, a school is not public simply because it is operated by the government. Even a school run by a city can be organized like a voluntary association, with school district boundaries, rather than admissions officers, defining who fits in. I consider a school public if it is open to the heterogeneity of American life and, as a result, enables its students to engage different types of people not simply in the curriculum but also in the classroom. As so defined, a public school influences the education students receive. Education has always been more than the transfer of nuggets of knowledge from teacher to student. Learning how to get along with one's peers is a central feature of the hidden curriculum of every school system, one as important as excellence in determining how well schools prepare their students for their future careers. Yet when a national commission on education told the country in 1983 that the deteriorating quality of the public education system had put the nation at risk, it focused only on the formal curriculum.

In my view, the same should have been said about the national need to improve our individual and collective capacity to get along with the kind of people who populate America's metropolitan areas, whoever they are.[4]

This conception of community building is based on, but modifies, the attempts in recent decades to reverse the divisive impact fostered by the predominant organization of American education. Since the 1950s, efforts to integrate the schools and to make school funding more equal have, in fact, become the principal vehicle for governmental efforts to reduce the fragmentation of American society. This oppositional policy, however, has faced two formidable obstacles that it has been unable to overcome. First of all, it has placed on education too great a share of the burden of combating racial and ethnic intolerance. Indeed, its success has been undermined by city, state, and federal policies on other matters that have worked in the opposite direction. For example, racial integration of the public schools has routinely been understood as an attack on the neighborhood school, but the neighborhoods themselves have been organized, through zoning and other government policies, in a way that has divided them into racially identifiable spaces. It is not surprising, therefore, that the adults who lived in areas understood as separate from—even hostile to—outsiders would be opposed to breaking barriers for their children that they were unwilling to break for themselves. The defense of the neighborhood school, after all, has always been a defense of the neighborhood as well as of the school. The same point can be made about crime policy. Fear of violence is one of the issues much in the minds of parents who are anxious about diversity in the public schools. But, as I argue in the next chapter, the principal way that parents have dealt with this fear for themselves is to isolate themselves from it. If so, it would be odd if they were willing to expose their children to the kind of violence that they have tried so hard to escape. Education, then, cannot be the central focus for solving urban problems. Community building has to be a strategy for organizing all city functions.

Recent efforts to diversify the public schools have also been hampered by being seen as a form of coercion ("forced busing"). This coercive element has been highlighted by the fact that integration was originally ordered by the courts: without judicial activism, it seemed, children would go to the school they "naturally" would go to—that is, their neighborhood school. These days, however, the school choice movement has made it clear that the neighborhood school itself is a form of coercion. Why should a child be forced to go to a neighborhood school rather than another one that seems better? By capitalizing on Americans' romance with the word "choice," proponents of school choice have made it seem even more natural than a neighborhood. Yet school choice is not natural either. Like the definition of a neighborhood for school attendance purposes, the mechanism that structures how parents' choices are made is a product of the legal system. No one proposes that the legal system treat education like a conventional market good. Defenders of school choice programs do not contend that people are free not to become educated if that's what they'd prefer, or free to refuse to pay taxes that support education because they don't believe in it. Although both ideas were controversial at their inception, required consumption and required purchase are part of all principal school choice proposals.[5] School choice advocates focus only on the selection of the school a child attends. Even on this issue, no proposal actually enables children to attend a school simply because their parents prefer it. Instead, as I discuss below, all of them rely on legal rules to allocate either to admissions officers or to school districts the power to determine the composition of the school population. The difference between efforts to promote homogeneity and efforts to promote diversity is itself produced by alternative structures of legal rules. As a result, a decision about which of these objectives to pursue does not require a choice between freedom and coercion. In fact, community building can be based on the very same devices—the organization of school funding and the assignment of students to schools—that are now used to promote metropolitan fragmentation.

Appeals to neighborhood and to choice often do have one thing in common: both are regularly invoked to foster the experience of sameness associated with voluntary associations, not the experience of a fortuitous association. And, many think, what people *want* are legal rules that produce homogeneous schools. But what people want is more complex than this claim suggests. First of all, most Americans support both neighborhood schools and school choice, at least for public schools, and these two starting points for educational policy conflict with each other. If outsiders could enroll in another neighborhood's school if they wanted to, it would no longer simply be a neighborhood school. A fully effective school choice program would undermine neighborhood schools more than "forced busing" ever did. Yet if neighborhoods had the power to exclude outsiders from their schools, the outsiders would not be free to choose where to go to school. Not only are these two policies contradictory but the decision parents make about which of them to prefer often turns on an evaluation of comparative educational quality. If parents thought that a diverse school would improve their children's education more than an homogeneous school would, they would want diversity. No doubt many parents now make a link instead between school quality and homogeneity. But this connection, currently under considerable attack in the educational literature, is itself fueled by the legal rules that limit the experience of diversity—in residential and commercial neighborhoods alike—in large parts of America's metropolitan areas. Even now there is considerable support in

America for integrated schools, from both whites and blacks, at least in principle. While most whites are unwilling to go to schools in which they are a minority—and most blacks are willing to be a minority only if they constitute more than a token presence in the schools—there is room for compromise, and no reason to think that these attitudes cannot be modified through further experience. In the minority of school districts in America with the most widespread and long-standing commitment to integrated education, there is considerable popular support for it.[6]

Interdistrict Community Building

An education policy designed to further community building can be based on an alteration of the legal significance now attributed to the state-created boundaries that define America's school districts. As the Connecticut Supreme Court declared in an important recent case, *Sheff v. O'Neill*, state districting statutes are "the single most important factor" determining the kind of students that attend the nation's public schools. Since they simultaneously define the location of the property that is taxed to support the schools, these statutes also are the single most important factor determining the resources available for public education. The most segregated school systems in America are located in those metropolitan areas that contain many small school districts easily distinguishable from each other by the extent of their exclusion of poor African Americans and Latinos—a common occurrence in America, one that has been blessed by Supreme Court decisions for more than twenty years. School district boundaries in these metropolitan areas function like city boundaries: they create a self-reinforcing mechanism that allocates school resources and middle-class students to some parts of the region rather than others. Real estate advertisements use schools as racial signals (the schools mentioned are always white schools), and these signals affect more than simply those who want to send their children to a racially homogeneous school. They also affect those who, while not opposing integration, do not want to send their children to schools in which they would be a racial minority, or that are filled with the social problems commonly associated with poverty. "If white families . . . face a choice between a central city area where all schools have 80 percent black . . . enrollments and dozens of virtually all-white suburban districts," as Gary Orfield puts it, "few will choose the city community." Few will choose a school populated predominantly by students from poor families as well. And America's segregated African American and Latino schools are dominated by poor children, while 96 percent of white schools have middle-class majorities.[7]

In *Sheff v. O'Neill*, the Connecticut Supreme Court became the first court in the nation to hold that a state districting statute—which in Connecticut had led to Hartford schools' becoming 92 percent black while suburban schools remained less than 10 percent black—violated a state constitutional prohibition of segregated education. The court's analysis of the impact of boundaries on educational segregation is convincing, but it would be a mistake, it seems to me, to assume that community-building efforts could be based on court cases of this kind. Decisions like *Sheff v. O'Neill* are unlikely to become common elsewhere in the country. There is bound to be considerable resistance to the integration of the schools unless the problems popularly associated with the public schools in poor neighborhoods—problems that the flight from these schools has itself helped bring about—are addressed. And these are not problems conventionally thought solvable by courts. The majority opinion in *Sheff v. O'Neill* was silent about the remedy for the constitutional violation it had found, while the dissenters argued, as do many commentators, that only a single metropolitan-wide school district would produce an integrated school system. But the creation of such a district, above all if court-ordered, would once again highlight the link between integration and coercive government action and once again place on education the entire burden of confronting racial and ethnic tension.

Overcoming the divisive impact of current school boundary lines, however, does not require court-ordered centralization of metropolitan school systems. Simply changing the location of school district boundary lines can open public schools to diversity in some areas of the country. There is nothing sacrosanct about the current location of these boundaries. The number of school districts in America has been declining for most of the century: from 127,531 in 1932 to 15,834 in 1992. And, particularly in the suburbs, the boundaries of these school districts regularly cross city lines. More than 75 percent of school districts are not contiguous with any other local boundary; only about one in ten tracks city boundaries.[8] These boundary lines have long been relied on—and schools have been located—to ensure the separation of different kinds of students. They could now be redrawn with the opposite result in mind. This technique will by no means work everywhere. In many parts of the country, housing segregation is now so complete that no redrawing of school boundaries, short of centralizing the school system, can open suburban schools to diversity. In these metropolitan areas, however, community building can concentrate not on changing the location of the district lines but on undermining the conception of local autonomy they seek to delineate.

Local government law now frustrates community building by providing an entitlement to those who move to prosperous suburbs: buying a house enables them to participate in the collective power to allocate educational resources and define public school admission requirements in a way that excludes the social problems and financial burdens associated with poverty. As I suggested above, this entitlement system analogizes school district boundaries to the boundaries of private property: whatever is located inside the boundary is "our" property, and the taxes derived from it can therefore be spent only on "our" children—at the very least, as a resource for supplementing the minimum level of education funded by the state. These references to "our" property and "our" children are references to a group, and the purpose of the regional negotiations over school funding that I envision is to expand the range of people that the group includes. When money is raised from a metropolitan region's property-owners—industrial and commercial property-owners as well as residential property-owners, nonresident property-owners as well as homeowners—whose money is it? And whose children should benefit from it? Currently, the legally imposed tie between the resources available to school districts and the value of the property located within their borders empowers some neighborhood schools while disempowering others, as the nationwide litigation challenging the traditional methods of public school funding has made clear. Many states have therefore struggled to improve educational opportunities for those disadvantaged by this system. But even in these states there has been insufficient effort to undermine the privatized idea that the property located within a school district's boundaries is a resource available solely to the people who live within the school district. Rejecting this notion does not necessitate equalized school spending throughout the region. A regional negotiation over school funding can allocate educational resources in countless ways. One possibility, for example, would be to reject the preference now given the localities that most effectively use their boundaries to defend their homogeneity, and to replace it with one that favors the region's most integrated neighborhoods. The reason for giving these neighborhoods a preference is not simply that they produce schools filled with different kinds of students. The reverse is also true: integrated schools generate support for diverse neighborhoods and, thereby, contribute to the task of community building.

Changing the rules that govern the allocation of educational resources is unlikely, standing alone, to produce heterogeneous schools. It is also necessary to revise the current entitlement that now enables school districts to define who is eligible for admission to their schools. One way to make such a revision is through school choice. Consider a system, for example, in which parents could choose to send their child to any public school in their metropolitan area as long as diversity, and not segregation, was promoted by their choice. To ensure that such a plan would produce the greatest possible heterogeneity, admission to every school in the region would be equally open to all metropolitan residents. In other words, no admission preference would be offered to students who lived within a school district's boundaries. Such an open admissions policy would resolve the conflict often asserted between self-interest and the allocation of school funding—why would anyone agree to allocate money to a diverse school rather than the one their own children attended?—by giving every child an equal chance of attending the best-funded school. It would also alter the structure of a number of current school choice programs, commonly called "controlled choice" plans, in order to make students' chances of being "insiders" and "outsiders" more equal. Under many current plans, such as the one adopted in Cambridge, Massachusetts, parents can choose to send their children to any public school as long as their choice promotes diversity. But they are largely limited to sending their children to schools within the school district in which they live because they can send them to another district's school only if there is "room" for them—that is, only if seats remain after all students who live in the district have been admitted—and only if the school district agrees to participate in the admission of outsiders. As a result, only a few "outsiders" are added to a student body predominantly entitled to admission as a matter of right.[9]

A decision to give an admission preference to district residents honors the school choice of some parents over that of others through the adoption of a state policy favoring neighborhood schools. It does not follow, however, that a regionwide school choice plan would establish the opposite policy, destabilizing neighborhood schools by bringing in a flood of outsiders. Its actual effect would depend on the outcome of regional negotiations over school funding because it would bring to the surface the conflict, mentioned earlier, between support for neighborhood schools and school choice. If it turned out that most people in the metropolitan area preferred neighborhood schools, the regional negotiation process would likely focus on making schools comparable enough so that most parents would choose to send their children to neighborhood schools. After all, a school choice program that offered no admission preference to neighborhood residents would undermine neighborhood schools (assuming most people preferred them) only if they substantially varied in quality. If, on the other hand, most people preferred to send their children to the best school in the region wherever it is located, the negotiations might focus instead on the dynamic that now makes residents of poor neighborhoods as reluctant to apply to out-of-district schools as residents of the more prosperous districts are to receive them.

Chances are, some elements of both of these agendas would be addressed. Many schools would become more integrated because children would no longer be disqualified from attending a school solely on the grounds that their parents cannot afford to buy a house nearby. Some parents would send their children to out-of-district schools either because they thought they were better or because (when a parent worked in the area, for example) they were more convenient. On the other hand, a regionwide school choice program—even if combined with a regional allocation of educational resources—is unlikely to generate many transfers from suburban schools to those of poor African American and Latino neighborhoods. And many residents of these neighborhoods might continue to send their children to neighborhood schools, rather than to a suburban school, because of fear of racial antagonism, loss of identification with African American or Hispanic culture, or the undermining of ties to neighborhood institutions. Indeed, critics have argued that allowing the voluntary transfer of African American and Latino students to privileged white schools would simply lure top students from neighborhood schools and, thereby, intensify the decline of the schools left behind.[10]

The community-building plan that I've just described is not, therefore, the equivalent of a metropolitan plan for integrating the region's schools. Rather than trying to desegregate the schools overnight, it attempts to avoid the problems that have historically been engendered by the effort to foster integration simply by changing the school system. It concentrates instead on revising local government law. The proposal rejects the current legal rules that rely on school boundary lines to divide the region into unequally funded school districts populated by students readily identifiable in terms of racial and class categories. And it installs in their place a system that makes both educational resources and students the responsibility of the region as a whole. These changes will increase the diversity of many metropolitan schools, but they clearly are only one ingredient in the task of doing so. Equally important community-building efforts must become an integral part of other city services. In poor African American and Latino neighborhoods, this includes initiatives such as regionwide efforts to promote economic development and, as described in the next chapter, effective crime control. In the outer suburbs, it includes organizing a transportation system that promotes the mobility of those who rely on public transportation as well as those who drive. Without a coordinated program of all city services, in my view, a single-minded commitment to school integration—an insistence, for example, that all schools have the same percentage of white and black students, with other concerns left unaddressed—could exacerbate, in the black community and white community alike, the very tensions that community building is designed to overcome.

My version of community building also abandons the historic reliance of integration proponents on government orders and court mandates. Instead, it creates an educational system that is no more (or less) coercive than the current system. Under both systems, taxpayers' contributions are allocated to other people's children as well as their own. And in both systems some parents will experience their children's school as chosen, while others will experience it as the only choice they have. To be sure, those who defend the current organization of public education will see my proposal as a scheme to reallocate the wealth and to undermine the ability of many parents to control the nature of their children's education. The element of truth in this reaction lies in the fact that every way of organizing public education affects the allocation of wealth and the composition of schools in America. The current organization of American education, when combined with other entitlements provided by local government law, such as the power to exclude the poor through zoning and to limit other city services solely to residents, powerfully affects the prosperity and life chances of Americans. The attachment to these current entitlements felt by many of those who benefit from them is not surprising. What is remarkable is that these benefits are so often considered to be the equivalent of property rights. There are no such property rights. On the contrary, it has been the fundamental understanding of local government law for almost a century that no one has a private right to benefit from the way America now organizes municipal governments. States are free to reorganize city boundaries and their attendant benefits at will, even if the reorganization makes some people's taxes go up.[11]

Such a reorganization is well worth the effort. Altering the rules that govern school funding and admission requirements would transform the reference to "our" property and "our" children into a gesture toward a heterogeneous group, and it would assign to an equally heterogeneous group the task of deciding how to strengthen the school system. The process of regional negotiations would itself contribute to the task of community building by focusing everyone in the region on the job of educating all of the region's children rather than on fortifying the barriers that separate them from each other. This regionwide focus is essential. A major ingredient in the powerful, sometimes violent, opposition to integration in the 1960s and 1970s was the fact that suburbanization allowed privileged whites not to participate in the transformation of the public schools. The greatest opposition to integration occurred when, with suburban neighborhoods exempted, integration efforts focused only on white neighborhoods experienced by their residents, because of their proximity to black neighborhoods, as transitional and easily vulnerable to change. The vast majority of people who live in America's metropolitan areas would benefit from the elimination of the legally created suburban escape hatch. School funding would become more fairly allocated. All residents of the metropolitan area—not just the most mobile—would have a choice about the best school for their children. The concentration of poor children into a limited number of schools would be reduced. All public schools would, once again, be open to everyone regardless of income. And, above all, parents and children from all income, racial, and ethnic categories would be able to develop more of a relationship with the variety of people who live in their metropolitan area, and thus benefit from the decrease in tension and increase in opportunities for learning that fortuitous associations offer. Once school systems became organized as fortuitous associations rather than as a series of separate voluntary associations, educational funding and innovation might even increase (thereby demonstrating the truth in the slogan "green follows white").

The Relationship between Public and Private Schools

Would the adoption of such a community-building plan for public education result in a massive flight from public to private schools? The answer is far from clear. A flight to private schools is already under way in some parts of the country, and a major change in the public education system could well accelerate it. On the other hand, in the areas of the country in which integration has been regionwide and thus worked most successfully—places like Wilmington (Delaware), Louisville (Kentucky), and Charlotte (North Carolina)—the enrollment of the public schools is increasing notwithstanding the existence of a private school alternative. Escaping to a private school is much harder than moving to the suburbs. In the country as a whole, private schools now educate only 12 percent of America's students, and many of them, such as Catholic schools in large central cities, are already quite diverse. Moreover, admission to the most "exclusive" private schools is a very expensive proposition. Few people in America can afford to pay for public schools and not use them. Besides, the rules of competition between public and private schools are themselves subject to change. Some metropolitan regions might decide, for example, to reexamine the continued public subsidization of private schools provided by tax-exemption and the funding of school transportation. It is not the task of community building, however, to make private schools unavailable. There are private alternatives for all city services, from private security to private transportation to private recreation, and draconian coercion would be required to eliminate them. The reason to organize city services to foster community building is not to abolish these private alternatives but to draw a distinction between them and city services: only public services would have the objective of fostering people's capacity to live in a diverse society. The result of the competition between truly open public schools and private schools will ultimately depend on the success of these community-building efforts. If a decrease in apprehension about diversity can be combined with an improvement in the quality of the public schools, the temptation to pay both taxes and school tuition might be reduced even for the wealthy.[12]

Some critics adopt a very different stance about the relationship between public and private schools. They argue that public support should be provided so that more people can send their children to private schools. From the perspective of these critics, my community-building proposal gives parents too limited a choice: no one is entitled to send a child to a private school or even to an out-of-district school if their child's admission makes the school more homogeneous. Why not, they might ask, give parents an absolutely free choice of schools that their children can attend? The answer is that no school choice proposal gives parents an absolutely free choice of schools. All of them offer only a "controlled choice," even though the label is now usually applied simply to a subset of school choice plans. The plans are distinguishable from each other only in terms of who exercises control, that is, whether admissions officers or government officials are given power to decide whether the child "fits in" to the school. School choice proponents who seek to limit the government's role in education insist that while children can apply to any school they like, wherever it is located, they should not get in unless the school officials decide to admit them. Some of these plans even allow a school to deny admission to those who cannot afford to pay the extra amount the school charges over the amount of public support for education. Of course, admissions officers, as well as local governments, can incorporate diversity rather than homogeneity into their definition of the kind of students they think will fit in to their school. And, as we have seen, government policy has long favored homogeneity over diversity. Still, the critical distinction among school choice plans is that advocates who favor allocating power to admissions officers justify doing so on the grounds that it allows individual schools to design their own student population. That way, the argument runs, different kinds of schools, made up of different kinds of students, can compete with each other for customers.[13]

By envisioning each school as a product offered in the market by those who run it, this consumer-oriented version of school choice adopts a privatized vision of educational services, whether or not the proposal includes private schools among those eligible to participate in government funding. Subject only to antidiscrimination laws, schools are encouraged to compete with each other by offering applicants a choice among voluntary associations to which they may apply for inclusion. The problem with this conception of school choice is not that it encourages competition—a metropolitan-wide open admissions policy would permit considerable competition. The problem is that it encourages a competition for exclusivity that separates and divides the population of the metropolitan area. Like the drawing of school district boundaries—and for the same reason—the ability of some schools to design "exclusive" admission standards destabilizes diverse schools throughout the school system. Antidiscrimination laws, which prohibit only "intentional" discrimination, have little impact on the dynamic that now splinters metropolitan school systems into distinct, even hostile, student bodies.[14] Only a metropolitan-wide commitment to community building can undermine this dynamic. That is why no public money should be given to a school that is not open to the entire range of people who live within the metropolitan area. Openness should be the defining characteristic of all public schools—not just schools to which parents apply under a school choice plan but neighborhood schools and charter schools as well.

Such a definition of public schools poses no threat to the continued existence of decentralized school systems. Individual public schools organized to foster community building can be as responsive to teachers, students, and parents, and have as much control over curriculum content, as current schools. Once changes in the composition of schools got under way, it even seems likely that teachers, students, and parents would become more involved than they are now to ensure that their newly designed school will provide quality education. The identity of the participants would have changed—as it does already, given the mobility of the American population—but the motivation to make "our" school a good one will not disappear with the erosion of the privatized vision of school district boundaries. School meetings would instead become an important forum for the exercise of public freedom, one that would take the diversity of the participants involved as a given.

My proposal raises many unanswered questions. If demand for any particular school is too high to include all those who want to attend, should more schools in that part of the region be built, or should students who do not get their first choice of school be assigned to their second-choice school? Should the effort be made to ensure that neighborhood schools exist everywhere in the region, or should some schools be abandoned in favor of greater openness elsewhere? What priorities should be given to siblings? The purpose of decentralizing educational decision making is to allow these kinds of questions to be answered in many different ways once exclusion and funding inequality are no longer assumed ingredients in public education.

Community Building within the Schools

Revising the rules governing school funding and admission criteria is essential to educational community building because many current schools are not diverse enough for community-building efforts even to get under way. But everyone knows that admitting different types of students into a school is not enough. Long-standing prejudices remain unaddressed, stereotypes are reinforced, tensions arise, cliques are formed. These phenomena now exist in diverse school systems throughout the country, and, later in life, graduates replicate them throughout the society as a whole. Education is a key ingredient in the task of dealing with these issues, not just for public school students but for their parents as well. Designing an educational process that is effective in doing so is an undertaking of great complexity. Here, I address only one of its components: confronting the widespread fear that diversity lowers the quality of education. This fear has not simply generated support for homogeneous schools. It also underlies the educational policy of segregating the student body in individual schools no matter how homogeneous or diverse they are.

The most important ingredient in this policy is academic tracking. The division of the student body into fast, average, and slow classes is pervasive in America's public schools—not just for English and math but, frequently, throughout the rest of the curriculum as well. This kind of categorization is based on a series of assumptions that link homogeneity and educational achievement. Students, it is thought, learn better when grouped with those who have similar academic abilities. Mixing students of different abilities holds the bright students back while undermining the confidence and learning capacity of the slow students. Therefore, bright students and slow students must be separated from each other, and they can be separated in a fair and reliable way. Every one of these assumptions is now being challenged in the education literature. Jeannie Oakes contends, for example, that there exist "virtually mountains of research evidence indicating that homogeneous grouping doesn't consistently help *anyone* learn better." Highest-achieving students in heterogeneous classrooms, she says, are not held back because, notwithstanding popular assumptions to the contrary, classes are not geared to the lowest common denominator but are designed to expose all students to the highest level of curriculum content. Top students do equally well regardless of the group in which they learn; a few studies even suggest they do better in heterogeneous settings.[15]

Oakes' position about the effect of heterogeneity on the highest-achieving students is the subject of considerable controversy. But there is little controversy about her observation that those now placed in lower tracks learn better in heterogeneous classes. Tracking denies those assigned to lower tracks exposure to a vast amount of educational material and creative analytical skills considered indispensable in the modern American economy. It therefore demoralizes lower-track students—and reduces their educational potential—considerably more than does the interaction with faster learners in heterogeneous classrooms. Moreover, it divides white students from students of color and, in racially homogeneous schools, separates students along class lines. Academic tracking is one of the ways Americans first learn that a heterogeneous group should be divided into categories, and that these categories should then be separated into different spaces—spaces not just for whites and blacks but for smart and dumb, college-bound and vocationally tracked, cool and nerd, blacks who identify with black culture and "brainiacs" who "act white." This process has helped Americans learn an important, and destructive, lesson: being in the same space with different kinds of people not only feels uncomfortable but also impedes personal advancement.[16]

Experiments with heterogeneous classes are now under way throughout the country. Even if advocates' descriptions of these classes are read skeptically, they suggest, at the minimum, that alternatives to homogeneous classrooms need to be seriously evaluated in every region of the country. The purpose of this evaluation is not to re-create the one big classroom of the little red schoolhouse. There are many ways to organize schools so that different kinds of students can encounter one another in the classroom. No doubt innovations in teaching techniques are required. And, clearly, the transition to heterogeneous classes has to be carefully managed, not only for students but for their parents as well. In fact, the most successful transitions to heterogeneous classrooms have included parent education as a major component—a process that itself contributes to community building. But experience has shown that, when successful, heterogeneous classrooms have a profound effect on students' learning experience. High-achieving students in some heterogeneous classrooms, for example, have been teamed with "slower" classmates, the joint goal being to raise the overall average of the group. In conventional schools, this kind of team effort is generally limited to participation in sports; only there are students offered the possibility of experiencing someone else's achievement as a victory for themselves. The extension of this kind of experience into the academic setting not only improves attitudes toward teaching and interpersonal skills but helps undercut the idea that educational achievement means celebrating the superiority of one's A over a classmate's C. As on sports teams, it would be a mistake to romanticize what this group interaction is like. Working with others produces tension, frustration, and disappointment. It would also be a loss for many parents—and many students—not to be able to celebrate a child's achievement of being placed in the track designed for only the most gifted. But heterogeneous classes need not be free of tension or conflict or problems to be preferable to homogeneous classes. It is enough if they can advance the education of the student body while simultaneously lessening the overall level of divisiveness within the school.[17]

An educational system that allocated resources in a way that reduced the current favoritism now given schools with homogeneous student bodies, that prevented school district boundaries from being used to exclude outsiders because they were different, and that taught students, from an early age, how to work with classmates of disparate talents and capacities would help overturn the divisive structure that now characterizes most of America's metropolitan school systems. Even if such a plan could unequivocally be shown to improve educational quality, however, it would generate opposition. The reason is that homogeneous schools and academic tracking are part of another strategy that affects city services across the board—one that has responded to the widespread fear of violence in America by dividing and separating the metropolitan population. The organization of American education functions as a zoning mechanism for the public schools: it creates a safe space that excludes, at least from the "highest" tracks and the "best" schools, students who are seen not merely as different but as threatening and dangerous. To some extent, the schools themselves can lessen the pervasive fear of violence by taking steps to ensure school safety. But to be successful, these efforts have to be linked with a more ambitious program designed to reduce the level of violence in the society as a whole.

10

Police

Fear of Crime and Its Response

Although the desire for good schools and the fear of crime are both powerful motivating factors leading people to move to, and away from, particular cities or neighborhoods, the impact of city services on these decisions is not the same. When education is the issue, the quality of city services significantly influences the decision to relocate ("we've moved here for the schools"). When security is the concern, by contrast, the caliber of the police department is not the focus of attention. Instead, people move (if they can) to a low-crime neighborhood and, once there, construct their houses and businesses to ward off criminals. They thus treat crime as largely beyond the ability of the police to control. And they are not alone. Experts agree that the principal methods that the police now employ— motorized patrolling, responding to emergency calls, and crime investigation—have little effect on the crime rate. "Police," as David Bayley succinctly puts it, "do not prevent crime." Even so, most people rely on the police, as well as on location, for protection. They treat the job of the police, however, as being not to eradicate crime but to reassure them that although crime will inevitably take place, it will take place elsewhere. In America, the predominant strategy individuals employ to deal with crime is to isolate themselves from it.[1]

The cost of relying on this strategy has been high. The government has incurred the cost of providing an escape route from crime, funding the highways and sewers and supporting the housing and commercial development that have enabled the creation and growth of America's low-crime suburbs. Those who live in these suburbs have paid for their escape through higher housing prices, the expense and strain of commuting, and the loss of a genuine option to live in large parts of the metropolitan area. Their reliance on avoidance as their principal method of crime control has itself been very expensive. Vastly more is spent in America on private efforts to provide security—through security guards, alarm systems, locks, window bars, surveillance cameras, doormen, armored cars, dogs, metal detectors, mace, homeowners insurance, and the like—than on city police. There are three times as many private security employees in America as there are city police officers—and the gap is widening. Residential security alone is a $5 billion business. Still, the greatest cost imposed by the current emphasis on escape as a response to crime has been borne by those who reside or work in America's less privileged suburbs and central-city neighborhoods. Not only have they had to buy their own security devices; they have suffered the consequences of being exposed to the violence that has not been eliminated, and that they have been unable to avoid. Whole neighborhoods have experienced an acceleration of social and economic decline; businesses have lost money because people are afraid to shop in them; crime victims have lost not just their property but their lives.[2]

Even after paying all of these costs, Americans still live with a pervasive fear of crime, and not only in the neighborhoods in which the crime rate is relatively high. Indeed, we can best see the true cost of the emphasis on isolation as a crime-control strategy by examining the impact of fear on people's daily lives. Virtually everyone in America organizes his or her life with crime in mind. In middle-class and upper-middle-class neighborhoods, people

> stay off the streets at night and lock their doors. If they go out, they walk only in groups and avoid certain areas of the city. They use taxis or cars to protect themselves from street crime. If they have to drive through high crime-rate areas of the city, they roll up their car windows and lock their doors. To avoid possible victimization, people do not use library and educational facilities at night, they stay away from meetings of social groups and organizations, and they keep out of parks and recreational areas. Some forfeit additional income by refusing overtime work which would force them to go home after dark. Some even carry firearms or knives. Many take security measures to protect their homes—additional locks on doors and bars on windows, brighter lights on porches and in the yards, burglar-alarm systems, and watchdogs.

Yet none of these forms of self-protection relieve—sometimes they increase—anxiety. Everyone feels so vulnerable, so alone. If crime strikes and the protective barriers don't work, all one can do is call the police. But by the time the police arrive, it will be too late ("the chances of making an arrest on the spot drop below 10 percent if even one minute elapses from the time the crime is committed").[3]

This widespread fear of crime is more than simply a reaction to the local crime rate. It is stimulated as well by the media, politicians, and word of mouth. The relentless daily portrayal of crime on television, in the headlines, in the movies, and at the dinner table feeds an anxiety that is disproportionate to the extent of the danger. People are more likely to be injured by cars than they are by criminals, but the threat posed by auto accidents produces relatively little anxiety. On the other hand, one well-publicized story, even of an event far away, is likely to generate fear regardless of the amount of local crime: 90 percent of Americans think that crime is rising even though it isn't. This is not to say that fear of crime is irrational: in America there is far too much crime everywhere. But crime is not the only problem: fear of crime is as destructive to America's social fabric as crime itself. One reason that this fear is so debilitating stems from the pervasive feeling that the people who commit crimes are vicious, uncontrollable—"other" in the strongest sense of the word. When engaged in defensive behavior, individuals and businesses are rarely thinking of white-collar crime, of the Mafia, of being attacked by friends or acquaintances, even of domestic violence. Especially in the neighborhoods of escape, fear of crime is associated with a burglary, robbery, rape, or assault perpetrated by a stranger. Fear of otherness, in short, helps generate the fear of crime.

And vice versa: fear of crime is a major ingredient fueling the fear of otherness—in fact, it is the language in which that fear is now usually articulated. If you ask people why they want to build a wall around their neighborhood, they'll say, "Security." And by "security" they will mean, more often than not, eliminating the danger epitomized in America today by young black males. Consider this description of how people behave when they see young black men on the street:

> When young black men appear, women (especially white women) sometimes clutch their pocketbooks. They may edge up against their companions or begin to walk stiffly and deliberately. On spotting black males from a distance, other pedestrians often cross the street or give them a wide berth as they pass. . . . Fellow pedestrians . . . avert their eyes from the black males, deferring to figures who are seen as unpredictable, menacing, and not to be provoked—predators.

This description, from Elijah Anderson's *Streetwise*, is not just of white reactions; Anderson is describing the conduct of other blacks as well. And he is describing behavior in a city neighborhood. In many white suburban neighborhoods, the reaction is even more intense. The presence of any black man on the street—let alone a group of young black males— generates alarm: *What is he doing here?* Many people in our society, to quote Anderson again, are "incapable of making distinctions between law-abiding black males and others . . . [and therefore] they rely for their protection on broad stereotypes based on color or gender, if not outright racism." Many are equally incapable of making distinctions among immigrants, Latinos, even the poor as a whole. This incapacity produces a stark we/they dichotomy that, in turn, enables people to condemn severely both criminals and those considered potential criminals. After all, they are not "condemning an important part of their own lives [or] the community in which they live." When combined with the general feeling that crime is out of control, this indiscriminate distrust of large categories of people explains why, after people move out of a diverse and bustling community full of friends and acquaintances into an isolated house or apartment far from their job, they so often breath a sigh of relief ("Safe, at last").[4]

No aspect of community building is more important than overcoming this mutual reinforcement between the fear of crime and the fear of otherness. Many current crime-prevention strategies, however, do the opposite: they intensify rather than undermine the divisiveness that the widespread fear of crime has generated. "There's no secret to fighting crime," one commentator says, summarizing such a strategy: "hire more police, build more prisons, abolish parole, stop winking at juvenile criminals, severely enforce public-nuisance laws, permit self-defense for the law-abiding, and put deliberate murderers to death."[5] This approach to crime imposes no obligations of any kind on law-abiding citizens: their strategy of withdrawal and their fear of otherness remain untouched. On the contrary, it pictures the police as the agents of these unreconstructed citizens, their job being to identify the bad guys and put them in jail. Nowhere is the sharpness of this boundary between "us" and "them" more striking than in the current enthusiasm for building prisons. Once imagined as places of rehabilitation, and even now occasionally thought of as instruments for deterrence, prisons have become the analogue in the crime-control area to the use of exclusionary zoning in the allocation of the nation's housing: prisons represent society's effort to deal with "them" by dividing and separating the metropolitan population. If only enough dangerous people can be locked up, it is thought, the rest of us will be safe.

The effect of such a "get-tough" attitude on the crime rate is a hotly debated issue. But even if we were to implement the dream of isolating criminals in a fortified ghetto by imprisoning everyone who satisfies a minimal test of dangerousness—thereby keeping in prison a substantial number of what "get-tough" advocates euphemistically call "false positives"[6]—it would be hard to lock up enough people to diminish the level of fear. Potentially threatening people will remain on the street. Unsolved crimes are inevitable. Violent offenders who have served their sentences will still have trouble finding a job. So will nonviolent offenders, some of whom will be more dangerous after their release from prison than they were when they entered it. Besides, no matter how many people are imprisoned, there will continue to be millions of unfamiliar-looking strangers in America's metropolitan areas who have never committed a crime, and more children—including more young black males—becoming teenagers every day. Since a "get-tough" strategy makes it no easier for individuals to distinguish a dangerous stranger from an innocuous one, building prisons is not likely to dampen their desire to build the opposite kind of walled communities at the same time—communities designed to protect insiders by walling off what frightens them on the outside.

A "get-tough" strategy threatens to exacerbate the current level of divisiveness in America in another way as well. It reinforces for all concerned the image of the police as an occupying army responsive to outsiders rather than to community residents. A primary objection voiced by African Americans to current crime-control efforts is that every black person, particularly every young black male, is viewed suspiciously by the police. This degree of surveillance has generated an antagonism between African Americans and the police that is much more fundamental than racial prejudice or excessive violence on the part of individual police officers or criminal acts perpetrated by individual African Americans—serious as these problems are. As David Bayley and Harold Mendelsohn put it, "there seems to be a reciprocating engine of resentment at work in the relations between police and minorities." This engine of resentment particularly infects the police-minority relationship in the poor African American neighborhoods most plagued by high crime rates. Residents of these neighborhoods are too familiar with examples of verbal abuse, brutality, and physical assaults to view police officers, in the manner of those who live in low-crime suburbs, as being there for their protection. Patrolling in low-crime suburbs may be designed to ward off crime, but in poor African American neighborhoods it too often provides an opportunity for routine harassment. And the reason for this harassment, many feel, is that the police are captured by an "us versus them" attitude—one that combines racial prejudice with an instinct to use excessive force even for a routine arrest. The police, on the other hand, see themselves as doing a tough, dirty job that the public doesn't understand or appreciate. They feel constantly threatened by potential violence and develop in response an omnipresent sense of mistrust. This mistrust is triggered most intensely in poor African American neighborhoods where, as police officers recognize, residents have a powerful suspicion, even hatred, of the police. The officers who work in these neighborhoods see them as filled with criminals and potential criminals who understand only toughness. Consequently, they define their job as requiring alertness to possible violence and a quick and authoritative response, rather than politeness or respect. It's not surprising, therefore, that they also come to believe that the only people they can trust while doing their job are their fellow officers. If so, it becomes critical to stand by them—no matter how they behave.[7]

Interlocal Community Building

There is a close relationship between the police-citizen antagonism in poor African American neighborhoods and the suspicion that separates residents of high-crime and low-crime areas: each source of conflict feeds and reinforces the other. As a result, redesigning law enforcement techniques to promote community building requires addressing both sources of conflict simultaneously. Reducing the tension between the police and those who live in high-crime communities involves substantial changes in the way police services are delivered—an issue to which I return below. But no matter how dramatic the changes in police behavior are, the specter of crime will continue to divide the nation's metropolitan areas unless the connection between the fear of crime and the fear of otherness is confronted directly. And this involves a fundamental change in law enforcement policy: crime prevention, rather than isolation and withdrawal, must become the basis of America's crime-control strategy.

Such a change must be based on a frank admission: in an important sense, the withdrawal approach has worked. Low-crime and high-crime areas within any metropolitan region can be located on a map, and usually the most privileged suburbs are low-crime areas, while poor suburban and central-city neighborhoods are high-crime areas. But, as the previous paragraphs were designed to demonstrate, it does not follow from this spatial allocation of crime that those who live in low-crime areas lack an incentive to decrease the crime rate elsewhere. The fear of crime and of high-crime areas touches the lives of everyone in the metropolitan region. This fear thus has the potential of being transformed into something other than an incentive for fortifying the barriers between different types of people. It can provide a basis for collaborative efforts across the region to solve a common problem: the high rate of crime plaguing specific neighborhoods within the metropolitan area. A metropolitan-wide effort to reduce crime in high-crime neighborhoods would do more than improve the lives of the people who live in these neighborhoods. Those who live elsewhere would feel less anxious about burglaries, car-jackings, and robberies whenever they went out. And large sections of the metropolitan area that are now too dangerous for insiders and outsiders alike would be reopened as places to go, even as places to live. The most important lines that currently divide American metropolitan regions—invisible lines that every metropolitan resident can locate—are the ones that mark off the areas associated with the threat of violence. African Americans don't enter neighborhoods where they will be harassed or treated as suspicious, and whites don't enter neighborhoods where they feel threatened or where crime rates are high. More than school district lines or any other metropolitan boundary, these lines reduce the opportunity for the kind of stimulation, variety, and growth that metropolitan life can offer in America. Diminishing the power of these lines to exclude outsiders is therefore essential to community building. Doing so requires no analogue to the proposal, sketched above, for school choice. No legally created mechanism now closes the border of American cities and neighborhoods to people from elsewhere in the region. What currently prevents freedom of movement is the fear of crime itself.

The vast public and private resources now devoted to helping people flee the residents of high-crime neighborhoods has exacerbated this fear. Isolation has limited the capacity of millions of Americans to develop a sense of personal security not dependent on isolation—a capacity that, following Richard Sennett, I have called "ego strength." Ego strength does not require people to learn how to accept the threat of violence. It requires instead building self-confidence and resilience so that one can feel comfortable with a wide variety of different kinds of strangers. And this, in turn, involves becoming familiar with the range of people who live in the metropolitan area, and knowledgeable about how to make distinctions when one is out on the street. Those who now live in the neighborhoods of escape could learn a great deal about these capacities from current residents of high-crime neighborhoods. They live with more crime than anyone should ever have to endure—vastly more than an effective crime-prevention program would tolerate. But although they too lock their doors and are worried about going out at night, unlike their suburban counterparts they have ideas, other than isolation, about how to protect themselves in public places. Residents of poor African American neighborhoods are not afraid of every black person they see. They learn how to identify and deal with potential troublemakers and therefore become more relaxed with a wide range of strangers. Young black males learn an additional form of behavior in public places—one designed to reassure the people they encounter on the street, above all whites, that they pose no danger to them. Residents of poor African American neighborhoods are now so segregated, however, that they too have only a limited scope for developing their capacity to deal with diversity—and even less scope for sharing their insights with outsiders. Regional negotiations over the allocation of crime-control resources have the potential of diminishing this isolation. They can also begin the process of reducing the widespread stereotyping of everyone who lives in high-crime neighborhoods, victim and perpetrator alike, as frightening and dangerous. Outsiders could learn that many of these individuals—including many young black males—are more afraid of crime than they are.[8]

No doubt many suburban residents will consider it a cost to give up the feeling of security that isolation has provided them. They have this feeling not only because they reside in a safe neighborhood but because they organize their lives to avoid places where they are likely to encounter anyone unconventional. When they go out, they limit themselves to a mall that feels comfortable, a business district filled with predictable-looking people, or a restaurant in a nice neighborhood. Only the homeless and the occasional street vendor threaten to jar them from the impression of safety they have derived from the purification of their environment. This process of purification, however, has imposed enormous costs on American society: it has enabled fear of crime to become a self-fulfilling prophecy. The widespread flight from crime has fueled the zoning, highway construction, and business investment decisions that have contributed to the acceleration of the economic decline in high-crime neighborhoods across the country, thereby helping to produce the conditions that have generated so much violence. Moreover, millions of metropolitan residents have moved to the suburbs for the very reason that they thereby escape paying taxes that, among other things, support programs designed to reduce crime in high-crime neighborhoods. And once across the border, they not only devote local resources solely to self-protection but treat crime in other cities as "their problem." Yet it should be clear—regardless of whether one thinks of crime as a rational choice made by desperate people, as a product of social conditions, as a personality disorder, or as a reaction to the inequities of America's social structure—that crime will continue to be a significant problem in America as long as our urban policy is based on isolating the poor into declining neighborhoods stripped of job opportunities while simultaneously fostering economic development elsewhere. If so, the resources now supporting the current crimogenic dynamic of escape should be directed instead to reducing the crime rate.

Crime prevention requires a regionwide focus. Local efforts tend not to eliminate crime but to shift it from neighborhood to neighborhood. Regional negotiations thus need to concentrate not only on moving resources from the patrolling of safe neighborhoods to crime reduction but on moving them from area to area as the need arises. But the justification for metropolitan-wide funding of police services is not simply to put more money into an efficient strategy for fighting crime. Like regional efforts to promote the economic development of poor neighborhoods, effective crime-prevention programs can generate support for other attempts to diminish the barriers that now divide America's metropolitan areas into neighborhoods that are prosperous and secure and neighborhoods that are declining and dangerous. For example, reduction in the crime rate can help bring about a change in current land-use policy, redirecting it from efforts to subsidize suburban sprawl to programs designed to rebuild existing neighborhoods—and build new neighborhoods—that foster interaction with different kinds of people. In chapter 7, I argued that this kind of modification of cities' zoning and redevelopment policy would promote community building. It would also contribute to crime prevention. There are, one should recognize, two different ways to construct a "defensible space" to ward off crime. One emphasizes building walls, speed bumps, gates manned by security guards, and alarm systems, thereby epitomizing and reinforcing the fear of outsiders. The alternative emphasizes designing streets that attract pedestrians rather than cul-de-sacs, well-located public squares rather than large, empty parking lots, and houses that facilitate "natural surveillance" of nearby areas instead of seclusion. Everyone knows, as Jane Jacobs says, that "a well-used city street is apt to be a safe street [while] a deserted city street is apt to be unsafe." These days, however, the level of trust in America is so low that even populated areas feel unsafe. It's hard to be confident that a stranger will help if a crime occurs because his or her own fear of being attacked generates a reluctance to "get involved," even if all that is needed is a call to the police. This lack of trust itself facilitates crime: "the more isolated people become and the less they share with others unlike themselves," to quote Peter Calthorpe once again, "the more they *do* have to fear."[9]

Community Policing

No one thinks that we can lessen the fear of crime without increasing the ability of the police to reduce the crime rate. A substantial literature argues that this requires redirecting police resources away from the traditional reliance on motorized patrolling, response to 911 calls, and crime investigation and toward what is commonly called "community policing." Community-policing programs seek to reinvigorate historical ideas about how city police should operate. At the time city police departments were first created in the United States, in the 1830s and 1840s, the police were not organized as a quasi-military force of trained outsiders designed to bring order to local neighborhoods. They were considered part of, and responsive to, the local community, and, as the visible representatives of "the city" on the street, they performed many services not directly related to crime control. At the turn of the twentieth century, however, Progressives, motivated in large part by their desire to end the control over police activity wielded by political machines, transformed the police into a "professional" organization—a centrally controlled, bureaucratic entity, specializing in the enforcement of the criminal law, and operated in a way that ensured independence from, rather than accommodation to, the diverse population of the city they patrolled.[10] Community policing advocates contend that the distance that this professional model has created between the police and the neighborhoods they patrol has impaired crime-prevention efforts in low-crime and high-crime areas alike.

According to the Department of Justice, community policing

> is, in essence, a collaboration between the police and the community that identifies and solves community problems. With the police no longer the sole guardians of law and order, all members of the community become active allies in the effort to enhance the safety and quality of neighborhoods.[11]

This approach to policing is applicable everywhere: the police regularly need the help of local residents when responding to crime. But the value of community policing will be tested, above all, by its impact in poor African American neighborhoods—the communities where, as we have seen, police-community relations are most in need of repair. The extent of police-community tension in these neighborhoods makes it clear, however, that the Justice Department's definition of community policing is far too idealistic. Rather than romanticizing the police-community relationship by describing it as being "active allies," a definition of community policing should acknowledge that the nature of the police-community collaboration being envisioned is ambiguous and has to be clarified in the process of implementation. Few people who live in poor African American neighborhoods will cooperate with the police as long as they remain a prime exemplar of interracial conflict. And, unlike 1960s-style proposals for "community control" of the police, community policing continues to grant the police a considerable degree of decision-making autonomy. The proposals offered in the 1960s attempted to transfer political authority over the police from the city as a whole to the neighborhood, thereby making the police an agent of the local community in a way comparable to the "get-tough" strategy's understanding of the police as an agent of law-abiding citizens.[12] When engaged in community policing, by contrast, the police will remain a force of outsiders—indeed, outsiders empowered to use violence against neighborhood residents.

Creating an effective police-community collaboration that is acceptable to both sides is, therefore, a tall order. The likelihood of doing so depends on the ability to forge a new police-community relationship out of the conflicts that now exist both within city police departments and within poor African American neighborhoods. Many police officers, including many current chiefs of police, want to purge their departments of their identification with an attitude of aggressive antagonism toward minority communities. These police officials are more frustrated with the ineffectiveness of current police methods than are their critics, and they have more reason than anyone to create a working environment that is less hostile. But their embrace of community policing is opposed within police departments by those who see such reform efforts as a mistaken attempt to transform police officers into social workers. At the same time, some residents of poor African American neighborhoods support efforts designed to lock up dangerous criminals. In fact, one common complaint voiced by neighborhood residents is that the police are ineffective when dealing with a crime committed by one resident against another: too often, the police do not take such crimes seriously. Others, however, think that the police should operate in black neighborhoods by settling disputes without making arrests. The existence of these internal conflicts does not suggest that a common vision of the future is shared by reformers on all sides. Quite the contrary. Community policing is a strategy for diminishing police-community antagonism by allowing people with very different views to participate in the effort to formulate crime-prevention programs. Like regional negotiations over the allocation of crime-control resources, its value lies in the creation of a mechanism for exploring how people can engage in cooperation to reduce the crime rate notwithstanding unresolvable feelings of tension between them.[13]

A major aspect of community policing not yet mentioned—one commonly called "problem-oriented policing"—provides a concrete illustration of the kind of issue that can profit from this kind of cooperative effort. Advocates of problem-oriented policing reject the traditional police practice of reacting to an endless stream of isolated, individual complaints, seeking instead to improve crime prevention by concentrating on clusters of similar or recurring problems associated with high-crime activity. These problems might be defined in terms of behavior (auto theft, drugs), locations generating multiple calls for help (a convenience store, a housing complex), specific kinds of offenders or victims (gangs, the elderly), or time periods (bar closing time, student housing during vacations). One prominent way to define community problems, for example, involves identifying the types of nonviolent disorder that mark a neighborhood as deteriorating and dangerous. Thus in New York City the mayor and police officials have singled out peddlers, panhandlers, squeegee cleaners, street prostitution, boom box cars, public drunkenness, reckless bicyclists, and graffiti as the kind of nonviolent disorder recognized by law-abiding citizens as "visible signs of a city out of control." Others have emphasized different kinds of disorder, such as vandalism, abandoned buildings, and litter and garbage. The first conception is consistent with, although certainly need not embrace, a "crackdown" attitude toward neighborhood residents. The second list of problems, on the other hand, demands much more than the invocation of the criminal law. The police need to work with other government officials, property-owners, and community activists to make any improvements last. Although the rubric of "community policing" allows for a wide range of choices from these different lists of problems—and there often is conflict both within the police department and within high-crime neighborhoods about priorities—we must recognize that the kinds of disorder that offend the sensibility of outsiders and the kinds of disorder that worry residents of high-crime communities are not likely to be identical.[14]

Still, the utility of community policing for community building does not depend on the specific problems selected for attention. It depends instead on the creation of a selection process that can both define relevant problems and diminish the hostility between the police and community residents. No problem solving will result in community building unless young residents of high-crime neighborhoods can begin to see the police, along with other city officials, as possible sources of help in their struggle with crime rather than as a source of oppression. Attitudes toward the police help shape the struggle for identity of teenagers who grow up in these neighborhoods. They inescapably form their own reaction to the idea that the way to respond to racism is to embrace the image of the black criminal as a hero. These days cooperation with the police, even for those now tempted by it, entails a very high cost: the appearance of collaboration with the enemy. Thus while community policing must do more than simply provide good PR for the police, good PR is an important ingredient for its success: police cannot reach out to community residents without changing their reputation.[15]

Will community policing actually reduce the crime rate? The honest answer, David Bayley says, is that we don't know.[16] But the same answer should also be given for every other proposal for reducing the crime rate, including the building of more and more prisons. What distinguishes these strategies is not the certainty of their effectiveness but their impact on the level of divisiveness in American society. It's not just that withdrawal, security devices, and prisons offer little prospect for diminishing the fracturing of the nation's metropolitan areas. The current police-community antagonism epitomizes, as it intensifies, the prevailing city-suburb tension. By contrast, the combination of a regional focus on crime prevention and community policing might generate a very different dynamic. Regional efforts to concentrate crime-prevention resources in high-crime communities could give impetus to the process of community policing and, thereby, increase its prospects for success in reducing the crime rate. And community policing, in turn, could transform the police into a new kind of role model: the police could demonstrate for the public at large how to lower the crime rate by working with people different from oneself.

11

Choosing City Services

Conventional City Services

It would try readers' patience, not to mention my own, if I were to canvas every city service in the detail just devoted to education and the police. But there is no need for me to do so. Given the impact of the desire for good schools and the fear of crime on the current fragmentation of American metropolitan areas, it would be surprising if cities committed to community building failed to include education and crime control in their efforts. Education and police protection are the two largest items in municipal budgets. Even those who want to privatize the police have a very limited view of what privatization would entail, and although the commitment to public education is more controversial, it too seems likely to remain significant for a long time to come. Only three other city services are close to being universal in American cities: fire departments, highway maintenance, and parks and recreation. Five additional functions—sanitation, health and hospitals, sewers, welfare, and courts—complete the standard list of conventional city services.[1] Few cities provide all of the these city services now. The critical question here is whether cities would provide them if they organized their services to promote community building.

There is no right answer to this question. Any of these conventional services could be organized to contribute to community building, but none of them has to be. Each metropolitan region needs to decide in its own context which of these services cities can most effectively utilize to nurture the capacity of their residents to live in a diverse society. Framing the issue in this way is important because it turns the conception of city services adopted by public goods theorists upside down. They treat city services as an option only if there is market failure: services should be allocated through private market transactions, they think, whenever possible. A community-building perspective, by contrast, refuses to limit city services to what's left over once private corporations have marketed whatever they can package as a consumer good. It gives cities their own mission to perform. Given limited resources, cities cannot do everything necessary to promote community building. The issue facing public decision-makers is: in our own metropolitan area, which city services can best further the objectives that city services are created to accomplish?

In addressing this issue, cities must decide, first of all, whether or not to organize a particular service to foster community building. Consider, for example, sanitation. Plainly one can think of sanitation services as simply the narrow task of picking up consumers' garbage and sweeping their streets. If so defined, these services could be provided by private refuse collectors as well as by the city. The choice between these two modes of delivery might even be decided solely through the determination of which entity can do the job more cheaply. But this is not the way that those who created America's sanitation departments thought about what they were doing. They considered municipal sanitation to be an ingredient in the creation of America's public health system and in the collective task of making city living desirable. As one group of early reformers put it:

DID YOU EVER STOP TO THINK THAT:
A clean town means a sanitary and healthful town.
A clean town means a more beautiful town.
A clean town means an increase in the value of our property.
A clean town brings business to our merchants.
A clean town induces a better class of people to locate here.[2]

Sanitation was thus another example of the patrician understanding that inspired city services generally—the desire to impose a civilized standard of behavior on city residents. If this nineteenth-century vision is, once again, revised so that its hierarchical overtones are eliminated, it suggests why a city might decide to organize its sanitation services to foster community building. Consumers' desires to have their own garbage picked up and their own street swept do not exhaust the need for sanitation. Unsanitary conditions elsewhere generate disease and impair the quality of life for those who live nearby, while inhibiting the freedom of movement for outsiders. Unclean streets are regularly seen as a sign of a bad neighborhood, and, many scholars contend, they therefore lower the general level of behavior wherever they are found. That's why they argue that improved sanitation contributes to crime prevention. Moreover, preserving a healthy environment is not the responsibility of city employees alone. Involving the public at large in the effort to maintain the cleanliness of city streets not only saves money but helps foster a cooperative spirit even among strangers ("I won't litter the streets because no one around here does"). Organizing sanitation services to promote community building might therefore contribute to changing attitudes toward other environmental threats to the public health as well, such as the notion that the problems generated by the location of hazardous waste sites and other sources of pollution are solved once they are put in someone else's neighborhood rather than one's own.

No matter what purposes sanitation services are designed to accomplish, cities need sanitation workers. And, some people argue, it does not follow from the decision to provide a particular city service that cities should deliver it themselves. Having private companies hire and supervise employees might make sense whatever the mission a city service adopts. Indeed, it might. But community building is a consideration when decisions are made as to who should perform city services as well as what their objectives should be. This is most obvious when one considers the hiring of police officers and schoolteachers: the kind of people who engage in community policing or who teach the area's children significantly affect what community policing and education actually mean. The same can be said about other city services as well. Citizens' attitudes toward all city employees are influenced by who they are. It should not be forgotten that minorities constitute a larger percentage of local government employees in the United States than they do of the private sector, and that the racial and ethnic composition of the city workforce is often taken as a sign of the city's openness to the diversity of its population.[3] Moreover, the employees' own attitudes toward their jobs depend on how they are defined, and those who seek to save money through privatization rely in large part on cheapening the cost of labor. Such a reduction in city workers' standard of living is bound to influence who is willing to work for the city and how they will perform on the job. So will any impact that privatization might have on the efforts of city workers to exercise more control over their own work product. It's not just schoolteachers and police officers whose status is diminished by low pay and lack of authority to work with others in the community to improve the quality of what they do. Finally, contracting out city services weakens the tie between the city and those who work for it and, with it, the extent of democratic control over city workers. This is not to say that private delivery of city services organized to promote community building is never a good idea. The point, instead, is that lowering the cost of city services is not the only factor that should be considered when deciding whether it is.

Privatization is also not the only alternative to direct delivery by cities. These days, as I have already noted, many city services are provided by public authorities and special districts—independent agencies, created by the state, designed to take public services "out of politics" and to be administered instead by professionals. There are now more districts and authorities in the United States than there are cities, and they deliver a wide range of services, including health care, housing, transportation, and parks. Education is one of the city services dominated by this organizational form; more than 90 percent of America's public schools are run by school districts. Public authorities and special districts merge features associated with the public and private sectors: they are public because they are state agencies, and they are private because they are managed, like business corporations, by "experts." But neither identity has made them helpful in promoting community building; on the contrary, these entities have contributed more to the fracturing of metropolitan areas than to their integration. Those with areawide jurisdiction have generally been limited to a single purpose, such as providing water or managing the airport, and they have dealt with their assigned task by concentrating on technical solutions to technical problems. Moreover, the people with decision-making authority are usually appointed officials or elected by property-owners, rather than elected by the public at large. As a result, although these regional authorities have had a significant impact on community-building concerns, they have not provided a mechanism for addressing them. Their major impact instead has been to lessen the pressure for intercity cooperation: by assigning to experts issues—such as water supply and airport management—that everyone concedes require a regional solution, they have helped prevent the pervasiveness of regional concerns from generating demands for regional decision making about more divisive issues, such as zoning, schools, and crime control. When districts and authorities—such as school districts—are created to deal with these more divisive issues, they rarely are organized on an areawide basis; more often, as described above, their boundaries have been relied on to separate different types of people. To promote the goals of community building, then, public authorities and special districts must be either radically restructured or replaced entirely by a more democratic form of organization—such as by the cities themselves.[4]

New City Services

Cities need not limit themselves to the conventional list of city services when designing community-building efforts. Quite the contrary. Reframing the mission of city services in terms of community building is likely to stimulate ideas about new services that cities might provide. One way to think about potential new city services is to enlarge one's vision of the tasks cities already perform. The three city services other than education and police most commonly provided by cities—fire fighting, highway maintenance, and parks and recreation—can serve as illustrations.

These days, fire services, along with police services, are the principal way in which cities present themselves to their residents as the place one should call when faced with a crisis. Even now fire departments respond to more than fires. A community-building orientation might lead to the development of other ways in which cities can serve as a fallback mechanism when disaster strikes. This would enable cities to build on the fact that city emergencies make city residents more open to each other: they produce empathy and stimulate conversations among strangers that otherwise would be unusual. Think of snow emergencies (the blizzard of 1978), electricity blackouts (New York, 1977), and natural disasters (floods, tornadoes, hurricanes). Consider too the astonishing popularity of stories about fires on television. No doubt events such as these make people more fearful as well. But this reaction also suggests that expanded city emergency services might promote community building. Such an expansion does not mean that every city has to be able to respond to every possible catastrophe. It would be better if individual cities took on different responsibilities, presenting themselves as willing to come to the aid of (and be funded by) the region as a whole. It would be equally important to ensure that ordinary citizens, and not just city employees, are involved in the assistance efforts. In this way, expanding city emergency services can contribute to improving the atmosphere associated with being part of a fortuitous association: they can help reassure metropolitan residents that it is possible to rely on strangers, no matter who they are, in a crisis.

Highway maintenance similarly raises issues broader than the need to fill potholes. Street repair is simply one of the many direct costs imposed on cities by America's auto-based society: cities spend money policing the streets, sweeping them, installing traffic signals, and sending the fire department and paramedic services when accidents occur. And highways are only one ingredient in a transportation system that can either link metropolitan residents together or divide them from each other. Decisions about the allocation of funds for highways, mass transit, and bicycle paths have had a major impact on the design of the area's streets, housing, and commercial life and, with it, the accessibility of jobs for the poor. Some cities and neighborhoods have excluded the region's mass transit system to prevent residents of poor neighborhoods from having easy access to them, and, as we have seen, highways have been located to separate the region into racially identifiable spaces. This history of isolating the poor makes it clear that a decision to shift resources from highways to a fully accessible mass transit system would affect the life of everyone in the region, not just those who ride the trains. A recognition of the effect that such a shift would have on the extent of car-generated pollution throughout the metropolitan area brings home the same point.

A reallocation of transportation resources could also focus on more than extending the transit system. It could lure people out of their cars by (for example) radically reducing the fares and, thereby, influence the kind of relationship with strangers that the region fosters. Mass transit and walkable streets are two of the major sources of public space in America: they facilitate the daily experience of crossing paths with different kinds of people. Driving, on the other hand, is a privatized affair: it facilitates focusing on oneself (daydreaming, putting on makeup), interaction with people one knows (car phones, carpools), or, at its most expansive, listening to the radio. Emphasizing alternatives to the car culture could therefore nurture an aspect of fortuitous associations different from the feeling of security I've associated with expanding cities' emergency services. It could foster a reaction that is common among people who live in big cities—and quite different from the feelings of discomfort or alarm so often experienced by suburban residents—when the girl with green hair and multiple piercings, the African American kids blasting hip-hop on a boom box, the gay couple holding hands, the panhandler, and the mentally ill person pushing a shopping cart pass by. That reaction is: Whatever.

City parks are another important source of public space in America—at least to the extent that they have not been replaced by private yards or abandoned by the general public because of criminal activity or drug dealing. Parks, like schools, are supported by local taxes yet, unlike schools, are open to residents and nonresidents alike. Thus creating and maintaining them, making them easily accessible, and ensuring users' safety are all activities that can contribute to community building. But they will not have this effect unless the parks are genuinely open to everyone. Parks must be attractive places not because they exclude undesirable people but because they appeal to as many people as possible. This can be accomplished in many ways: through the creation of empty spaces that invite different kinds of unstructured activity, through the building of playgrounds that invite interaction among the children (and parents) who happen to be there, and through the organizing of concerts and "happenings." City efforts of this kind also need not be located solely in parks. Hundreds of thousands of people congregate along the river in Boston for the Fourth of July celebration, in Atlanta for Freaknik, in New Orleans for Mardi Gras, in Las Vegas, as well as Times Square, on New Year's Eve, and for gay pride parades throughout the country. Some view these events with apprehension: so much traffic congestion, so many people, so scary. But cities devoted to community building might decide to expand their support for these kinds of activities because they make palpable the experience of living in a world filled with different kinds of people and promote an aspect of fortuitous associations different from the feeling of security or indifference mentioned above: they help demonstrate that contact with different kinds of people can be fun.

As these ideas suggest, the range of possible city services is limited only by the extent of citizens' unwillingness to override the constraints that the current vision of city services now imposes upon them. These days, the city (understood as an institution or governmental entity) has a relatively narrow impact on the life of the city (understood as a place). Local economic vitality depends largely on private initiative and national and state governmental decision making rather than on city policy. Cities do not provide jobs or job training to their unemployed, build housing for those who need it, or provide food in areas that the large private grocery chains have abandoned. Nor are the traumas of family life much affected by city policy. Family problems that cannot be resolved by the affected individuals are in the hands of voluntary organizations or officials (whether local, state, or federal) implementing state or national governmental policies. Even the cultural forms—such as professional sports teams—that give citizens their sense of devotion to the metropolitan area in which they live are largely controlled by private organizations. Cities committed to community building could decide that some or all of these areas of concern are a priority. Simply as illustrations, consider six activities that a regional legislature might empower one or more of the region's cities to perform:

1. A city could operate banks or other financial institutions. It is widely recognized that investment decisions have a major impact on the region's economic life. A city-owned bank, if properly organized, could ensure that these decisions were made with a different sense of priorities from that adopted by, say, Citibank. A bank responsible to democratic control might, for example, prefer investment within the region to investment abroad, and it might also take different positions on matters such as plant closings, the democratic organization of work, and the job opportunities afforded racial and ethnic minorities. It is crucial that the bank be organized in a way that promotes the regional economy, not the limited concerns of one city's residents. Moreover, there is no reason for such a city bank to be a monopoly. It could compete for customers and deposits with private banks and, perhaps, other city-owned banks—and build its competitive appeal on its connection with community building.

2. A city could run a cable television system (as some now do). The purpose of city ownership would be to organize the system in a way that would facilitate the ability of people within the region to communicate with each other. A city-run cable system could enable schools to educate adults as well as children, local music and drama groups to increase their audience, and community organizations to produce programs of interest to others. Given the number of alternatives that cable television can simultaneously offer, these kinds of programs need occupy only some of the channels. There still will be room for sports, news, and sitcoms.

3. A city could build or acquire significant amounts of residential housing, particularly apartment houses and other multiple-family dwellings. This does not require replicating the model of "public housing." The city's property interest could be limited to taking title to the property, with all decisions regarding the housing itself—who should live there, the nature of the relationship among those who do, the amount of money to be spent for maintenance, and the like—made by the residents themselves. The city, in other words, could simply be a landlord—one that receives no rent—and a corporation consisting of (and controlled by) all current occupants could be the tenant. In this way, the housing could be run like a condominium, with one exception: the legal ownership of the property would be lodged not in the residents but in the city. The reason for placing title in the city would be to ensure that the housing remains dedicated to residential purposes and to prevent profit making when a unit is transferred to new residents. The city, as a landlord, could thus preserve housing units in the city, control the rate of gentrification, and encourage democratic control over the operation of multiple-family housing units.

4. A city could own cooperative grocery stores. Once again, as in the case of housing, the city need not be given complete control of these stores; it could allow most of the prerogatives of property ownership to vest in the cooperative itself. In fact, the stores could be required to use their revenues to pay off the city's costs over a few years, thereby preventing them from becoming a permanent drain on the city's resources. These city grocery stores could serve a number of purposes: they could ensure that stores exist in city neighborhoods where they are needed, aid in providing food to people at lower costs, and generate and promote information about nutrition. And, as in the other examples presented above, cities could use these grocery stores as vehicles for promoting the democratic organization of an important aspect of daily life.

5. A city could assume ownership (or part ownership) of the major regional sports team—either by purchasing it or, if necessary, by taking it by eminent domain. Cities now spend billions of dollars to construct and improve sports stadiums and install nearby roads and other infrastructure, often in an effort to prevent the team from leaving town. A city-owned team would not threaten to leave town. It might even make money rather than—as in the case of the costs a city incurs when it outbids another city's offer to lure the team away—be a burden on the city treasury. This is not to say that it would make sense in every regional area to spend money in this way. Everywhere a decision has to be made as to whether it would be better to use city resources on the other activities—museums, music festivals, and so forth—that stir the loyalty and devotion of regional residents. The form of legal ownership can also vary: the Green Bay Packers, for example, are now owned by local residents themselves. Whatever the details, the justification for any such effort is the importance of connecting the enthusiasm for local teams and cultural centers with community-building efforts.

6. A city could support community organizations devoted to easing the burdens on family life. As Philippe Ariès has argued, a principal reason for the current sense of crisis felt by so many families is the fact that the nuclear family is now expected to satisfy a host of needs that were once supplied, in large part, by neighbors and others in the surrounding community. In traditional city neighborhoods, adults other than parents participated in supervising and influencing neighborhood children, and the children, in turn, had emotional connections with a variety of people to whom they could turn in a crisis. For adults as well, city life provided a form of social interaction different from the worlds

of work and family that now so often occupy the entirety of people's lives. Ariès insists that it is impossible for families to shoulder the burden of being the only locus for child rearing, emotional connection, and social interaction; "the real roots of the present domestic crisis," he says, "lie not in our families but in our cities." Expanding the forms of personal interaction in the modern metropolis is clearly no easy task. And there is no reason to assume that direct city programs are the best way to do so. But cities could help stimulate and fund attempts to address these needs—an effort that could make an important contribution to community building.[5]

No one is likely to think that all of these suggestions are a good idea. The task here is not to nail down the list of city services—that must be accomplished through decentralized decision making region by region— but to provoke readers to generate their own ideas for services that have the potential of furthering community-building objectives. Besides, I suspect that there is another issue that, at the moment, is more pressing in the reader's mind than the list of city services: *Who is going to pay for all of this?* This, of course, raises a central question of American politics: how much money should we devote to government and its services? Nothing I have suggested in this book mandates an increase in the amount cities now spend on city services: a reorientation of these services can be achieved without their being expanded. In fact, cities so disposed could allocate more money to some services while contracting out or abandoning those that they decided were not helpful to community building. Admittedly, a metropolitan region that took community building seriously enough to consider the suggestions made in last few paragraphs would increase the role of city services in metropolitan life. The important point to emphasize here is that if they decided to do so, they could. There is enough money in every metropolitan region in the country to support a significant increase in community-building efforts. We need not wait for the federal government to act before changing the nature of America's metropolitan areas. Even if other metropolitan regions maintained the status quo, there is no reason to think that a metropolitan region's decision to promote community building would reduce its economic competitiveness rather than increase it: businesses, like people, are more influenced by the quality of life provided by a metropolitan area than by its tax rate.[6] The barrier standing in the way of community building is not the lack of funds but the fact that these funds are now allocated to fortifying the boundaries that separate prosperity from poverty—even (perhaps especially) when they are walking distance from each other.

The standard understanding of the role of local governments in the economy rejects the possibility of this kind of local initiative.[7] It insists that only the federal government can engage in decision making about the distribution of resources across local boundaries in America. This stance is based on the assumption that decentralization means the defense of local autonomy, and, therefore, that the only way to overcome the competition and divisiveness that this autonomy generates is through centralization. A community-building perspective embraces neither the notion of local autonomy nor the idea that centralization is the solution to metropolitan conflict. It therefore offers a mechanism for strengthening city services without the necessity of a federal handout. No doubt, the federal government—representing people from every region in the country—can contribute to the community-building enterprise. It might, for example, take a leadership role in establishing the definition of metropolitan regions.[8] If it undertakes this responsibility, however, it must prevent regional boundaries from reproducing on a larger scale the current effect of city boundaries. The difficulty of drawing regional boundaries in many parts of the country should be treated as a virtue: from the neighborhood level to the national level, the objective should be to reduce the impact that geographic boundaries have on people's lives.

I expect the proposals made in this chapter to generate a variety of reactions from my readers. But I think most of them will agree that if these kinds of proposals were all adopted, cities would gain significantly in the power they exercised in American life. Their new power would extend to many critical aspects of daily life: economic investment, housing, food supply, mass communications, family life, and cultural activities. Cities would therefore recapture an important role in American society without relying on the equation of decentralization with local autonomy. It will certainly take energy and imagination to transform our current city institutions into vehicles for promoting the values I have associated with city life. And it will take equal energy and imagination to overcome our current preference for having a conglomerate, rather than a city, own a combination of financial, housing, food supply, and television businesses. But if cities are, once again, to become vital institutions, they need to be freed from the current legal conception that limits them to a narrow definition of what city services can entail. City services need to recapture and redefine the role of "the public" in American life. To do so, they need to become a vehicle for building connections among the people who live in the same geographic area, and for enabling ordinary people to participate in the design of the world in which they live.

Afterword _____

IN THIS BOOK, I have suggested a number of ways to expand the exercise of public freedom: using juries to decide controversial issues of public policy; introducing public participation into the work of regional authorities and special districts; broadening the new urbanists' idea of "charrettes" to widen public involvement in land-use decisions; diversifying the parents, teachers, and students involved in decision making about individual schools; strengthening the role of community policing; involving ordinary people in an expansion of city-run emergency services; creating cooperatives to run city-owned housing and grocery stores. I have argued for the development of more public space in order to enable metropolitan residents to gain a greater level of comfort with, and knowledge of, their region's diversity. And I have proposed a new legal definition of cities, one designed to open the city borders that are now closed not only by local government law but by the widespread feelings of unease—and fear—that people experience when they are crossed. All of these efforts, if combined, would significantly enlarge the role of public life in American society, making it an important counterpart—one might say antidote—to the increasing privatization that gated communities, shopping malls, and office parks, and the long commute between them, now epitomize. Moreover, by substituting community building for the defense of local autonomy, these initiatives would provide a role for cities in everyday life that is not vulnerable to the well-developed attack on local autonomy, and, at the same time, facilitate the kind of intercity cooperation necessary to build a defensible form of decentralized power.

Supporters and critics, including students and colleagues, have raised three objections to these ideas, and I conclude this book with a brief response to each of them. "Let's get real," those who raise the first objection say. "I admit that I think it would be *possible* to reorient the legal concept of cities to promote public freedom, community building, and public space. In fact, I even think it would be desirable to do so. But let's face it, it's just not going to happen. People aren't interested in engaging with unfamiliar strangers. And they also aren't interested in experiments in public freedom. They like privatization and the immunity from contact with different kinds of people that city boundaries now provide. And they are going to continue to like these things. No one is going to want to end the reliance on the autonomy model for American cities. The separation of different kinds of people is so well established in American society that we can't even think about turning it around."

In response, I ask the reader to consider what it will be like if privatization continues to accelerate in America, so that in the twenty-first century the country will have more and more gated communities, consumer-oriented city services, and suburbs built to ensure isolation from those who live across the city border. I doubt that most readers, or most Americans, would endorse this urban policy with enthusiasm. Instead, I think most people are divided about this vision of the future. Of course people like their private space, their ability to isolate themselves from the intensity of living in a metropolis, and the sense of security that being surrounded by familiar-looking strangers provides them. Yet they also want to feel more comfortable when they leave their protected space to work, visit friends, or go out; they worry about the impact of suburbanization on the costs of housing, commuting, and child care; and they regret the narrowness of their daily lives imposed by the current design of American metropolitan areas. The choice between our current urban policy and community building cannot be made by referring to "what people want." Both the status quo and a more public life appeal to versions of ourselves.

The problem we face is that local government law has nurtured one version of the self over alternatives. It has organized cities in a way that provides fewer and fewer people the experience of collective decision making, of living in diverse cities and neighborhoods, and of using public space on a daily basis. By reducing the availability of these aspects of life, the legal system has helped make alternatives to the status quo seem impossible. We seem caught in a self-perpetuating dynamic: local government law—a system of state-created legal rules—not only fosters city autonomy and metropolitan fragmentation but reinforces the notion that withdrawal, self-protection, and personal advancement define what it means to exercise human freedom. Earlier in the book, I referred to Tocqueville's view that we can resist the seductive temptation to reduce our life experience to the comfort of friends, family, and material prosperity only through political engagement on the local level. For him, local institutions provided a mechanism through which people were able to engage in, and take pleasure from, the process of working with strangers on common problems—the aspect of liberty that I've called public freedom. "Local institutions are to liberty what primary schools are to science," he said, "they bring it within people's reach, they teach people to use and enjoy it."[1] Now, 150 years after Tocqueville wrote, these schools are largely closed.

"But that's the problem with your ideas," the second objection goes. "How do you get people who have learned to accommodate themselves to privatization—more than that, learned to like it—to engage in the political effort necessary to change the status quo? If politics represents the will of the people, and that will now favors privatization, it doesn't matter whether their will has been nurtured by a historical process, or even by governmental action. We are where we are. What kind of political vision do you have for getting from here to there?"

The change in urban policy is unlikely to be successfully confronted, it seems to me, simply by appeals to the virtues of openness, tolerance, and diversity. Some people respond to these appeals. But it is important also to speak in the language of privatized self-interest that has become so dominant in our contemporary political discourse. Like suburbanization itself, the change has to be built on concerns people have about their daily lives: their fear of crime, their anxiety about the future of public education, the distress they experience when they attempt to combine work and family, their inability to retire and stay in the community in which they live. The key ingredient, therefore, is to organize people in terms of these kinds of issues and, by so doing, gradually loosen the grip that the city/suburb distinction has on our way of understanding American politics. We have heard far too much about how "the suburbs" now control political decision making in America, and, as a result, about how "the cities" have lost the ability to change its course. There is no unified political entity in the United States called "the suburbs" or "the cities." As I have argued at length above, the suburbs are now divided into inner suburbs and outer suburbs, prosperous suburbs and declining suburbs, heterogeneous suburbs and homogeneous suburbs, white suburbs and black suburbs, and America's central cities are diverse as well. To replace our obsession with the city/suburb distinction, the political strategy, like the legal strategy, should disregard current city boundary lines. In chapter 7, I suggested focusing on the problems facing women, residents of the inner suburbs, the elderly, and African Americans as a way to do so. In some areas of the country, however, the effect of suburban sprawl on the environment might be a better source of political energy. Environmental concerns have generated support for an urban growth limit in Portland, Oregon (and in other places as well), with the result that, although Portland's metropolitan population has grown by 25 percent since 1980, the size of the urban area has grown only 1 percent. (In metropolitan Chicago, by contrast, while the population has grown only 4 percent, the area's land-size has grown 46 percent during the same period.) In other parts of the country, concentrating on the public expense involved in the expansion of the outer suburbs, and the consequent drain on the resources of inner suburbs and central cities alike, might also be effective (as it has been, to some extent, in Minneapolis–St. Paul). Even the Bank of America, which has financed more than its share of suburbanization, has argued that development costs, highway costs, and social tensions make further suburban expansion too expensive: "we cannot afford," the bank has said, "another generation of sprawl."[2]

This brings us, finally, to the third objection. "In the book, you regularly disclaim the notion that your vision of public life is romantic. But your disclaimers are simply unconvincing. Any attempt to improve human relationships, particularly with strangers—even in the diminished sense embodied in your definition of community—is utopian. The same can be said about your notion of fostering alliances among women, residents of the inner suburbs, the elderly, and African Americans. These alliances would be nice, but to think they can happen is a fantasy. Your proposals are designed to inspire, to be evangelical, but they are not in touch with the realities of practical politics."

It is true that a good deal of this book has been romantic, even evangelical, in tone. But the suburban dream has been equally romantic and evangelical. To inspire our current urban policy, it has relied on the appeal of nature, of home ownership, of privacy, and of escape. I don't think that we can displace the appeal of this dream without an alternative. Romantic images have considerable practical effect: the suburban dream has had an enormous impact on American life. In fact, it has worked, and still works, despite the fact that it is unachievable. The traffic, the density of many suburban developments, the detailed restrictions on individual freedom that these developments impose, the office parks that feel even bleaker than "downtown"—none of these aspects of suburban life detract from its appeal. We need to replace the suburban dream with one that builds on what city life offers American society. Such a dream is not a new invention: the vision of an America that can deal with its diversity has had a long history. Moreover, adopting such a goal doesn't require eliminating the enjoyment of nature, home ownership, privacy, and escape. These values can coexist with an increased emphasis on the importance of public life; they don't depend on our making separateness the organizational principle of the metropolitan landscape.

No doubt, there lurks in every dream a nightmare. I have devoted a good deal of this book to detailing the nightmare of suburbanization by stressing the costs it has generated both for those who live in the inner and outer suburbs and for those who have remained in the central cities, especially poor African Americans. For most people, the nightmare raised by my proposals, I think, is triggered by their fear of otherness. And by this I mean, above all, their fear—in middle-class black neighborhoods as well as white neighborhoods, in central-city neighborhoods as well as in the suburbs—of the poor African Americans who are now concentrated in selected parts of the metropolitan area. Only 11 million people live in these urban ghettos—less than 5 percent of the country's urbanized population. Why must we construct our metropolitan areas by simultaneously isolating and running away from those who live in these neighborhoods? Sure, it would cost a lot of money—and require considerable effort—to confront the problems in these neighborhoods that our current urban policy has helped bring about. But running away has cost a lot of money and has required considerable effort too. It seems to me that we can begin to deal with this issue only if we do not set the standard of community too high. The African Americans who now control important American cities aren't willing to fuse with those who have fled to the suburbs, and those who have fled are not willing to fuse with those they have left behind. But there is no reason to think that the choice facing America is between local autonomy and regional (or state or national) government—between separation from others and being overwhelmed by them in the name of togetherness. There is considerable room for maneuver between separation and unity, between local autonomy and centralization, between balkanization and assimilation. I have described one form this intermediate space can take through my notions of public freedom, community building, and public space. But I have not written this book because I think I can define once and for all the form of human relationship that cities should foster in America. Perhaps you, my reader, can think of a better definition. My goal has been to stimulate thinking about how we might replace the urban policy of fragmentation and division with one that can accommodate American diversity. Only if we do can we, at long last, begin to rebuild what we have for so long sought to eradicate: the variety, temptation, stimulation, challenge, and vitality of city life.

Notes

Introduction

1. Andrew Hacker, *Two Nations: Black and White, Separate, Hostile, Unequal* (1992); Robert Fishman, *Bourgeois Utopias: The Rise and Fall of Suburbia* 198–205 (1987).

2. John Dewey, "Logical Method and Law," 10 *Cornell L.Q.* 17, 26 (1924).

3. Michel Foucault, *Language, Counter-Memory, Practice* 221 (Bouchard ed. 1977).

4. Iris Young, *Justice and the Politics of Difference* 237–238 (1990).

5. Timothy Egan, "Many Seek Security in Private Communities," *New York Times*, September 3, 1995, p. 1.

Chapter 1
City Powerlessness

1. For an overview of these doctrines of local government law, see Gerald Frug, *Local Government Law* 52–81, 107–169 (2d ed. 1994). The case quoted is *Hunter v. City of Pittsburgh*, 207 U.S. 161, 178–179 (1907).

2. Recent attempts by the United States Supreme Court to limit federal power over the states restrict it only at the margin. For a general description of federal restraints on city power—and the cases that have sought to limit it—see Gerald Frug, supra note 1, at 169–251; for a discussion of federal controls over state taxation, see Lawrence Tribe, *American Constitutional Law* 441–468 (2d ed. 1988); for a discussion of debt limitations, see U.S. Advisory Commission on Intergovernmental Relations, *State Constitutional and Statutory Restrictions on Local Government Debt* 27–30 (1961).

3. On the private law exception, see Gerald Frug, supra note 1, at 78–85; on city profit making, see id. at 676–709. For a discussion of public authorities, see chapter 11.

4. Hannah Arendt, *On Revolution* 30–31, 114–115, 119–120 (1962). My reference to the critique of Western thought is to a vast literature—ranging from Thomas Carlyle, "Sign of the Times," in 7 *Collected Works* 314 (1869), and John Ruskin, "The Nature of Gothic," in 2 *The Stones of Venice* 152 (1881), to Max Weber, *From Max Weber* 196–244 (Gerth and Mills eds. 1956), and Karl Marx, *Capital: A Critique of Political Economy* (Fowkes trans. 1977), to Charles Lindblom, *Politics and Markets* (1977), and Roberto Unger, *Knowledge and Politics* (1975).

5. Alexis de Tocqueville, *Democracy in America* 506 (Lawrence trans. 1969); see generally id. at 62–63, 68–70, 87–98, 189–195, 231–245, 667–705; John Dewey, *The Public and Its Problems* 143–184 (1972); Hannah Arendt, supra note 4, at 215–281. See also Aristotle, *Politics* bk. 7, 255–298 (Sinclair trans. 1962),

Montesquieu, *The Spirit of the Laws* bk. 8, ch. 16, at 176–177 (Carrithers ed. 1977), and Jean-Jacques Rousseau, *The Social Contract* bk. 2, §§ 9–10, bk. 3, §§ 1, 3, 4, at 40–44, 48–53, 55–58 (Bair trans. 1974). The modern argument is exemplified by works such as Robert Dahl, *A Preface to Economic Democracy* (1985), Benjamin Barber, *Strong Democracy* (1984), John McMurtry, *The Structure of Marx's World View* (1978), and Carole Pateman, *Participation and Democratic Theory* 1–44 (1970). I have written on this topic as well. Jerry Frug, "Administrative Democracy," 40 *U. Toronto L.J.* 559 (1990).

6. Karl Mannheim, *Ideology and Utopia* 192–204 (Wirth and Shils trans. 1936). On the American Revolution, see Gordon Wood, *The Creation of the American Republic 1776–1787*, 3–124 (1969); on Marxism, see John McMurtry, supra note 5; on the size of cities, see Charles Adrian and Ernest Griffith, *A History of American City Government: The Formation of Traditions 1775–1870*, 20–21 (1983); A.H.M. Jones, *Athenian Democracy* 8–9 (1977).

7. Compare Henri Pirenne, *Medieval Cities* 193 (Halsey trans. 1925) ("the air of the city makes free"), with *The Federalist Papers* 69 (No. 10) (Bourne ed. 1901) (on the dangers that small groups pose to individual liberty); Tocqueville, supra note 5 (cities as the source of individual development), with Georg Simmel, "The Metropolis and Mental Life," in *The Sociology of George Simmel* 409–424 (Wolff ed. 1950) (cities as the source of the atrophy of individualism); "Letter from Thomas Jefferson to Samuel Kercheval" (July 12, 1816), quoted in Hannah Arendt, supra note 4, at 250 (cities as expression of rationalism), with 4 *Works of Thomas Jefferson* 86 (Ford ed. 1904) (Notes on Virginia of 1782) (cities as threat to rationalism).

8. The word "state" has two meanings. It is the traditional term for the liberal concept of the sovereign, the person(s) or institution(s) that wield governmental power over individuals in "civil society." See, e.g., Roberto Unger, *Law in Modern Society* 58–61 (1976). Machiavelli is generally considered the originator of this sense of the word (*"lo stato"*). Hannah Pitkin, *Wittgenstein and Justice* 310–313 (1972). In America, however, the term also refers to each of the fifty states within the federal system. This duality of meaning is troublesome, but it cannot be helped. Since the city has become subordinate to the state in both senses of the word, I usually do not attempt to distinguish them.

9. For an account of the public/private distinction in modern political and legal thought, see, e.g., Lawrence Tribe, supra note 2, at 1688–1720; Roberto Unger, supra note 4, at 63–103; Sheldon Wolin, *Politics and Vision* 286–351 (1960). Compare 1 John Dillon, *Commentaries on the Law of Municipal Corporations* §§ 9–12, 24–30 (4th ed. 1890) (cities are part of the state), with Frederick Maitland, *Township and Borough* (1898), and Henri Pirenne, supra note 7 (cities are part of civil society).

10. See *City of Cleburne v. Cleburne Living Center*, 473 U.S. 432 (1985) (Fourteenth Amendment); *Printz v. United States*, 117 S.Ct. 2365 (1997) (Tenth Amendment); *Monell v. Department of Social Services*, 436 U.S. 658 (1978) (Eleventh Amendment); *Community Communications Co. v. Boulder*, 455 U.S. 40 (1982) (antitrust law).

Chapter 2
A Legal History of Cities

1. Octavio Paz, *Claude Lévi-Strauss: An Introduction* 6 (Bernstein and Bernstein trans. 1970).

2. The principal sources for this section include Fernand Braudel, "Towns," in *Capitalism and Material Life 1400–1800,* 373 (Kochan trans. 1967); Otto Gierke, *Associations and Law* 95–142 (Heiman trans. 1977); Otto Gierke, *Political Theories of the Middle Ages* (Maitland trans. 1958); Otto Gierke, *The Development of Political Theory* (Freyd trans. 1966); Frederic Maitland, *The Constitutional History of England* 39–54 (1909); Frederic Maitland, *Township and Borough* (1898); Henri Pirenne, *Economic and Social History of Medieval Europe* (Clegg trans. 1936); Henri Pirenne, *Medieval Cities* 193 (Halsey trans. 1925); Colin Platt, *The English Medieval Town* (1976); and Max Weber, *The City* (Martindale and Neuwirth trans. 1958). Also useful were Ernst Freund, *The Legal Nature of Corporations* (1897); Ernst Kantorowicz, *The King's Two Bodies* (1957); Lewis Mumford, *The City in History* 243–343 (1961); Carl Stephenson, *Borough and Town* (1933); and James Tait, *The Medieval English Borough* (1936).

3. Fernand Braudel, supra note 2, at 402–403.

4. Id. at 399.

5. Henri Pirenne, supra note 2, at 199–201.

6. Frederic Maitland, *Township and Borough*, supra note 2, at 11–12.

7. Id. at 18.

8. On rural developments, see Marc Bloch, *Feudal Society* (Manyon trans. 1961); Fernand Braudel, supra note 2; Barrington Moore, *Social Origins of Dictatorship and Democracy* 3–100, 413–508 (1966). On the king himself, see id. at 63; Ernst Kantorowicz, supra note 2. Gierke calls the development of modern political thought the development of the "theory of natural law." Otto Gierke, *Natural Law and the Theory of Society 1500–1800* (Barker trans. 1935). The quotation is from Otto Gierke, *Political Theories of the Middle Ages,* supra note 2, at 87.

9. For examples of medieval corporations, see 1 William Blackstone, *Commentaries* *467–471. For Gierke's analysis of the development of modern thought, see his *Natural Law and the Theory of Society,* supra note 8, at 162–165, 180–195. The quotation about fraternal associations is from Max Weber: "More than anything else the fully developed ancient and medieval city was formed and interpreted as a fraternal association." Max Weber, supra note 2, at 96.

10. The principal sources for this section include Philip Abrams and E. A. Wrigley, *Towns in Societies* (1978); Perry Anderson, *Lineages of the Absolutist State* 15–42, 113–142 (1974); Fernand Braudel, supra note 2, at 373–440; Peter Clark and Paul Slack, *Crisis and Order in English Towns 1500–1700* (1972); Peter Clark and Paul Slack, *English Towns in Transition 1500–1700* (1974); Thomas Hobbes, *Leviathan* (Oxford ed. 1909); Jennifer Levin, *The Charter Controversy in the City of London, 1660–1688, and Its Consequences* (1969); John Locke, *Second Treatise of Civil Government* (1924); and Max Weber, supra note 2. Also useful were 8 William Holdsworth, *A History of English Law* 192–222 (1925); Michael Landon, *The*

Triumph of the Lawyers (1970); C. B. MacPherson, *The Political Theory of Possessive Individualism: Hobbes to Locke* (1962); and Jon Teaford, *The Municipal Revolution in America* (1975).

11. Perry Anderson, supra note 10, at 41.

12. The quotation is from Jennifer Levin, supra note 10, at 80. For a definition of quo warranto, see 1 William Blackstone, supra note 9, at *485.

13. Thomas Hobbes, supra note 10, at 256–257.

14. John Locke, supra note 10, at 187–188.

15. 1 William Blackstone, supra note 9, at *485; 2 William Blackstone, supra note 9, at *37.

16. 1 William Blackstone, supra note 9, at *470–471; Stuart Kyd, *Law of Corporations* (1793–1794).

17. The principal sources for this section include Howard McBain, "The Legal Status of the American Colonial City," 40 *Pol. Sci. Q.* 177 (1925); the works of Otto Gierke, supra note 2; Ernest Griffith, *History of American City Government: The Colonial Period* (1938); *Town and Country: Essays on the Structure of Local Government in the American Colonies* (Daniels ed. 1978); and Michael Zuckerman, *Peaceable Kingdoms* (1970). Also useful were Edward Allinson and Boies Penrose, *The City Government of Philadelphia* 10–33 (1886); Carl Bridenbaugh, *Cities in the Wilderness* (1960); Carl Bridenbaugh, *Cities in Revolt* (1955); Robert Brunhouse, *The Counter-Revolution in Pennsylvania 1776–1790* (1942); George Haskins, *Law and Authority in Early Massachusetts* (1968); Kenneth Lockridge, *A New England Town: The First Hundred Years* (1970); Sam Bass Warner, *The Private City* 3–45 (1968).

18. On Charleston, see Richard Waterhouse, "The Responsible Gentry of Colonial South Carolina: A Study in Local Government 1670–1770," in *Town and Country*, supra note 17, at 160; on Philadelphia, see Sam Bass Warner, supra note 17, at 9.

19. 1 William Blackstone, supra note 9, at *473. On colonial religious bodies, see Julius Goebel, "Editor's Introduction," in Shaw Livermore, *Early American Land Companies* x–xix (1939).

20. Oscar Handlin and Mary Handlin, *Commonwealth* 100 (1947); Ernest Griffith, supra note 17, at 71.

21. 1 Adam Smith, *Wealth of Nations* 133–146 (Cannon ed. 1965); Thomas Hobbes, supra note 13. For a description of the images of the state and the individual in late-eighteenth-century America, see Gordon Wood, *The Creation of the American Republic 1776–1787*, 3–45, 159 (1969).

22. This process is described in Joseph Davis, *Essays in the Earlier History of American Corporations* (1917); Edwin Merrick Dodd, *American Business Corporations until 1860* (1954); Oscar Handlin and Mary Handlin, supra note 20; Oscar Handlin and Mary Handlin, "Origins of the American Business Corporation," 5 *J. Econ. Hist.* 1 (1945); Hendrik Hartog, *Public Property and Private Power: The Corporation of the City of New York in American Law, 1730–1870* (1983); Louis Hartz, *Economic Policy and Democratic Thought: Pennsylvania 1776–1860* (1948); James Willard Hurst, *The Legitimacy of the Business Corporations in the Law of the United States, 1780–1970* (1970); and Jon Teaford, supra note 10.

23. *Trustees of Dartmouth College v. Woodward*, 17 U.S. (4 Wheat.) 518 (1819).

24. Oscar Handlin and Mary Handlin, supra note 20, at 173.

25. 17 U.S. (4 Wheat.) at 668–669 (Story, J., concurring). Justice Story's earlier opinion was *Terret v. Taylor*, 13 U.S. (9 Cranch) 43, 51–52 (1815).

26. 2 James Kent, *Commentaries on American Law* 275 (3d ed. 1836). Kent's first edition more closely follows Story's original language. 2 James Kent, *Commentaries on American Law* 222 (1st ed. 1827).

27. Compare Aristotle, *Politics* bk. 7, 255–298 (Sinclair trans. 1962), Montesquieu, *The Spirit of the Laws* bk. 8, ch. 16, at 176–177 (Carrithers ed. 1977), and Jean-Jacques Rousseau, *The Social Contract* bk. 2, §§ 9–10, bk. 3, §§ 1, 3, 4, at 40–44, 48–53, 55–58 (Bair trans. 1974), with *The Federalist Papers* 69 (No. 10) (Bourne ed. 1901) and David Hume, "Idea of a Perfect Commonwealth," in 1 *Essays, Moral, Political, and Literary* 480, 480–481, 492 (Green and Grose eds. 1875).

28. The first of Jefferson's remarks is quoted in Hannah Arendt, *On Revolution* 235 (1962); the second is from 4 *The Writings of Thomas Jefferson* 86 (Ford ed. 1904). For Tocqueville's views, compare 1 Alexis de Tocqueville, *Democracy in America* 62, 68–70, 262–263 (Lawrence trans. 1969), with id. at 278, note 1. On Chancellor Kent's views, see Marvin Meyers, *The Jacksonian Persuasion* 239–240 (1957).

29. See Howard McBain, *The Law and Practice of Municipal Home Rule* 5–12 (1916).

30. John Dillon, *Treatise on the Law of Municipal Corporations* (1st ed. 1872).

31. After serving as a prominent state and federal judge, Dillon became a leading corporate lawyer and was elected president of the American Bar Association in 1892. For selections from his speeches, see Arnold Paul, *The Conservative Crisis and the Rule of Law* 28–29, 78–81 (1960). For Dillon's own writings, see, e.g., John Dillon, "Property—Its Rights and Duties in Our Legal and Social Systems," 29 *Am. L. Rev.* 161 (1895); John Dillon, *The Laws and Jurisprudence of England and America* (1894).

32. John Dillon, "Property—Its Rights and Duties in Our Legal and Social Systems," supra note 31, at 173; John Dillon, *Treatise on the Law of Municipal Corporations*, supra note 30, at 21–25.

33. John Dillon, supra note 30, at 82–83, 21–22.

34. John Dillon, *The Laws and Jurisprudence of England and America*, supra note 31, at 16; John Dillon, supra note 30, at 25–26, 72.

35. 1 Chester Antieau, *Municipal Corporation Law* §§ 2.00, 5.04, 5.06 (1980).

36. Thomas Cooley, *A Treatise on the Constitutional Limitations Which Rest upon the Legislative Power of the States of the American Union* (1868); *People ex rel. LeRoy v. Hurlbut*, 24 Mich. 44, 93 (1871) (Cooley, J., concurring); Amasa Eaton, "The Right to Local Self-Government" (pts. 1–3), 13 *Harv. L. Rev.* 441, 570, 638 (1900); (pts. 4–5), 14 *Harv. L. Rev.* 20, 116 (1900).

37. McQuillin's first edition was Eugene McQuillin, *A Treatise on the Law of Municipal Corporations* (1st ed. 1911). Quotations are from the second edition, 1 Eugene McQuillin, *The Law of Municipal Corporations* 679–681, 514–516 (2d ed. 1928).

38. 1 John Dillon, *Commentaries on the Law of Municipal Corporations*, § 98, 154–156 (5th ed. 1911); Howard McBain, "The Doctrine of an Inherent Right of Local Self-Government" (pts. 1–2), 16 *Colum. L. Rev.* 190, 299, 300–301 (1916).

39. William Munro, *The Government of American Cities* 53 (1923); 2 Eugene McQuillin, *The Law of Municipal Corporations* § 4.82, at 182 (1988).

40. *Santa Clara County v. Southern Pac. R. R.*, 118 U.S. 394 (1886).

41. See Gerald Frug, *Local Government Law* 141–149 (2d ed. 1994). The case referred to in the text is *Ponder v. State*, 141 Tenn. 481, 212 S.W. 417 (1919).

42. Gerald Frug, supra note 41, at 70–85, 110–130.

43. Samuel Orth, *The Boss and the Machine* vii (1919). The quotations from the Progressive critique are from Richard Hofstadter, *The Age of Reform* 183 (1955). For other histories of this period, see James Weinstein, *The Corporate Ideal in the Liberal State: 1900–18*, 92–116 (1968); Robert Wiebe, *Businessmen and Reform* (1962).

44. 1 John Dillon, *Commentaries on the Law of Municipal Corporations*, § 15, at 34 (4th ed. 1890) (citing 1 James Bryce, *American Commonwealth* 625 [1888]). McQuillin resisted this reformulation of city status, insisting that cities should retain their identity as miniature states. 1 Eugene McQuillin, supra note 37 (2d ed.), at 302–306.

45. Frederick Howe, *The City: The Hope of Democracy* (1905).

46. Arthur Schlesinger, *The Rise of the City 1878–1898* (1933).

Chapter 3
Strategies for Empowering Cities

1. This is the vision of society expressed by Rousseau. Jean-Jacques Rousseau, *The Social Contract* bk. 2, §§ 9–10, bk. 3, §§ 1, 3, 4, at 40–44, 48–53, 55–58 (Bair trans. 1974). The critique of Rousseau's vision is a mainstay of the literature on political theory. See, for example, Andrew Levine, *The Politics of Autonomy* (1976); Carole Pateman, *Participation and Democratic Theory* 1–44 (1970).

2. On the family as a corporation, see Henry Maine, *Ancient Law* 184 (1861). Examples of legislation designed to protect individuals from corporate power include Title VII of the Civil Rights Act of 1964, 42 U.S.C. §§ 2000e-1 to 2000e-17 (1998) and the National Labor Relations Act, 29 U.S.C. §§ 151–169 (1998). For examples of legislation designed to protect individuals from family members, see *The Legal Response to Violence against Women* (Maschke ed. 1997); Inger Sagatun and Leonard Edward, *Child Abuse and the Legal System* (1995); Mary Ann Glendon, *State, Law, and Family: Family Law in Transition in the United States and Western Europe* (1977).

3. On the history of the attempt to protect private corporations through constitutional interpretation, see Lawrence Tribe, *American Constitutional Law* 560–586 (2d ed. 1988). The quotation concerning political decentralization is from Bernard Bailyn, *The Ideological Origins of the American Revolution* 206 (1967) (quoting James Otis). The classic statement on the problem of dual sovereignty is that of Hobbes. Thomas Hobbes, *Leviathan* 131–132 (Oxford ed. 1909). It might be thought that the premise of a unified sovereign has been rejected in the United States and replaced with the notion of federalism. But those who created the fed-

eral system envisioned retaining one absolute sovereign by placing sovereignty "in the people." It is "the people" who retain final say on all political issues in the United States. Gordon Wood, *The Creation of the American Republic 1776–1787*, 462, 530–532, 544–547, 590–591, 599–600 (1969). For two centuries, those who created American constitutional law have struggled to determine what this idea means. In the late nineteenth century, the courts seemed to settle on the view that the people, the federal government, and the states could all exercise political sovereignty without conflict, all exercising "absolute power within their sphere." See Duncan Kennedy, *The Rise and Fall of Classical Legal Thought* ch. 5 (October 1975) (unpublished manuscript). It is that notion that underlay late-nineteenth-century efforts to create an area of home rule for cities, making the city absolute within its sphere as well. In the twentieth century, however, the idea that state and federal authority can coexist without one's having superior political power over the other has collapsed. For all practical purposes, the unified sovereign has become the federal government (absent a constitutional convention), exercising power by virtue of the Commerce Clause, section 5 of the Fourteenth Amendment, the spending power, or, if necessary, another source. The recent attempts by the United States Supreme Court to assert the immunity of state sovereignty from the federal commerce power (based again on the notion of "absolute power within their sphere") in *Printz v. United States*, 117 S.Ct. 2365 (1997), has created, overall, only a minor deviation from this proposition.

4. See, e.g., Robert Hessen, *In the Defense of the Corporation* (1979) (freedom of association); Arthur Okun, *Equality and Efficiency* 38–39 (1975) (individual rights); Kingman Brewster, "The Corporation and Economic Federalism," in *The Corporation in Modern Society* (Mason ed. 1970) (virtues of federalism).

5. See, e.g., Robert Ellickson, "Cities and Homeowners Associations," 130 *U. Pa. L. Rev.* 1519 (1982); Gregory Alexander, "Dilemmas of Group Autonomy: Residential Associations and Community," 75 *Cornell L. Rev.* 1 (1989).

6. Richard Briffault, "Our Localism: Part II—Localism and Legal Theory," 90 *Colum. L. Rev.* 382, 444–445 (1990); Joan Williams, "The Constitutional Vulnerability of American Local Government: The Politics of City Status in American Law," 1986 *Wisc. L. Rev.* 83, 105–120.

7. *Schad v. Mt. Ephraim*, 452 U.S. 61, 85, 87 (1981) (dissenting opinion).

8. On the regulation of the suburbs, see *Dolan v. City of Tigard*, 512 U.S. 374 (1994) (property); *Citizens Against Rent Control v. Berkeley*, 454 U.S. 290 (1981) (speech); *Larkin v. Grendel's Den*, 459 U.S. 116 (1982) (religion); *Southern Burlington County N.A.A.C.P. v. Township of Mt. Laurel*, 336 A.2d 713 (N.J. 1975) (zoning); *Edgewood Independent School District v. Kirby*, 777 S.W.2d 391 (1989) (school financing). On the regulation of corporations, see the Securities Act of 1933, 15 U.S.C. 77a–77aa (1997) and the 1934 Securities Exchange Act, 15 U.S.C. 78a–78kk (1997); for commentary on corporate power, see e.g., John Galbraith, *The New Industrial State* 61–97 (1971); Adolph Berle, "Constitutional Limitations on Corporate Activity—Protection of Personal Rights from Invasion by Economic Power," 100 *U. Pa. L. Rev.* 933 (1952); Adolf Berle and Gardiner Means, *The Modern Corporation and Private Property* (1932). On the regulation of homeowners associations, see David Kennedy, "Residential Associations as State Actors: Regulating the Impact of Gated Communities on Nonmembers," 105 *Yale*

L.J. 761 (1995); Evan McKenzie, *Privatopia: Homeowners Associations and the Rise of Residential Private Government* (1994).

9. See Richard Briffault, supra note 6; Joan Williams, supra note 6.

10. On the public responsibility of private corporations, see Adolf Berle, *Power without Property* (1959); Carl Kaysen, "The Social Significance of the Modern Corporation," 47 *Am. Econ. Rev.* 311, 313–314 (1957).

11. *Associated Building and Construction Trades Council v. Associated Builders and Contractors*, 507 U.S. 218 (1993) (federal preemption does not apply); *White v. Massachusetts Council of Construction Employees*, 460 U.S. 204 (1983) (Commerce Clause does not apply).

12. Richard Briffault, supra note 6, at 444–445.

13. *Brown v. Board of Education*, 347 U.S. 483 (1954); *Community Communications v. Boulder*, 44 U.S. 40 (1982). For the quotation, see Alexis de Tocqueville, *Democracy in America* 251 (Lawrence trans. 1969).

14. On developments in family law, see sources cited supra note 2; on developments in property law, see Thomas Grey, "The Disintegration of Property," in *Property: Nomos XXII* 69 (Pennock and Chapman eds. 1980); on community, see Iris Young, *Justice and the Politics of Difference* (1990).

15. Frederick Nietzsche, *The Will to Power* §§ 370, 481, at 199, 267 (Kaufmann trans. 1967). On the ways in which the narrative form itself affects what is included and excluded in any account of the self, see Hayden White, *The Content of the Form: Narrative Discourse and Historical Representation* (1987); W.J.T. Mitchell, *On Narrative* (1981).

16. Seyla Benhabib, *Situating the Self: Gender, Community and Postmodernism in Contemporary Ethics* 5 (1991).

17. Michel Foucault, *Power/Knowledge: Selected Interviews and Other Writings 1972–1977*, 98 (Gordon ed. 1980).

18. Michel Haar, "Nietzsche and Metaphysical Language," in David Allison, *The New Nietzsche: Contemporary Styles of Interpretation* 17–18 (1977).

19. Quoted in Kenneth Gergen, *The Saturated Self: Dilemmas of Identity in Contemporary Life* 155 (1991).

20. Barbara Johnson, *A World of Difference* 178 (1987).

21. Anthony Appiah, "Race, Culture, Identity: Misunderstood Connections," in Anthony Appiah and Amy Gutmann, *Color Conscious: The Political Morality of Race* 64 (1996) (race); Judith Butler, *Gender Trouble: Feminism and the Subversion of Identity* (1990) (gender); Eve Sedgwick, *Epistemology of the Closet* (1990) (homosexuality).

22. See Benedict Anderson, *Imagined Communities: Reflections on the Origin and Spread of Nationalism* (1983) (defining a nation).

Chapter 4
The Situated Subject

1. Kenneth Gergen, *The Saturated Self: Dilemmas of Identity in Contemporary Life* 157 (1991).

2. Michael Sandel, *Liberalism and the Limits of Justice* 150 (1982); Charles Taylor, "Atomism," in Charles Taylor, *Philosophical Papers: Philosophy and the Human*

Sciences 187, 205–209 (1985); Michael Walzer, "The Communitarian Critique of Liberalism," 18 *Political Theory* 6, 21 (1990).

3. Michael Walzer, supra note 2, at 21; Frank Michelman, "Law's Republic," 97 *Yale L.J.* 1493, 1503–1528 (1988); Frank Michelman, "The Supreme Court, 1985 Term, Forward: Traces of Self-Government," 100 *Harv. L. Rev.* 4, 26–27 (1986); Hannah Pitkin, "Justice: On Relating Private and Public," 9 *Pol. Theory* 327, 344 (1981).

4. Roberto Unger, *Knowledge and Politics* 215–216 (1975); Roberto Unger, *Passion: An Essay on Personality* 20–37 (1984). See also Roberto Unger, *Politics: A Work in Constructive Social Theory* (1987); Roberto Unger, *The Critical Legal Studies Movement*. (1986).

5. Carol Gilligan, *In a Different Voice* 35, 62, 173 (1982).

6. Martha Minow, "The Supreme Court, 1986 Term, Forward: Justice Engendered," 101 *Harv. L. Rev.* 10, 75–95 (1987). For a more complete statement of her views, see Martha Minow, *Making All the Difference: Inclusion, Exclusion, and American Law* (1990).

7. Robert Fishman, *Bourgeois Utopias: The Rise and Fall of Suburbia* 26 (1987).

8. Gregory Weiher, *The Fractured Metropolis: Political Fragmentation and Metropolitan Segregation* 188 (1991). Illustrative cases include *Cadoux v. Planning & Zoning Comm'n*, 162 Conn. 425, 294 A.2d 582, cert. denied, 408 U.S. 924 (1972); *MacNeil v. Town of Avon*, 386 Mass. 339, 435 N.E.2d 1043 (1982); *Village of Arlington Heights v. Metropolitan Housing Development Corp.*, 429 U.S. 252 (1977); *James v. Valtierra*, 402 U.S. 137 (1971).

9. M. P. Baumgartner, *The Moral Order of a Suburb* 10–13 (1988); Carol Gilligan, supra note 5, at 42; William Whyte, *The Organization Man* 310 (1956).

10. *Southern Burlington Township N.A.A.C.P v. Township of Mt. Laurel*, 67 N.J. 151, 174–177, 336 A.2d 713, 724–726 (1975) (*Mt. Laurel I*). See also *Southern Burlington Township N.A.A.C.P. v. Township of Mt. Laurel*, 92 N.J. 158, 456 A.2d 390 (1983) (*Mt. Laurel II*).

11. Gregory Weiher, supra note 8, at 167.

12. For developments in New Jersey after *Mt. Laurel*, see *Hills Development Co. v. Bernards Township in Somerset County*, 103 N.J. 1, 510 A.2d 621 (1986).

13. Alexis de Tocqueville, *Democracy in America* 515 (Lawrence trans. 1969).

14. *Steinbergh v. Rent Control Board of Cambridge*, 406 Mass. 147, 546 N.E.2d 169 (1989); *Greater Boston Real Estate Bd. v. Boston*, 397 Mass. 870, 494 N.E.2d 1301 (1986); *Bannerman v. City of Fall River*, 391 Mass. 328, 461 N.E.2d 793 (1984); *Marshal House, Inc. v. Rent Review and Grievance Board of Brookline*, 357 Mass. 709, 260 N.E.2d 200 (1970). The Massachusetts cases are not unusual. Other state courts have also invalidated local efforts to restrict condominium conversions. See, e.g., *City of West Hollywood v. Beverly*, 52 Cal.3d 1184, 805 P.2d 329 (1991); *Miami Beach v. Rocio Corp.*, 404 So.2d 1066 (Fla. App. 1981); *Rockville Grosvenor, Inc. v. Montgomery County*, 289 Md. 74, 422 A.2d 353 (1980); *Hampshire House Sponsor Corp. v. Ft. Lee*, 172 N.J. Super. 426, 412 A.2d 816 (1979). For a case rejecting an attack on the exclusion of the poor generated by gentrification, see *Asian Americans for Equality v. Koch*, 72 N.Y.2d 121, 527 N.E.2d 265, 531 N.Y.S.2d 782 (1988).

15. E.g., National Health Planning and Resources Development Act of 1974, P.L. 93-641, 88 Stat. 2225, 2232–2235 (repealed, P.L. 99-660, 100 Stat. 3799 [1986]); Housing and Urban Development Act of 1968, P.L. 90-448, 82 Stat 476, 526–532 (repealed P.L. 97-35, 95 Stat. 398 [1981]); Comprehensive Health Planning and Public Health Services Amendments of 1966, P.L. 89-749, 80 Stat. 1180, 1180–1190, 42 U.S.C. § 246 (1992); Public Works and Economic Development Act of 1965, P.L. 89-136, 79 Stat. 552, 564–569 (repealed, P.L. 97-35, 95 Stat. 766 [1981]). A similar idea was embraced by the Intermodal Surface Transportation and Efficiency Act of December 18, 1991, P.L. 102-240, 105 Stat. 2006.

16. Sources as varied as the history of New England towns and Marx's analysis of the Paris Commune suggest ideas for organizing regional legislatures to frustrate the dynamic of centralization. These include requiring legislators to appear regularly before neighborhood meetings to report on legislative activity, allowing those at the meeting to vote on the kinds of compromises that the legislators are authorized to make, enabling neighborhood residents to control legislative salaries and perks, and establishing term limits for those serving in the legislature. See Michael Zuckerman, *Peaceable Kingdoms* 19–28 (1970); Karl Marx, "The Civil War in France," in *The Marx-Engels Reader* 526, 554–557 (Tucker ed. 1972).

17. Alexis de Tocqueville, supra note 13, at 274.

18. Martha Minow, supra note 6, at 95; Michael Sandel, supra note 2, at 183; Roberto Unger, *Passion*, supra note 4, at 88–89; Kenneth Gergen, supra note 1, at 6.

Chapter 5
The Postmodern Subject

1. Mikkel Borch-Jacobsen, "The Freudian Subject, from Politics to Ethics," in *Who Comes after the Subject?* 61, 66 (Cadava, Connor, and Nancy eds. 1991); Kaja Silverman, *The Subject of Semiotics* 158 (1983).

2. Emile Benveniste, *Problems in General Linguistics* 224 (Meek trans. 1971); Roland Barthes, *The Rustle of Language* 51, 53 (Howard trans. 1986).

3. Judith Butler, *Gender Trouble: Feminism and the Subversion of Identity* 136–140 (1990).

4. Jean-François Lyotard, *The Postmodern Condition: A Report on Knowledge* 15, 81 (Bennington and Massumi trans. 1984).

5. I think of the postmodern attitude as that of a man who loves a very cultivated woman and knows he cannot say to her, "I love you madly," because he knows that she knows (and that she knows that he knows) that these words have already been written by Barbara Cartland. Still, there is a solution. He can say, "As Barbara Cartland would put it, I love you madly." At this point, having avoided false innocence, having said clearly that it is no longer possible to speak innocently, he will neverthe less have said what he wanted to say to the woman: that he loves her, but he loves her in an age of lost innocence.

Umberto Eco, *Postscript to the Name of the Rose* 67 (Weaver trans. 1983).

6. Jean Baudrillard, "The Ecstasy of Communication," in *The Anti-Aesthetic: Essays on Postmodern Culture* 132–133 (Foster ed. 1983); Brian McHale, *Postmodernist Fiction* 9–10, 16 (1987). See also Frederic Jameson, *Postmodernism, or, The Cultural Logic of Late Capitalism* 16–31 (1991); Rosalind Krauss, "The Originality of the Avant-Garde," in Rosalind Krauss, *The Originality of the Avant-Garde and Other Modern Myths* 151 (1985).

7. Michel Foucault, *Language, Counter-Memory, Practice* 161–162 (Bouchard ed. 1977); Michel Foucault, *Power/Knowledge: Selected Interviews and Other Writings, 1972–1977*, 98 (Gordon ed. 1980); Michel Foucault, "The Subject and Power," in Hubert Dreyfus and Paul Rabinow, *Michel Foucault: Beyond Structuralism and Hermeneutics* 216 (1982); Jean-François Lyotard, supra note 4, at 15.

8. Angela Harris, "Race and Essentialism in Feminist Legal Theory," 42 *Stan. L. Rev.* 581, 584, 608 (1990); Patricia Williams, *The Alchemy of Race and Rights: Diary of a Law Professor* (1991): bell hooks, "Postmodern Blackness," in bell hooks, *Yearning: Race, Gender, and Cultural Politics* 15–40 (1990).

9. Robert Fishman, *Bourgeois Utopias: The Rise and Fall of Suburbia* 6 (1987).

10. Christopher Leinberger, "Business Flees to the Urban Fringe," 255 *The Nation* 10, 11 (July 6, 1992); Robert Fishman, "America's New City: Megalopolis Unbound," 14 *Wilson Quarterly* 25, 27 (Winter 1990); Joel Garreau, *Edge City: Life on the New Frontier* 7 (1991). Joel Garreau has coined a new term, "Edge City," to describe areas, overwhelmingly residential or rural thirty years ago, that now are single-end destinations for jobs, shopping, and entertainment. To qualify as an Edge City, the area must have, according to Garreau, at least five million square feet of office space, at least six hundred thousand square feet of retail space, and a population that increases during the workday ("more jobs than bedrooms"). Id. at 6–7, 425.

11. James Vance, *The Continuing City: Urban Morphology in Western Civilization* 508 (1990). Clayton is the county seat of St. Louis County; it surrounds, but does not include, the central city.

12. Robert Fishman, supra note 9, at 185, 203; Joel Garreau, supra note 10, at 3, 8.

13. David Rieff, *Los Angeles: Capital of the Third World* (1991).

14. Robert Fishman, supra note 10, at 26; Joel Garreau, supra note 10, at 25; Michael Sorkin, "Introduction: Variations on a Theme Park," in *Variations on a Theme Park: The New American City and the End of Public Space* xi (Sorkin ed. 1992).

15. The phrase is Christopher Lasch's. Christopher Lasch, *Haven in a Heartless World: The Family Besieged* (1977).

16. *Poletown Neighborhood Council v. City of Detroit*, 410 Mich. 616, 304 N.W.2d 255 (1981); Robert Caro, *The Power Broker* 850–877 (1975); Jane Jacobs, *The Death and Life of Great American Cities* (1961).

17. *Holt Civic Club v. City of Tuscaloosa*, 439 U.S. 60, 69 (1978). For a discussion of ways to open city services to nonresidents, see chapters 9 and 11.

18. *Edgewood Independent School District v. Kirby*, 777 S.W.2d 391, 392–393 (Sup. Ct. Texas 1989).

19. *San Antonio Independent School District v. Rodriguez*, 411 U.S. 1, 49–50 (1973); *Edgewood Independent School District v. Kirby*, 1991 Tex. Lexis 21, 34 Tex. Sup. J. 368 (February 25, 1991); *Rose v. Council for Better Educ.*, 790 S.W.2d 186, 212 (Sup. Ct. Ky. 1989); *Abbott v. Burke*, 575 A.2d 359, 410 (Sup. Ct. N.J. 1990); *Helena Elementary School v. State*, 769 P.2d 684, 690–691 (Sup. Ct. Mont. 1989).

20. *Matthews v. Bay Head Improvement Association*, 95 N.J. 306, 471 A.2d 355 (1984), cert. denied, 469 U.S. 821 (1984); Gerald Frug, *Local Government Law* 412–435 (2d ed. 1994).

21. See, e.g., *Dean Milk Co. v. City of Madison*, 340 U.S. 349 (1951).

22. *Holt Civic Club v. City of Tuscaloosa*, 439 U.S. 60, 82 (1978).

23. *Ortiz v. Colon*, 385 F. Supp. 111 (D. PR 1974), vacated as moot, 429 U.S. 1031 (1977); *Kramer v. Union Free School District*, 395 U.S. 621, 630 (1969).

24. For an argument advancing the usefulness of ad hoc organizations, see Warren Bennis, *Organizational Development: Its Nature, Organization, and Prospects* (1970); Warren Bennis, *Changing Organizations* (1966).

25. David Osborne and Ted Gaebler, *Reinventing Government: How the Entrepreneurial Spirit Is Transforming the Public Sector* (1992).

Chapter 6
Community Building

1. Iris Young, *Justice and the Politics of Difference* 237–238 (1990).

2. Lyn Lofland, *A World of Strangers* 3 (1973) (italics omitted); Hadley Arkes, *The Philosopher in the City: The Moral Dimensions of Urban Politics* 324 (1981).

3. Richard Sennett, *The Uses of Disorder: Personal Identity and City Life* 39 (1970).

4. Iris Young, supra note 1, at 238–240.

5. Iris Young, supra note 1, at 250–256.

6. Richard Sennett, supra note 3, at 39, 36, 134.

7. See, e.g., Richard Sennett, *Flesh and Stone: The Body in Western Civilization* (1994); Richard Sennett, *The Fall of Public Man: On the Social Psychology of Capitalism* (1974); Richard Sennett, supra note 3.

8. Richard Sennett, supra note 3, at 123–132. See also Richard Lerner, *On the Nature of Human Plasticity* (1984); Robert Jay Lifton, *The Protean Self: Human Resilience in an Age of Fragmentation* (1993); Herbert Hermans, Harry Kempen, and Rens van Loon, "The Dialogical Self: Beyond Individualism and Rationalism," 47 *American Psychologist* 23–33 (January 1992); Harry Stack Sullivan, *The Interpersonal Theory of Psychiatry* 308 (1953) ("maturity").

9. Roland Barthes, "Semiology and the Urban," in Mark Gottdiener and Alexandros Lagopoulos, *The City and the Sign: An Introduction to Urban Semiotics* 96 (1986).

10. Iris Young, supra note 1, at 240–241; Morton and Lucia White, *The Intellectual versus the City* 222 (1962).

11. Leo Marx, *The Machine in the Garden: Technology and the Pastoral Ideal in America* 5–11, 121 (1964); Raymond Williams, *The Country and the City* (1973); Joel Garreau, *Edge City: Life on the New Frontier* (1991).

12. Jane Jacobs, *The Death and Life of Great American Cities* (1961); Richard Wright, "How 'Bigger' Was Born," in *Twentieth Century Interpretations of "Native Son"* 39 (Baker ed. 1972); Elizabeth Wilson, *The Sphinx in the City: Urban Life, the Control of Disorder, and Women* 158 (1991).

13. The key works include Georg Simmel, "The Metropolis and Mental Life," in *The Sociology of Georg Simmel* 409–424 (Wolff ed. 1950); Robert Ezra Park, "The City: Suggestions for the Investigation of Human Behavior in the Urban Environment," in Robert Ezra Park, *Human Communities: The City and Human Ecology* 13–51 (1952); Louis Wirth, "Urbanism as a Way of Life," in Louis Wirth, *On Cities and Social Life* 60–83 (Reiss ed. 1964). These essays, among others, have been collected in *Classic Essays on the Culture of Cities* (Sennett ed. 1969).

14. See, e.g., Claude Fischer, *The Urban Experience* 173–199 (2d ed. 1984); Richard Dennis, "The Rural-Urban Continuum: Real but Relatively Unimportant," 66 *Am. J. of Sociology* 60–71 (1960).

15. Robert Park, supra note 13, at 50–51; Louis Wirth, supra note 13, at 69, 79, 66.

16. Claude Fischer, supra note 14, at 35–39; Herbert Gans, "The Balanced Community: Homogeneity or Heterogeneity in Residential Areas?" in *Housing Urban America* 135, 137–141 (Pynoos, Schafer, and Hartman eds. 1973).

17. Lyn Lofland, supra note 2; David Karp, Gregory Stone, and William Yoels, *Being Urban: A Sociology of City Life* 107–131 (2d ed. 1991); Thomas Wilson, "Urbanism and Tolerance: A Test of Some Hypotheses Drawn from Wirth and Stouffer," 50 *Am. Soc. Review* 117–123 (February 1985); Erving Goffman, *Behavior in Public Places: Notes on the Social Organization of Gatherings* 84 (1963).

18. M. P. Baumgartner, *The Moral Order of a Suburb* 104, 126, 133 (1988).

19. Georg Simmel, supra note 13, at 416–418; Louis Wirth, supra note 13, at 69; Robert Park, supra note 13, at 47–49, 14.

20. Claude Fischer, supra note 14, at 35–39, 113–171; David Karp et al., supra note 17, at 100–103; Jane Jacobs, supra note 12, at 70.

21. Raymond Williams, supra note 11, at 144; Robert Ellickson, "Controlling Chronic Misconduct in City Spaces: Of Panhandlers, Skid Rows, and Public Space Zoning," 105 *Yale L.J.* 1165, 1169 (1996).

22. Douglas Massey and Nancy Denton, *American Apartheid: Segregation and the Making of the Underclass* 1–114 (1993) (the quotation is at 46). For a richly detailed history of the process Massey and Denton describe, focused on a single city, see Thomas Sugrue, *The Origins of the Urban Crisis: Race and Inequality in Postwar Detroit* (1996). See also Richard Alba and John Logan, "Minority Proximity to Whites in Suburbs: An Individual-Level Analysis of Segregation," 98 *Am. J. Sociology*, 1388, 1421–1425 (May 1993).

23. Douglas Massey and Nancy Denton, supra note 22, at 83–185 (the quotation is at 91). The term "concentration of effects" is from William Julius Wilson, *The Truly Disadvantaged: The Inner City, the Underclass and Public Policy* 59 (1987). For the debates on the reasons for this concentration of effects, see, e.g., Carl Nightingale, *On the Edge: A History of Poor Black Children and Their American Dreams* 1, 5 (1993); *The Urban Underclass* (Jencks and Peterson eds. 1991);

Elijah Anderson, *Streetwise: Race, Class and Change in an Urban Community* (1990); Daniel Fusfeld and Timothy Bates, *The Political Economy of the Urban Ghetto* (1984); Charles Murray, *Losing Ground: American Social Policy, 1950–1980* (1984); Douglas Glasgow, *The Black Underclass: Poverty, Unemployment, and Entrapment of Ghetto Youth* 1–15 (1981); Edward Banfield, *The Unheavenly City* (1970). For a discussion of the positive aspects of the culture, see Steven Gregory, *Black Corona: Race and the Politics of Place in an Urban Community* (1998); Regina Austin, " 'A Nation of Thieves': Securing Black People's Right to Shop and to Sell in White America," 1994 *Utah L. Rev.* 147; Regina Austin, " 'The Black Community,' " Its Lawbreakers, and a Politics of Identification," 65 *S. Cal. L. Rev.* 1769 (1992); Carol Stack, *All Our Kin: Strategies for Survival in a Black Community* (1974); Elliot Liebow, *Tally's Corner: A Study of Negro Streetcorner Men* (1967).

24. U.S. Department of Justice, Bureau of Justice Statistics, *Highlights from Twenty Years of Surveying Crime Victims: The National Crime Victimization Survey, 1973–92*; U.S. Department of Justice, Bureau of Justice Statistics, *Crime Victimization in City, Suburban and Rural Areas* (1992); U.S. Department of Justice, Bureau of Justice Statistics, *Murder in Large Urban Counties* (1988).

25. Peter Hall, *Cities of Tomorrow* 290–292 (1988); Kenneth Jackson, *Crabgrass Frontier: The Suburbanization of the United States* 190–218 (1985); Ann Markusen and Robin Bloch, "Defensive Cities: Military Spending, High Technology, and Human Settlements," in *High Technology, Space, and Society* 115–118 (Castells ed. 1985).

26. Arnold Hirsch, *Making the Second Ghetto: Race and Housing in Chicago, 1940–1960* (1983); Mike Royko, *Boss: Richard J. Daley of Chicago* 132–133 (1971) ("Containing the Negro was unspoken city policy. Even expressways were planned as man-made barriers, the unofficial borders. The Dan Ryan, for instance, was shifted several blocks during the planning stage to make one of the ghetto walls").

27. Richard Ford, "The Boundaries of Race: Political Geography in Legal Analysis," 107 *Harv. L. Rev.* 1841, 1860–1878 (1994). Representative cases include *Village of Arlington Heights v. Metropolitan Housing Development Corporation*, 429 U.S. 252 (1977) (exclusionary zoning); *San Antonio Independent School District v. Rodriguez*, 411 U.S. 1 (1973) (school financing); *Martinez v. Bynum*, 461 U.S. 321 (1983) (preferring residents to outsiders).

28. Jane Jacobs, supra note 12; Martin Anderson, *The Federal Bulldozer: A Critical Analysis of Urban Renewal, 1949–1962* (1964); Herbert Gans, *The Urban Villagers: Group and Class in the Life of Italian-Americans* 323–377 (1982). Representative statutes and cases limiting central-city power include California Revenue and Taxation Code § 17041.5 (nonresident taxes); *Ash v. Attorney General*, 418 Mass. 344, 636 N.E.2d 229 (1994) (rent control); *Nance v. Mayflower Tavern, Inc.*, 106 Utah 517, 150 P.2d 773 (1944) (racial discrimination).

29. Representative cases limiting suburban immunity include *Board of Supervisors of Sacramento County v. Local Agency Formation Commission*, 3 Cal.4th 903, 838 P.2d 1198 (1992) (municipal incorporation); *Edgewood Independent School District v. Kirby*, 777 S.W.2d 393 (Sup. Ct. Texas 1989) (school financing); *South-*

ern Burlington County N.A.A.C.P. v. Township of Mt. Laurel, 67 N.J. 151, 336 A.2d 713 (1975) (exclusionary zoning). The Supreme Court position upholding limits on city autonomy was most importantly articulated in *Hunter v. City of Pittsburgh*, 207 U.S. 161 (1907).

30. Thomas Edsall and Mary Edsall, *Chain Reaction: The Impact of Race, Rights, and Taxes on American Politics* (1991).

31. Robert Park, supra note 13, at 47.

32. *Report of National Commission on Civil Disorders* 1–2 (1968).

33. Richard Sennett, *The Fall of Public Man*, supra note 7, at 340.

Chapter 7
City Land Use

1. *Village of Belle Terre v. Boraas*, 416 U.S. 1, 13, 14 (1974); *Village of Euclid v. Ambler Realty*, 272 U.S. 365, 391, 364 (1926).

2. Seymour Toll, *Zoned American* 143–187 (1969); *Ambler Realty Co. v. Village of Euclid*, 297 F. Supp. 307, 316 (1924); Frank Popper, *The Politics of Land-Use Reform* 54 (1981).

3. *Village of Arlington Heights v. Metropolitan Development Corporation*, 429 U.S. 252, 269 (1977); Constance Perin, *Everything in Its Place: Social Order and Land Use in America* 32–128 (1977).

4. Bernard Frieden and Lynne Sagalyn, *Downtown, Inc.: How America Rebuilds Cities* 15–37, 265, 288–289 (1989); Roger Friedland, *Power and Crisis in the City: Corporations, Unions and Urban Policy* 60–77 (1983).

5. *Berman v. Parker*, 348 U.S. 26, 32–38 (1954).

6. Lawrence Friedman, *Government and Slum Housing: A Century of Frustration* 151 (1968); Bernard Frieden and Lynne Sagalyn, supra note 4, at 29–37, 288–289, 41; Larry Bennett, *Fragments of Cities: The New American Downtowns and Neighborhoods* 35 (1990).

7. Bernard Frieden and Lynne Sagalyn, supra note 4, at 133–172, 227–236, 297; *Lloyd Corp. v. Tanner*, 407 U.S. 551 (1972).

8. Lynne Sagalyn, "Explaining the Improbable: Local Redevelopment in the Wake of Federal Cutbacks," 56 *American Planning Assoc. J.* 429, 432 (Autumn 1990).

9. Paul Peterson, *City Limits* (1981); Stephen Elkin, *City and Regime in the American Republic* (1987); John Logan and Harvey Molotch, *Urban Fortunes: The Political Economy of Place* (1987).

10. For a discussion of Houston's land-use policy, see, e.g., Richard Babcock, "Houston: Unzoned, Unfettered, and Mostly Unrepentant," 48 *Planning: The ASPO Magazine* 21 (1982); Bernard Siegan, "Non-Zoning in Houston," 13 *J. L. & Econ.* 71 (1970).

11. Jane Jacobs, *The Death and Life of Great American Cities* 252, 254, 409 (1961); Vincent Scully, *American Architecture and Urbanism* 254 (1969).

12. Daniel Solomon, *ReBuilding* 6 (1992); Peter Calthorpe, *The Next American Metropolis: Ecology, Community, and the American Dream* 18 (1993); Andres Duany and Elizabeth Plater-Zyberk, "The Second Coming of the American Small

Town," *The Wilson Quarterly* 19, 29 (Winter 1992). See generally Peter Katz, *The New Urbanism: Toward an Architecture of Community* (1994).

13. Peter Calthorpe, supra note 12, at 16, 27, 47; Daniel Solomon, supra note 12, at 7.

14. Peter Calthorpe, supra note 12, at 30; Andres Duany and Elizabeth Plater-Zyberk, supra note 12, at 31–35.

15. Peter Calthorpe, supra note 12, at 37.

16. Jerry Adler, "Bye-Bye Suburban Dream," *Newsweek*, May 15, 1995, at 41–53; Andres Duany and Elizabeth Plater-Zyberk, supra note 12, at 47.

17. Dolores Hayden, *Redesigning the American Dream: The Future of Housing, Work, and Family Life* 3–40 (1984); Gwendolyn Wright, *Building the Dream: A Social History of Housing in America* 96–113 (1981).

18. Bureau of the Census, U.S. Dept. of Commerce, Series P-20, No. 437, *Household and Family Characteristics: March 1988*, 96, table 18 (1989); Nancy Dowd, "Stigmatizing Single Parents," 18 *Harv. Women's L.J.* 19, 22–23, notes 13, 20 (1995).

19. Dolores Hayden, *The Grand Domestic Revolution: A History of Feminist Designs for American Homes, Neighborhoods, and Cities* (1981); Doreen Massey, *Space, Place and Gender* (1994); Barbara Hooper, " 'Split at the Roots': A Critique of the Philosophical Sources of Modern Planning Doctrine," 13 *Frontiers* 45 (1992).

20. Andres Duany and Elizabeth Plater-Zyberk, supra note 12, at 46–47.

21. Rob Gurwitt, "The Quest for Common Ground," 11 *Governing* 16 (June 1998).

22. Thomas Bier, *Cuyahoga County Outmigration* (March 1993); Thomas Bier et al., *Moving Up and Out: Government Policy and the Future of Ohio's Metropolitan Areas* (1994); Thomas Bier and Ivan Maric, "IRS Homeseller Provision and Urban Decline," 16 *J. of Urban Affairs* 141 (1994).

23. Myron Orfield, "Talk Radio Called Him a Commie and Put Him on Hold," *Minneapolis Star Tribune*, May 23, 1995, at 13A. For a description of the successes and failures of Orfield's proposed legislative reform, see Myron Orfield, *Metropolitics: A Regional Agenda for Community and Stability* (1997).

24. Lewis Mumford, "For Older People—Not Segregation but Integration," in *Housing the Elderly* 39, 44 (Hancock ed. 1987). See also *Housing and the Aging Population: Options for the New Century* (Folts and Yeatts eds. 1994).

25. Paul Jargowsky, "Ghetto Poverty among Blacks in the 1980s," 13 *J. of Policy Analysis and Management* 288, 294–302 (1994).

26. Nancy Denton, "Are African Americans Still Hypersegregated?" in *Residential Apartheid: The American Legacy* 49–81 (Bullard ed. 1994); Joe Feagin and Melvin Sikes, *Living with Racism: The Black Middle-Class Experience* 223–271 (1994); Charles Banner-Haley, *The Fruits of Integration: Black Middle-Class Ideology and Culture, 1960–1990*, 7–9 (1994).

27. The phrase is from John Logan and Harvey Molotch, supra note 9, at 9.

28. Richard Ford, "The Boundaries of Race: Political Geography in Legal Analysis," 107 *Harv. L. Rev.* 1841, 1914 (1994).

Chapter 8
Alternative Conceptions of City Services

1. See, e.g., Richard Musgrave and Peggy Musgrave, *Public Finance in Theory and Practice* 41–45 (5th ed. 1989).

2. Charles Tiebout, "A Pure Theory of Local Expenditures," 64 *J. Pol. Econ.* 416 (1956); Wallace Oakes, "On Local Finance and the Tiebout Model," 71 *Am. Econ. Rev.* 93 (1981).

3. Bruce Hamilton, "Zoning and Property Taxation in a System of Local Governments," 12 *Urban Studies* 205 (1975); James Buchanan, "Principles of Urban Fiscal Strategy," 11 *Public Choice* 1, 13–16 (1971); Clayton Gillette, "Opting Out of Public Provision," 73 *Denver U.L. Rev.* 1185, 1204 (1996).

4. Mark Sagoff, "At the Shrine of Our Lady of Fatima or Why Political Questions Are Not All Economic," 23 *Ariz. L. Rev.* 1283, 1286 (1981).

5. Robert Nozick, *Anarchy, State and Utopia* 297–331 (1974).

6. Eric Monkkonen, *America Becomes Urban: The Development of U.S. Cities and Towns* 89 (1988); Eric Monkkonen, *Police in Urban America 1860–1920*, 4–15, 30–64 (1981); David Tyack, *The One Best System: A History of American Urban Education* 74, 28–77 (1974); 2 *The Papers of Frederick Law Olmsted* 235 (Beveridge ed. 1981).

7. William Fischel, "Property Taxation and the Tiebout Model: Evidence for the Benefit View from Zoning and Voting," 30 *J. of Econ. Literature* 171, 176 (1992).

Chapter 9
Education

1. *Brown v. Board of Education*, 347 U.S. 483, 493 (1954). For a discussion of education that emphasizes the search for academic excellence, see John Chubb and Terry Moe, *Politics, Markets and America's Schools* 6, 70 (1990).

2. John Dewey, *Democracy and Education* 20–21 (1916); Lawrence Cremin, *Traditions of American Education* 50 (1976).

3. David Tyack, *The One Best System: A History of American Urban Education* 229–255 (1974); Amy Gutmann, *Democratic Education* (1987). See also *Plyler v. Doe*, 457 U.S. 202, 222 n. 20 (1982) ("Schools are an important socializing institution, imparting those shared values through which social order and stability are maintained").

4. On the hidden curriculum, see Robert Dreeben, *On What Is Learned in School* (1968); Michael Walzer, *Spheres of Justice* 215 (1983) ("The content of the curriculum is probably less important than the human environment in which it is taught . . . [S]o much of what we know we learn from our peers"). The 1983 report referred to is National Commission on Excellence in Education, *A Nation at Risk: The Imperative for Educational Reform: A Report to the Nation and the Secretary of Education* 5 (1983).

5. On the history of compulsory education, see David Tyack, supra note 3, at 68–71 and Michael Katz, *School Reform: Past and Present* 65–87 (1971); on the

controversy over tax-supported education, see Carl Kaestle, *Pillars of the Republic: Common Schools and American Society, 1780–1860*, 148–151 (1983). For the contemporary relevance of this history on the evaluation of school choice proposals, see James Liebman, "Voice Not Choice," 101 *Yale L.J.* 259 (1991).

6. On attitudes toward school integration, see Gary Orfield and Susan Eaton, *Dismantling Desegregation: The Quiet Reversal of Brown v. Board of Education* 106–112 (1996); Jennifer Hochschild, *The New American Dilemma: Liberal Democracy and School Desegregation* 179–187 (1984).

7. *Sheff v. O'Neill*, 678 A.2d 1267, 1274 (1996). Representative Supreme Court cases include *Milliken v. Bradley*, 418 U.S. 717 (1974) and *Missouri v. Jenkins*, 115 S.Ct. 2038 (1995). The quotation and statistics are from Gary Orfield and Susan Eaton, supra note 6, at 309, 53.

8. David Tyack and Larry Cuban, *Tinkering toward Utopia* 19 (1995); 1992 Census of Governments, *Vol. 1: Government Organization* 34–35 (1994).

9. For a discussion of "controlled choice," see *Public Schools by Choice: Expanding Opportunities for Parents, Students, and Teachers* (Nathan ed. 1989); Michael Alves and Charles Willie, "Controlled Choice Assignments: A New and More Effective Approach to School Desegregation," 19 *Urban Review* 67 (1987). For a discussion of the Cambridge plan, see Cambridge Public School Department, *The Cambridge Controlled Choice School District Desegregation Plan* (1992); Charles V. Willie, Michael Alves, and George Metzger, *Planning Report on Controlled Choice and School Facilities* 5, 29–31, 34 (1996). For an overview of the school choice literature, including a state-by-state survey of controlled choice plans, see Peter Cookson, *School Choice: The Struggle for the Soul of American Education* (1994).

10. See *Who Chooses? Who Loses? Culture, Institutions, and the Unequal Effects of School Choice* (Fuller and Elmore eds. 1996).

11. *Hunter v. Pittsburgh*, 207 U.S. 161 (1907).

12. For an analysis of successful integration plans, see Gary Orfield and Susan Eaton, supra note 6, at 111, 179–206, 316–317. On private school enrollment, see National Center for Educational Statistics, *Private Schools in the United States: A Statistical Profile, with Comparison to Public Schools* 33 (1991).

13. John Chubb and Terry Moe, supra note 1, at 221–222 (insisting on schools' making their own admission decisions but forbidding extra charges); Milton Friedman, *Capitalism and Freedom* 89 (1962) (allowing schools to charge more). Compare John Coons and Stephen Sugarman, *Education by Choice: The Case for Family Control* 135–145 (1978) (refusing to allow schools to set their own admission requirements).

14. Reliance on antidiscrimination law is conventional in school choice proposals; see, e.g., John Chubb and Terry Moe, supra note 1, at 211. But the authors rarely take into account the development of antidiscrimination law after the Supreme Court adopted the intent test of *Washington v. Davis*, 426 U.S. 229 (1976), a development that dramatically limits its impact.

15. Jeanie Oakes, *Keeping Track: How Schools Structure Inequality* 7 (1985).

16. For criticism of Oakes' position, see, e.g., Maureen Hallinan, "Track Mobility in Secondary School," 3 *Social Forces* 983, 984 (1996); on brainiacs and acting

white, see Signithia Fordham and John Ogbu, "Black Students' School Success: Coping with the Burden of 'Acting White,' " 18 *The Urban Review* 176 (1986).

17. Hugh Mehan, Irene Villanueva, Lea Hubbard, and Angela Lintz, *Constructing School Success: The Consequences of Untracking Lower Achieving Students* (1996); Anne Wheelock, *Crossing the Tracks: How "Untracking" Can Save America's Schools* (1992).

Chapter 10
Police

1. David Bayley, *Police for the Future* 3 (1994). See also Herman Goldstein, *Problem-Oriented Policing* (1990); Malcolm Sparrow, Mark Moore, and David Kennedy, *Beyond 911: A New Era for Policing* (1990); Jerome Skolnick and David Bayley, *The New Blue Line* (1986).

2. On the cost of private security, see David Bayley, supra note 1, at 10, and William Cunningham and Todd Taylor, *Crime and Protection in America: A Study of Private Security and Law Enforcement Resources and Relationships* 14 (May 1985); on the cost to victims, see Albert Reiss and Jeffrey Roth, *Understanding and Preventing Violence* 4 (1993); on the impact on high-crime neighborhoods, see Randall Kennedy, *Race, Crime and the Law* 11 (1997) (collecting authorities).

3. John Conklin, *The Impact of Crime* 6 (1975); Jerome Skolnick and David Bayley, supra note 1, at 5.

4. Elijah Anderson, *Streetwise: Race, Class, and Change in an Urban Community* 164–165 (1990); John Conklin, supra note 3, at 33.

5. Jeff Jacoby, "Crime Is Down; So Why Don't We Feel Safe?" *Boston Globe*, August 17, 1995, p. 19, col. 1.

6. Richard Wright, *In Defense of Prisons* 123–131 (1994).

7. David Bayley and Harold Mendelsohn, *Minorities and the Police: Confrontation in America* 108 (1969). See also Randall Kennedy, supra note 2, at 136–163; Charles Ogletree et al., *Beyond the Rodney King Story: An Investigation of Police Conduct in Minority Communities* (1995); Stan Shernock, "An Empirical Examination of the Relationship between Police Solidarity and Community Orientation," 16 *J. of Political Science and Administration* 182 (1988); Jerome Skolnick, *The Police and the Urban Ghetto* (1968).

8. Elijah Anderson, "The Code of the Streets," 273 *The Atlantic* 80 (May 1994).

9. Jane Jacobs, *The Death and Life of Great American Cities* 44 (1961); Oscar Newman, *Creating Defensible Space* (1996); Peter Calthorpe, *The Next American Metropolis: Ecology, Community, and the American Dream* 37 (1993).

10. Alexander von Hoffman, "An Officer of the Neighborhood: A Boston Patrolman on the Beat," 26 *J. of Social History* 309, 317 (1992); Roger Fogelson, *Big-City Police* (1977).

11. U.S. Department of Justice, Bureau of Justice Assistance, *Understanding Community Policing: A Framework for Action* vii (1994). See also works cited supra, note 1.

12. See, e.g., Jerome Skolnick, "Neighborhood Police," *The Nation*, March 22, 1971, at 372.

13. On the conflicts within police departments, see David Bayley, supra note 1, at 56–75; on the conflicts within African American neighborhoods, see Randall Kennedy, supra note 2, at 19–21, Roger Dunham and Geoffrey Alpert, "Neighborhood Differences in Attitudes toward Policing: Evidence for a Mixed-Strategy Model of Policing in a Multi-Ethnic Setting," 79 *J. of Criminal Law and Criminology* 504 (1988), and William Whyte, *Street Corner Society* 136 (1943).

14. Herman Goldstein, supra note 1; Wesley Skogan, *Disorder and Decline: Crime and the Spiral Decay in American Neighborhoods* 89–93 (1990); James Q. Wilson and George Kelling, "Making Neighborhoods Safe," *The Atlantic Monthly,* February 1989, at 46; James Q. Wilson and George Kelling, "Broken Windows: The Police and Neighborhood Safety," *The Atlantic Monthly,* March 1982, at 29; New York City Police Department, *Police Strategy No. 5: Reclaiming the Public Spaces of New York* 5 (1994).

15. Carl Nightingale, *On the Edge: A History of Poor Black Children and Their American Dream* 166–185 (1993); Regina Austin, " 'The Black Community,' Its Lawbreakers, and a Politics of Identification," 65 *S.Cal. L. Rev.* 1769, 1776 (1992); Emily Frug, *Walking a New Beat: A Study of the Community Policing Program in New Haven* (1996).

16. David Bayley, supra note 1, at 117.

Chapter 11
Choosing City Services

1. 1992 Census of Governments, *Vol. 4: Government Finances* 2, table 1; Roland Liebert, *Disintegration and Political Action: The Changing Functions of City Governments in America* 18–22 (1976).

2. Martin Melosi, *Garbage in the Cities: Refuse, Reform, and the Environment, 1880–1980,* 112 (1981).

3. John Zipp, "Government Employment and Black-White Earnings Equality, 1980–1990," 41 *Social Problems* 363, 369 (1994); Robert Suggs, *Minorities and Privatization: Economic Mobility at Risk* (1989).

4. Nancy Burns, *The Formation of American Local Governments: Private Values in Public Institutions* (1994). For a comparable analysis of interlocal agreements, see Gary Miller, *Cities by Contract: The Politics of Municipal Incorporation* (1981).

5. Philippe Ariès, "The Family and the City in the Old World and the New," in *Changing Images of the Family* 29, 41 (Tufte and Myerhoff eds. 1979). On sports teams, see Matthew Mitten and Bruce Burton, "Professional Sports Franchise Relocations from Private Law and Public Law Perspectives: Balancing Marketplace Competition, League Autonomy, and the Need for a Level Playing Field," 56 *Md. L. Rev.* 57 (1997).

6. See Peter Enrich, "Saving the States from Themselves: Commerce Clause Constraints on State Tax Incentives for Business," 110 *Harv. L. Rev.* 378, 391–393 (1996). Some scholars argue that a region's cities are highly interdependent and that increasing the welfare of those that are worst off improves the competitiveness of the metropolitan region as a whole. See, e.g., H. V. Savitch, David Collins, Daniel Sanders, and John Markham, "Ties That Bind: Central Cities, Suburbs, and the New Metropolitan Region," 7 *Economic Development Quarterly* 341

(1993); Richard Voith, "City and Suburban Growth: Substitutes or Complements?" *Business Review: Federal Reserve Bank of Philadelphia* 21 (September–October 1992). See also Henry Cisneros, *Regionalism: The New Geography of Opportunity* (1995).

7. The most influential source for this proposition is Paul Peterson, *City Limits* (1981).

8. The census defines regional areas and is therefore a place to begin. Its definition relies on factors such as commuting patterns, density, and the amount of space that is urbanized. The 1990 census, however, recognized the complexity of this task by distinguishing between a primary metropolitan statistical area (PMSA) and a consolidated metropolitan statistical area (CMSA)—the latter being an area including more than one PMSA.

Afterword

1. Alexis de Tocqueville, *Democracy in America* 63 (Lawrence trans. 1966).

2. David Rusk, *Cities without Suburbs* 104 (1993); Myron Orfield, *Metropolis: A Regional Agenda for Community and Stability* 104–172 (1997); Bank of America, *Beyond Sprawl: New Patterns of Growth to Fit the New California* 2 (1995).

Index